D1712239

ISO 9000
AND
MALCOLM
BALDRIGE

IN
TRAINING
AND
EDUCATION

A PRACTICAL
APPLICATION
GUIDE

C.W. RUSS RUSSO

CHARRO PUBLISHERS, INC./LAWRENCE, KANSAS

ISBN 0-9646992-5-7

Library of Congress Catalog Card Number 95-069520

Topics: Total Quality Management
          Malcolm Baldrige National Quality Award
          ISO 9000
          Training and Education

First Edition. First Printing 1995.

Printed in the United States of America by
Constable-Hodgins Printing Co., Kansas City, Kansas

Cover design: Bananagraphics, Inc., Evanston, IL

Acknowledgments

Many people have influenced my thinking and supported my efforts over the years. These few acknowledgments pale in comparison to the list of all the people I wish to thank. I offer thanks to:

Payson, Barbara, and Gene, who helped transform this material into a book;

Marie, who always helped me value my successes;

Rosie and Charley simply for always being there for me;

Stephanie and Izzy for the joy they bring me;

all the trainers and educators in my life who have shared their enthusiasm and love for their work;

and my darling wife Tracy, who understood it all from the beginning twenty-five years ago.

Disclaimer

There are no guarantees in this life. There are certainly no guarantees given or implied in this book. The ISO 9000 Standards and Malcolm Baldrige criteria and their respective organizations, the International Organization for Standardization (ISO) and National Institute of Standards and Technology (NIST), are the final authorities for interpretation of their standards and criteria. Trainers and educators should learn as much as possible about the standards and criteria and interpret them in their own organizations. The suggestions offered in this book are ideas for trainers and educators to use to begin thinking about their needs and to develop strategies and tactics to meet their goals and objectives.

Contents

Foreword

This book may be most effective read either from cover to cover or as a source for information in specific areas. The following tables may help readers find the information they are seeking.

Table 1 identifies types of readers and their needs, then identifies chapters of particular interest to them.

Table 2 will help users decide whether Baldrige or ISO—or both—meet their needs by highlighting some similarities and differences between the Malcolm Baldrige National Quality Award criteria and the ISO 9000 standards.

A third and fourth table are topic/page locators for trainers. More than an index of topics, they help trainers compare and contrast Baldrige and ISO sections.

TABLE 1	
Needs Locator	
This table will help readers identify which chapters address their particular needs.	
If You:	**Then Look In:**
Are trying to help your training organization choose between applying the Baldrige or the ISO standards,	Chapters 1 and 2 and Table 2 in the Foreword.
Need to develop a glossary of terms for your training procedures,	Chapter 3.
Need help to plan a quality implementation project,	Chapter 4.
Need to create an internal audit process and write a procedure for your team,	Chapters 22 and 36.
Need information about the ISO standard,	The first two sections of each chapter in Part Two.
Are knowledgeable about the ISO standard but need information about the guideline,	Sections three and four of the chapters in Part Two.
Need to compare a particular training issue in both the Baldrige and ISO,	Tables 3 and 4 in the Foreword.

TABLE 2

The Baldrige and ISO
Similarities and Differences

This table compares and contrasts the purpose of and thinking behind the MBNQA and the ISO 9000. It can be used to help trainers understand the advantages inherent in both and decide which they should apply to their training organization.

The Malcolm Baldrige Award Criteria	The ISO 9000 Standards
Limited to United States.	Used in 100+ countries around the world.
An award. Maximum six per year.	Any company that meets the standard can apply and be registered.
Integrates all process and interrelationships throughout the organization.	Focuses on 20 elements and specific activities.
High quality orientation.	High quality orientation.
Emphasis on leadership and vision.	Emphasis on executive oversight and a quality manual to describe practices.
Emphasis on quality philosophy.	Emphasis on quality practice.
Customer Service: encourages surveys and partnering.	Customer Service: requires contract review, verification and validation of design to satisfy needs.
Benchmarking best practices.	No benchmarking.
Requires employee empowerment and training.	Requires training; no employee empowerment.
Generic, non-prescriptive. Raises issues and expects company to devise own best practice.	Generic, non-prescriptive. Raises issues and expects company to devise own best practice.
World class; industry leader.	Highest common denominator.
Right-brained culture—integrative.	Left-brained culture—linear, structured, hierarchical.
Process oriented. Education organizations (new award) may apply but not for training departments within organizations.	Process oriented. Training organizations within organizations may be registered.
Criteria may be used as a way to self-evaluate internal processes without applying for award.	Standards may be used as a way to self-evaluate internal processes without applying for registration.
Focuses on continuous improvement.	Focuses on internal audit, corrective and preventive action.

TABLE 3
Comparison of the Baldrige Educational Pilot Criteria and the ISO Z-1.11 Education and Training Guideline

Baldrige Education Pilot Criteria	ISO Z-1.11 Education and Training Guideline	Page
1.0 Leadership	4.1 Management Responsibility	49
2.0 Information and Analysis	4.20 Statistical Techniques	198
2.1 Management of Information and Data	4.5 Document and Data Control	89
2.3 Analysis and Use of School-Level Data	4.4.7 Design Verification	78
3.0 Strategic and Operational Planning	4.2.3 Quality Planning	58
4.0 Human Resource Development and Management	4.18 Training	184
5.0 Education and Business Process Management	4.9 Process Control	116
5.1 Education Design	4.4.1 Design Control	75
5.3 Education Support Service Design and Delivery	4.6 Purchasing	99
5.6 Business Operations Management	4.9 Process Control	116
6.0 School Performance Results	4.10 Inspection and Testing	143
7.0 Student Focus and Student Stakeholder Satisfaction	4.1.1 Quality Policy	50

TABLE 4

Comparison of the ISO Z-1.11 Education and Training Guideline (draft 9/28/94) to the Baldrige Educational Pilot Criteria (1995)

ISO Z-1.11 Education and Training Guideline	Baldrige Education Pilot Criteria	Page
4.1 Management Responsibility (Administration Responsibility)	1.0 Leadership	222
4.1.1 Quality Policy	1.2 Leadership System and Organization	225
4.1.2 Organization (School or Training Company)	1.1 Senior Administration Leadership	222
4.1.3 Management Review	1.2 Leadership System and Organization	225
4.2 Quality System	5.0 Educational and Business Process Management	258
4.2.3 Quality Planning	3.1 Strategy Development	239
4.3 Contract Review	5.3 Education Support Service Design and Delivery	266
4.4 Design Control	5.1 Education Design	259
4.5 Document and Data Control	2.0 Information and Analysis	230
4.6 Purchasing	5.3 Education Support Service Design and Delivery	266
4.9 Process Control	5.0 Educational and Business Process Management	258
4.10 Inspection and Testing	5.2 Education Delivery 6.0 School Performance Results	293 279
4.14 Corrective and Preventive Action	Item "c" in each area to address	
4.18 Training	4.3 Faculty and Staff Development	251
4.20 Statistical Techniques	2.0 Information and Analysis	230

Preface

Total Quality Management and other quality principles and programs have been attracting interest among managers for several years. In 1990, when the Malcolm Baldrige
National Quality Award winners first began advertising their
achievements in the media, interest in Total Quality
Management (TQM) and related quality programs surged.
Although quality assurance ideas are not new, TQM came to
be seen as a way for companies to compete more effectively
in the face of domestic and international competition and
economic pressures. As more and more companies began
exploring quality programs, many trainers found themselves
teaching quality management topics, such as statistical
process control and team empowerment. This was the first
connection between quality assurance concepts and training.

In light of increasing acceptance of the Baldrige
Award and its underlying ideas, it seemed evident to me that
training and education organizations would gain considerable advantage and credibility within their companies if they
modeled their processes on the MBNQA criteria. However,
when I asked colleagues if they were adopting these criteria
into their training processes, I discovered they were not

using them and they did not plan to do so. This seemed to me a lost opportunity.

More recently, another major quality movement—ISO 9000—has received wide acceptance. Like the Baldrige, the ISO 9000 model focuses on specific elements to help companies produce quality products. Thus, manufacturing companies around the world are applying the ISO 9000 quality assurance model to their production methods. Very recently, some service organizations also have adopted ISO 9000, since they have come to understand that quality assurance is critical in meeting their strategic goals. And now, most encouraging of all, education and training organizations are beginning to adopt both the Baldrige criteria and the ISO standards as a basis for their own activities. Organizing training processes around either the MBNQA or ISO gives trainers both the support of a demonstrated system to contribute to corporate goals and the credibility to harness organizational resources toward this goal.

Adopting the Baldrige criteria or ISO standards offers trainers a means to address three pervasive problems.

- First, trainers too frequently have taken a back seat in their companies, receiving little attention and limited resources. In many of these cases, this is because management does not appreciate the value training adds to the organization, especially how it can help the company meet strategic goals. This may be because these managers have not made the connection between the training efforts and company goals or because trainers have been unable to demonstrate training's value to the organization.
- Second, sometimes trainers' credibility with line managers and employees has suffered because training has not always met employees' needs. The training literature frequently identifies inaccurate or incomplete communication and unmet expectations

among trainees, managers, and trainers as causes. In the end, however, employees and managers want and need practical ways to become more productive.

■ Third, many training organizations have been less-well organized than they could or should be, and trainers have been too busy with the press of their tasks to worry about how their own processes are functioning. They see training as a service function, responding to the needs of other groups. Therefore, it is difficult for trainers to see the benefits of having a structured foundation for their efforts. The reality is, however, that poorly organized training processes, just like other poorly organized processes, work against everyone's best efforts to succeed.

The single most powerful solution to all three problems is to adopt a structured training process. The ISO standards or MBNQA criteria, separately or together, provide a solid framework for this change. They can provide other benefits to the entire organization as well. First, because company leaders have come to understand the value of quality and its underlying ideas, they should appreciate the advantages of applying this approach to training. Second, applying quality concepts, such as customer service, in their own processes gives the training organization credibility with line managers and employees. Third, adopting the MBNQA criteria or ISO standards helps trainers do their own tasks more effectively and efficiently.

I believe training organizations will gain credibility, become more effective and efficient, and be better able to support their organizations' strategic goals if they adopt either MBNQA or ISO as a foundation for their activities. This book is a tool to help trainers meet that end.

The increasing interest in ISO and MBNQA by many training and educational organizations encourages me because I believe training is pivotal to organizational success. This book is designed to help trainers develop a plan to transform their processes to meet the Baldrige criteria or ISO 9000 Standards. It combines explanations of the criteria and standards with pragmatic and practical suggestions about how to align training to the standard or criteria, including a series of action items for each element of the standard. Quality Project Teams should address each of these action items in turn and decide how they can be adopted or adapted to the team's goals. Experience has shown that these often critical points apply broadly across companies. They are useful in triggering critical decision making and reconciling the human dynamics in a company in order to meet the spirit and letter of the standards.

The material in this book is useful for trainers and human resource staff responsible for training in commercial organizations, including service industries and manufacturers, as well as nonprofit organizations, including government, academic, and charitable organizations. In other words, this book is for everybody in the training and education business.

This volume really is two books in one because it presents two distinct topics: first, the ISO standards and, second, the Baldrige criteria. There are similarities between Baldrige and ISO, but, to my mind, their differences are more significant than their similarities. The Baldrige focuses primarily on education institutions such as schools and colleges. The ISO standards, however, are strongly oriented toward industry training.

The ISO standards are very practical and pragmatic. They will help an organization devise a solid foundation to organize their processes. The Baldrige criteria represent a more complex change program, providing a way to integrate both training's internal operation and its relationships with the rest of its organization. Despite the differences, both educational institutions and industry training groups can use either criteria or standards for their own needs. Generally, I encourage trainers and educators to start with the ISO standards to establish a more pragmatic foundation. Once the ISO standards are in use, the process of adopting the Baldrige becomes significantly simplified and easier. I encourage readers who wish to skip the ISO 9000 standards and go straight to the Baldrige criteria to revisit their assumptions and plans. The time, energy, and resources invested in ISO—before addressing Baldrige—will pay significant dividends.

How the Book is Organized

The book is organized into a foreword and four parts. Part One introduces basic ideas and terms. Because a great deal of information is available about the origin and philosophies of ISO and Baldrige, I have kept this discussion short and focused on information pertinent to trainers. Its purpose is to provide a foundation for ideas and discussion throughout the remainder of the book.

The foreword contains four tables, the first to help trainers identify their needs and explain how this book can help them. The second highlights similarities and differences between the Baldrige criteria and the ISO standards, which are further discussed in Chapter 1. Tables 3 and 4 relate and compare sections of the Malcolm Baldrige Criteria and ISO Guidelines to help trainers and educators see how both address similar issues.

Chapter 2 presents a short history of ISO and MBNQA and a discussion of the philosophy underlying both the ISO registration process and the Malcolm Baldrige National Quality Award. It provides general information about registration and award schemata.

Chapter 3 contains a series of definitions trainers will need to handle in the process of implementing a quality assurance program. This is more than a glossary. These definitions reflect the importance and role of key conceptual terms. Training team members will find agreeing on terms will help them as they work to implement a quality assurance project.

The final chapter in Part One has two sections. The first section provides some tools to help organize a registration or award project. Any organizational transformation project is lengthy and complex. An ISO or Baldrige Q-Project frequently takes a year and more often 18 months. When good project management principles are used, process improvement strategies are employed, and team-based processes are in place, such an undertaking goes smoothly and is successful. The second section presents an overview of a registration audit or award visit to help trainers prepare for this event.

Part Two focuses on the 1994 version of the ISO 9001 Standard and the ISO Z-1.11, Education and Training Guideline. The guideline offers interpretations of how to apply the standard to education and training. There are 21 chapters in Part Two. Please note: copyrights protect the ISO standards and guidelines, and therefore they are not reproduced here. Readers should obtain copies of the Z-1.11 guideline to use as reference. This guideline contains the standard, so a separate copy of the standard is not necessary.

In Part Two, the first chapter explains introductory materials in both the ISO 9001 Standard and Education and Training Guideline. Then each of the following 20 chapters covers one element in the ISO 9001 Standard. Each chapter includes:

- Information about the element's purpose and how it might be applied in a quality assurance program.
- Discussion of what the ISO 9001 Standard requires and what an ISO auditor might look for during an audit.
- How the Z-1.11 Guideline adapts the standard to training and what a training assessor might look for.
- Q-Project action items to spark discussion and give

a training team some ideas to begin transforming their organization.

- Some final remarks to help trainers adopt a practical perspective, acknowledging political and operational realities, when applying their ideas.

The Q-Project Action Items are suggestions. They may or may not fit a particular organization. Neither the standard nor the guideline specifies a right or wrong way to apply the standard to a particular organization. Each organization must decide how to apply the standard and guideline to its own particular needs. Adapting these generic elements is one of the most frustrating parts of every ISO 9000 project. The ISO standard identifies what issues must be addressed, but it does not provide any specifics on how to address them. These Action Items are offered as a way to help trainers begin to find ways to apply the generic standard.

Part Three discusses the Malcolm Baldrige National Quality Award criteria. It is organized similarly to Part Two, in eight chapters. The first chapter discusses the MBNQA criteria introductory material, and the remaining seven chapters look at sections in the criteria. Each chapter is organized into three parts:

- A comparison of the Baldrige criteria to the newly published 1995 Education Pilot Criteria.
- An interpretation of what a training examiner might look for.
- A discussion offering some ideas about how to structure education processes to meet the criteria.

As in Part Two, these suggestions are idea starters. The team's job is to find specific ways to apply the generic criteria to their own organizations.

The five chapters in Part Four address the quality assurance guidelines in the ISO 9000 series. There is a fundamental difference between a guideline and a standard. Standards are *contract auditable*, which means that an organization must address and meet each element in the standard, or, if it pursues formal ISO registration, resolve why it will not meet each element. In contrast, a *guideline* is a guide to thinking. Auditors cannot audit against guidelines, and there is no expectation the organization will necessarily meet each element of the guideline. The guidelines discussed in this part include:

- ISO 9000-x, guidelines that help management decide to which standard (9001, 9002, 9003) they should register their company.
- ISO 9004-x, guidelines that help management understand how they should organize and manage a quality system.
- ISO 9004-2, the guideline for service industries to help them apply the ISO standard.
- ISO 10011-1, 10011-2, and 10011-3, guidelines on how to structure and manage quality auditing systems. This section is meant to help readers understand how to organize and conduct internal audits.
- ISO 8402, the vocabulary guideline.

Each guideline focuses on issues and concerns trainers need to address to meet the standards or to apply the guideline to their organization. The final chapter of the book addresses issues after an ISO registration or Baldrige Award project. Does a company move upward and onward to greater heights? Or do letdown and disappointment await the training organization? A few concluding thoughts may help trainers and educators maintain a realistic perspective as they work within an established quality system.

Some Thoughts to Begin

In companies where training is perceived as integral, applying Baldrige or ISO to the training function will support trainers' best work. A training process based on outcomes that can be measured and processes that can be examined gives trainers credibility. The focus on customer service and careful planning presents training to both trainees and management as effective and efficient. Many senior managers have come to understand the contributions that quality assurance actions make to their companies, and the clear links between quality assurance programs and training are powerful. In companies where training is seen as an ancillary activity and a cost center, applying Baldrige or ISO to the training function should produce a cultural shift in which this critical activity is perceived as a valuable contributor to strategic objectives and as a profit center.

Perhaps the most important idea in the array of quality is the belief that good customer service is a hallmark of a high quality organization. In keeping with that idea, I always ask my workshop participants what they wanted or expected to gain from the workshop that they did not, what needed more emphasis, or should be excluded. I want to know what additional information they need to do their jobs more effectively. Those same questions will provide a way to assess the value of this book. Therefore, I am including my address and encouraging you, as my customers, to contact me with your ideas and suggestions.

So with all that, two final words: Good Fortune! I am enormously enthusiastic about the prospect of training and education organizations applying ISO 9000 and Baldrige to their processes. I hope this book is a valuable tool to aid you and your organization to meet your goals.

Dr. C. W. Russ Russo
The Trainers Workshop
4700 Carmel Court
Lawrence, KS 66047-1842
913-865-4306
913-865-4311 fax

Part One
ISO 9000 and Baldrige Award in Training and Education

This section of the book describes the philosophy behind the Malcolm Baldrige Criteria and ISO 9000 Standards and discusses practical ideas about how to organize a project to implement either quality system.

CHAPTER 1

ISO 9000 and Malcolm Baldrige in Training and Education

In 1995, the National Institute of Standards and Technology (NIST) began a pilot program to expand the Malcolm Baldrige National Quality Award to include education. Also in 1995, the International Organization for Standardization (ISO) published a guideline explaining how to apply the ISO 9001 Standard to education and training.

Trainers have been in the forefront in helping their companies initiate quality programs. Employees gain the skills and knowledge necessary to carry out and sustain a quality program through effective and efficient training programs. Quality management and quality assurance practitioners recognize the critical need to train employees in quality principles and methods. Now, these new initiatives from MBNQA and ISO are helping educators and trainers practice what they teach. These initiatives recognize the need for training organizations to meet established quality standards. Training, just like other elements of the organization, needs to be structured on the basis of quality assurance principles.

Three major issues, one cultural and two philosophi-

3

cal, have hindered some training organizations from achieving excellence through a quality assurance process. The cultural issue in many organizations is that upper management sees training as a cost center and separate from the corporation's core functions or strategic objectives. Although the organization must invest resources, including employees' time away from work, to support training activities, there may be no immediately visible payoffs for this investment. Without evidence of value, training resources may seem wasted. When organizations do not understand how training adds value and supports the company's strategic and financial missions, they frequently give training short shrift. Too often, the practical result of this mind-set is trainers who are not included in strategic planning. As a result:

- Insufficient lead time is available for trainers to prepare effective programs to meet strategic needs.
- Insufficient resources are allocated to training.
- Insufficient time is allowed for employees to attend training.
- Training programs are not adequately focused on desired strategic corporate goals.

Management will more easily perceive value in training if its goals and activities are determined through the same types of decision-making processes supporting other organizational decisions. A well-structured, business-based decision-making process helps a company devise a training strategy that:

- Identifies and addresses employee training needs adding to employee productivity.
- Selects training activities and materials to meet specific employee training needs.
- Aids management's understanding of payoffs for resource expenditures.

The first goal, identifying training which adds to employee productivity, is satisfied when trainers ensure that

4

every training activity has a specific job purpose. The step need not be expensive or complex. However, it is necessary for the company to understand the job requirements and identify the desired training outcomes. Ensuring that there is a match between needed job skills and training is possible when based on clearly specified job needs.

The second goal, selecting training to meet employees' needs, is satisfied when employees understand how training will help them improve their job performance. Besides giving employees skills they need to do their jobs, a well-conceived and well-executed training program sends two clear messages to employees:

- The company wants them to be able to do a good job.
- Employees are valued contributors to the company's strategic mission.

Training helps companies gain more productive employees, reduce errors and downtime, manage risks, achieve higher quality products and services, and, finally, achieve greater profitability. In addition, employees gain self-confidence when they possess skills to do their tasks.

Two philosophical issues drive organizations' response to training. The first is whether training is a science or an art form. And the second is whether the product of training is the training program or the skilled employee. Although it is possible, theoretically, to see training as either art or science, training as an art form cannot be structured, and results may not meet needs or reflect effort invested. In contrast, trainers who see training as a science focus on job performance. In this view, trainers can structure processes to analyze training needs, design and develop materials, and deliver and evaluate training results. This is straightforward in teaching measurable skills where learning outcomes are readily observable. The proof is the trainee's ability to perform the learned task. Outcomes are less easily demonstrated from a scientific perspective when teaching so-called soft-skills, such as leadership or communication, because the learner's performance is not easily observed or measured.

Trainers who have always seen training as an art form sometimes express concern that attempts to structure it and apply procedures will inhibit their creativity and spontaneity. They resist a scientific approach based on procedures because they feel it may inhibit creativity in their work. An additional real concern when applying ISO 9000 procedures is such structures will blossom into a predominantly bureaucratic exercise where more time is spent writing procedures than on the real work of providing effective and efficient instruction.

The documentation nightmare is not an unfounded fear. There is a real need to think carefully and design procedures which are sufficiently structured to be accessible to everyone and still flexible enough to help rather than hinder the individuals who use them. The secret to success is to write good, short, useful procedures. This is more easily said than done.

A hidden benefit of spending time to develop useful procedures is that they help trainers understand what is expected of them, how they should go about their tasks, and what they need to do to be successful. Beyond providing structure and order to the organization, procedures send a clear message that the company has made an effort to understand what tasks must be accomplished and to provide guidance to accomplish their tasks. The message is that management cares about trainers and has spent resources necessary to help them do their jobs successfully and contribute value to the corporation's strategic goals.

The second philosophical question concerns the training product. Is the training product represented by programs, that is, the lesson materials and all the attendant physical manuals and documentation created and taught? Or is the product a skilled and trained employee who can do a job? The answer is both. It is important to recognize there is a double nature to the product (both trainees and materials) and to consider how to structure processes to account for both products. There are several places in the ISO guideline where this issue is raised and must be resolved.

Despite these philosophical issues, the new MBNQA and ISO initiatives make now the time for trainers and educators to align their activities to quality assurance standards. The Baldrige criteria and ISO 9000 Standards are excellent tools to accomplish such a transformation. An established quality assurance process will help trainers and educators ensure their training is effective and efficient. Additionally, trainees will view these programs as credible if they meet the same quality assurance standards that their own departments follow. Perhaps more importantly, training processes will have a firm foundation from which to gain management support. Because management understands the language and outcomes of the quality movement, a training process meeting ISO 9000 or Baldrige will be recognized as a valuable contributor to the strategic success of the entire organization.

ISO 9000 is not a panacea. Both the ISO process and the standards themselves have shortcomings. One shortcoming of the standards is that the process has no directly defined requirements for continuous improvement. However, an ISO guideline does address continuous improvement, and several elements in the current standard support continuous improvement programs.

Another problem occurs when a company attempts to meet ISO standards through a formula or cookbook approach or a purchased pre-packaged system. These shortcuts are a waste of time, money, and effort. The nature of quality assurance systems is that they must be designed, developed, and implemented by the employees who use them. It remains their responsibility to enact their quality process and adjust it to fit changing needs, improving it every day. People who live the system must own the system, being part of the creative process from the beginning. A consultant-generated system might look pretty, but too often it will sit unused on a shelf. More importantly, the ISO 9000 registrar will quickly recognize it for what it is and will not grant registration.

A significant challenge for companies using ISO standards is the requirement to establish written procedures and keep records. Unfortunately, some individuals like to "pencil-whip" a process and can turn ISO into a paperwork boondoggle. Registrars have reported that some fundamental problems experienced by companies seeking ISO registration are in documentation and record keeping. The secret to making ISO a valuable tool is to structure the paperwork carefully. The primary challenge is to Keep It Simple and Keep It Useful.

Finally, the process in the United States is relatively new. Countries in Europe and elsewhere have used ISO for many years and have quasi-governmental boards with broad representation from manufacturing and service industries, government agencies, nonprofit organizations, and educational bodies. In the U.S., additional work and time are needed to reach this level of integration and support.

CHAPTER 2

Background and History

Many manufacturing and service industries are discovering benefits from aligning their quality programs with either the ISO 9000 Standards or the Malcolm Baldrige National Quality Award Criteria. Perceived benefits for pursuing such a business strategy include improved competitive market position, quality products and services, and control over internal quality assurance processes. These standards and criteria help companies take a closer look at their operations and goals and lead to noticeable results in customer satisfaction, improved productivity, reduced waste, cost savings, and increased profitability.

The Malcolm Baldrige National Quality Award (MBNQA) has become a benchmark of world-class companies in the United States. Award winners have shown that quality management results in high quality products and services. In addition to MBNQA, the ISO 9000 Standards, accepted in more than 100 countries around the world, provide a practical way of focusing company activities to meet customer needs. Importantly, its global acceptance makes it a recognized signal both in the U.S. and abroad that the ISO

9000 registered company has focused its quality process to meet customer requirements.

This chapter provides some background information about both MBNQA and ISO, their application and purpose, their organization and administration, and some general information about registration and accreditation. The chapter is useful for trainers and educators looking for background information to decide which standard or criteria to adopt and for support arguments about the merits of using ISO standards or the MBNQA criteria in their organization.

The International Organization for Standardization (ISO)

More than 100 countries are members of the International Organization for Standardization (ISO), headquartered in Geneva, Switzerland. The American National Standards Institute (ANSI) is the U.S. member of ISO. ISO's basic mission is to provide manufacturing and performance standards for a variety of products and devices. The ISO 9000 series, comprised of three standards and several guidelines specifically focused on quality assurance processes, is one of several thousand standards published by ISO. Whereas other ISO standards are product specific, the ISO 9000 standards are generic and therefore can be used by a wide range of companies to help maintain an effective and efficient quality assurance system. ISO 9000 allows each company to build its own quality processes based on the ISO framework.

In the last five years or so, ISO 9000 has gained increasing acceptance in the United States for several reasons. ISO-registered companies are perceived by the marketplace as having a quality process in place and producing quality products and services. ISO 9000 is not a pie-in-the-sky, flavor-of-the-month approach to quality. Instead, it provides a focused and structured approach to organize a quality assurance program based on customer needs. The standards' simplicity provides a practical model to ensure that all employees and management understand what must be done to produce high quality products and provide high quality service based on customer requirements. Primary advantages of ISO are improved competitive market position, increased control over internal operations, and improved efficiencies. In addition, improved customer satisfaction as well as a reduction in both costs and waste are benefits of having an ISO system in place.

The ISO 9001 Standard contains 20 elements a company must address to become registered. The basic idea underlying the ISO standard is simple: SAY what you do, DO what you say, RECORD what you did, CHECK the results, and ACT on the difference. The assumption is if the company's quality process is functioning, they are producing a quality product.

The Malcolm Baldrige National Quality Award (MBNQA)

In 1987, Congress created the Baldrige Award to promote quality awareness and thereby help improve the U.S. economy. The award criteria are composed of seven criteria based on a series of values and concepts. Each criterion has an assigned number of points, and examiners score each criterion against three dimensions: how the company addresses a criterion, the extent to which the company meets all of the requirements in the criterion, and the company's success in achieving the purpose of the criterion.

The Baldrige Award is administered by the U.S. Department of Commerce through the National Institute of Standards and Technology (NIST). No more than six companies in three categories can win the award in one year. Award winners are seen as representing world class and best of class. In contrast, ISO is not an award. It is a standard for a quality assurance system. Any company meeting the standard can achieve registration.

Registration and Award Schemata

As with other registration and award processes, the credibility and authority for ISO 9000 registration or the Baldrige Award come from individuals or companies who subscribe to their philosophies. As ideas underlying these quality assurance programs gain acceptance and credibility, more companies gain confidence that the extent to which organizations reflect them represents a good measure of the subscribers' or members' credibility. So it becomes a self-perpetuating, circular process. The registrar or award gains credibility from those adopting its tenets, and its members gain acceptance and credibility from each other and by association with the registrar or award.

There are additional general similarities among registrations and award schemata:

- Registration or award schema are generally generic rather than specific. They establish criteria or standards, but do not give direction on how to meet their criteria.
- Different schemata contain different levels of detail concerning specific items that must be accomplished or achieved.
- Registration schemata usually subscribe to their own super-registration bodies, often called accreditation bodies. These accreditation bodies ensure that their member registrars are meeting a set of standards which allows them all to present themselves as competent registrars.
- Quality assurance registrars around the world often are recognized through a governing body established by their country's government. Usually these

governing bodies have wide representation from government, educational organizations, and industry groups and companies.

- Most companies who decide to implement an MBNQA or ISO quality assurance process find the process results in a major organizational transformation process.

- Many organizations adopt the standards or criteria without intending to apply for the Baldrige Award or ISO registration. They perceive the process as valuable in its own right as a way to improve their business results.

CHAPTER 3

Training and Quality Terms and Concepts

Many books have a glossary of terms in an appendix. This chapter presents terms in a more elaborate way than a glossary, establishing a framework of understanding necessary for meaningful discussions of the Baldrige criteria and ISO standards.

Practitioners have found as they transform their training organizations to meet either the criteria or standards that they engage continually in discussions concerning terms and their meanings. Change projects, process analyses, and procedure writing activities can be fraught with frustrations and misunderstandings which are essentially failures to define meanings carefully. Trainers need clear definitions and distinctions among terms, some of which are synonymous and others which seem synonymous but are not. Agreeing on specific definitions and using them carefully help build a foundation philosophy that in turn underpins a workable and focused process.

It is important for teams to consider and discuss these

terms and accept, adapt, change, or refine their definitions to their own organization. The point is that teams should make a specific effort to agree on definitions of terms. These agreements will be particularly helpful in designing training processes and writing procedures which explain them. It is useful to come back to this chapter from time to time in a quality assurance implementation project so use of the terms stays consistent. Additional information on terms appears in Chapter 37, which contains a discussion of ISO Guideline 8402, Vocabulary.

This chapter is organized in two sections: terms related to training and terms related to quality assurance. Terms are presented in a logical progression for understanding and readability, rather than alphabetically.

Terms Related to Training

STUDENT VS. TRAINEE

Individuals who attend academic institutions are *students*. They attend to become educated, and their emphasis is on theory and broad application. There is an implied element of delayed gratification, that if the student works hard in school, someday the effort will be rewarded.

Employees who attend work-related training programs are *trainees*. They attend to satisfy a specific job purpose, and the emphasis is on practical application rather than theory. There should be no element of delayed gratification; trainees expect to use newly gained knowledges and skills immediately upon returning to their jobs.

Additionally, the term *trainees* implies that these individuals are adults. Their role is not as a person subservient to a teacher who possesses information and bestows it to underlings. Trainees are customers, and they expect to gain an advantage from a training transaction. More importantly, trainers and trainees are equal participants in this transaction. Both have something to contribute to the process, and both are responsible for its success.

PROCESS VS. FUNCTION

The term *process* is used throughout this book because the terms *function, department,* or *organization* are too limiting. Something happens in a training process. The thing that happens—the process—is what is important. Further, these terms frequently refer to physical structures that may be static and bureaucratic. The term *process* recognizes that much learning happens throughout the organization, even when it is not part of a specific department or occurs in a non-traditional setting.

CONTENT TRAINING VS. PERFORMANCE TRAINING

Content training focuses on the transfer of knowledge to trainees. The typical school model used for content training attempts to educate trainees or help them learn how to think. *Performance training* helps trainees learn how to do something, a task or job. It focuses on skills, knowledges, and attitudes necessary to do a job. This learning is something trainees can use immediately at work.

SKILLS, KNOWLEDGES, AND ATTITUDES (SKAs)

These are three kinds of learning described by learning theory. The categories are called domains of learning. Using learning domains is important to instructional developers who must create learning interventions to help trainees do their jobs. Learning domains are particularly important when considering ISO 9001, Element 4.4, Design Control.

- *Skills,* or the psychomotor domain, refers to physical manipulation or use of the physical person or body to do something.
- *Knowledges,* or the cognitive domain, refers to mental processes.

16

■ *Attitudes,* or the affective domain, refers to values and beliefs individuals hold that guide their behavior.

Within each domain is a hierarchy of subcategories. For example, there are six levels in the cognitive domain, from simple understanding to highly refined judgment processes. There are several levels, from gross to fine psychomotor skills. Individuals hold various degrees of attitudes ranging from simply being aware and accepting a value to being committed to and willing to act upon the value.

Depending upon desired outcomes, an instructional developer selects strategies from the appropriate domain to design the lesson materials. For example, if the trainee must accurately read a meter or fine-tune a gauge, the trainer will use strategies to improve trainees' psychomotor skills. If safety precautions are a necessary part of a job, the developer must plan activities emphasizing the affective or attitudes domain. Other elements of the affective domain include courteous customer service, attention to safety precautions, appropriate team member behaviors, and willingness to follow established procedures.

Two notes are appropriate here. First, there is an "s" in knowledges, as there is an "s" in attitudes and skills, because instructional analysis will identify several different kinds and levels of knowledges an individual must master in order to perform a task. Second, sometimes the "A" in SKAs is incorrectly called abilities. There is no ability learning domain. Moreover, there is no distinction between a skill and an ability in terms of learning theory.

INSTRUCTIONAL SYSTEMS DESIGN (ISD)

ISD is a five-step training process. The steps are:
■ *Analysis:* decide what job skills the organization needs its employees to master in order for the organization to reach its strategic goals. Define which SKAs individuals need to do their jobs.

17

- *Design:* determine appropriate activities to help individuals acquire needed SKAs.
- *Develop:* produce whatever materials they need, i.e., lesson plans, job-aids, re-engineered work processes.
- *Deliver:* do it, teach it, make it happen.
- *Evaluate:* go back and make sure the process worked. Evaluate throughout each of the five steps.

The ISD five-step process is a road map to help trainers and an organized, structured way for them to succeed. The ISO Education and Training Guideline does not specifically require an ISD, but it does refer frequently to these five steps, and ISO requirements are easy to apply if trainers use an ISD model. Other instructional models also are available and can be adopted. The key is that training team members agree on whatever process they adopt.

SUBJECT MATTER EXPERT (SME)

An *SME* is an individual who is knowledgeable and skillful in a particular job or task. Usually these individuals have considerable experience with the company and are called upon frequently by their fellow workers to help figure out what to do or how to do it. They are usually not supervisors—although they might be—but they are often informal leaders. Training organizations do well to cultivate help and support from SMEs. These are the people who can help figure out what training is needed and how best to do a job. They can also enhance the credibility of training activities with their supervision and management.

PROGRAM, COURSE, LESSON

These three terms often overlap, and organizations can use them as they wish. For this book the following definitions serve:

- A *program* consists of several courses.

A program is an entire body of information that an

individual masters to become completely competent in one major set of tasks or job. For example, an Introductory Supervisor Program would prepare the individual to perform duties as a supervisor. An Electronic Technician Program might be designed to prepare the individual to become a journeyman electrician.

- A *course* consists of several lessons.

A course is a coherent body of skills, knowledges, and attitudes an individual must possess to perform major activities within a specific job. For example, a basic course on troubleshooting malfunctioning meters would fit within an Electronic Technician Program. A typical course would require several days, weeks, or months to complete.

- A *lesson* is a subset of a course.

Again, a lesson is a coherent body of skills, knowledges, and attitudes an individual must possess to perform a task or series of tasks within an activity. For example, how to wire a meter would be a lesson within an Electronic Technician Program. A lesson would require several hours or days to complete.

NEEDS ANALYSIS AND JOB-TASK ANALYSIS

The first step in the ISD process is to figure out what needs to be done. The analysis step allows organizations to decide if a training activity is an appropriate solution for a perceived job performance problem, and if so, what the training activity should achieve. There are two types of analyses: needs analysis and job-task analysis.

A *needs analysis* is done for a particular company or a particular individual. The needs analysis, or gap-analysis, is a comparison of what the individual currently knows or can do and what he or she needs to be able to do. On a department or company-wide basis, the needs analysis identifies the gap between available capability and needed capability. The needs analysis helps an organization through a change process because it shows where it currently is and where it needs to go to meet its goals.

A *job-task analysis* is a list of all tasks associated with a particular job. A *job* is a series of tasks a person does. A *task* is an activity with a start, a finish, and some steps in between. A *job-task analysis* is a list of all the skills, knowledges, and attitudes individuals must possess to complete tasks successfully. With a task analysis in hand, the developer can create activities, and structure and organize training.

Finally, a *wants analysis* is a wish list usually based on surveyed requests from individuals who believe a training program would be useful or interesting to them.

TEST-ITEM ANALYSIS

A *test-item analysis* is a statistical technique showing correlations between total scores achieved on examinations and scores achieved on particular questions or items. In theory, examination items are supposed to distinguish trainees who understand the material from those who do not. If there is a positive correlation, individuals who score highly on the examination will answer the question correctly. Those who do not understand the material will answer the question incorrectly.

A negative correlation would indicate that capable trainees missed the question and suggests the question is confusing, poorly written, or not adequately reflecting the objective. Also, a negative correlation might suggest a problem with instruction. That is, the material was not adequately presented so trainees are confused. An absence of correlation would also suggest the question is either confusing or the material was not adequately presented. Either a negative or no correlation is a signal that there is an opportunity for improvement somewhere in the training process.

FORMATIVE, SUMMATIVE, AND IMPACT EVALUATIONS

Trainers obtain these kinds of evaluations as part of

the ISD evaluation process. The ISO Education and Training Guideline introduction defines these three terms.

- *Formative* evaluation refers to any evaluation of trainees, trainers, or the instructional program while training is taking place. In the vernacular, formative evaluation is a pop-quiz for trainees or, for instructors, a drop-in assessment of instructor performance by a training supervisor.

- *Summative* evaluations are conducted at the conclusion of a training program. They are also known as final exams.

- *Impact* evaluation focuses on the value of training to trainees. Sometimes impact evaluation is referred to as transfer of training. The idea is to determine if employees have internalized learning and taken newly learned SKAs back and applied them in their work, i.e., transferred the learning from classroom to work. Trainers usually obtain impact evaluations through post-training surveys of trainees or interviews with their supervisors.

Terms Related to Quality Assurance

STANDARD, GUIDELINE, NOTE

A *standard* is a contractual or compliance document. A company is audited against and registered against a contractual standard. ISO 9001, 9002, and 9003 are compliance standards. A *guideline* gives readers some ideas and examples on specific topics that may help them apply a standard. ISO 9000-x and 9004-x are guidelines to help readers understand the 9001, 9002, and 9003 standards. In some standards notes are attached to various elements. These *notes*, like guidelines, provide additional information and are not auditable.

ELEMENT, CRITERIA, CLAUSE

ISO 9000 is composed of 20 *elements*, and the Baldrige

is composed of seven *criteria*. Using the terms carefully and consistently helps trainers distinguish between the two approaches. *Clauses* are sub-paragraphs within either an element or criteria. Training team procedure writers should strive to ensure consistent use of terms throughout their procedures.

SUPPLIER, CUSTOMER, SUBCONTRACTOR

There has been some confusion about these terms; however, the ISO 1994 version has standardized the language.

- The *supplier* is the company registered to the ISO 9000 standard.
- The *customer* is the entity that buys products or services from an ISO 9000 registered supplier.
- The *subcontractor* sells parts or services to suppliers who in turn incorporate those parts or service into finished products provided to customers.

SHALL, SHOULD, WILL, REQUIRES, SPECIFIES

Shall is a requirement. *Should* is a recommendation. Avoid the term *will* because it cannot be defined. Care should be taken using these three terms when writing procedures because auditors distinguish specifically among them. Auditors must assess performance against procedures. If the procedure says *shall*, then auditors expect to see every instance of the requirement performed. Unfortunately, a procedure writer cannot escape this trap by using only the term *should* because auditors will rightly judge the process as not sufficiently in control to meet the ISO 9000 standard. Careful understanding, definition, and use of these terms help avoid arguments and confusion in an audit evaluation.

Generally, the ISO standard is contract auditable and therefore *requires* certain actions. A guideline is not contract auditable. It provides insight into ways to address issues. The Z-1.11 is a guideline, so most discussion is couched in the term *specifies*. The reality is, however, that companies apply-

ing the Education and Training Guideline will need to
address these issues regardless of whether the guideline specifies or requires.

QUALITY CONTROL, QUALITY ASSURANCE

These frequently confused terms should be clearly
distinguished. *Quality Control* (Q.C.) is an inspection process
in which each item produced, or a sample of items, is
inspected. A key concept in Q.C. is that this process does not
address the root of problems. Q.C. only fixes problems after
they are discovered. Even the most thorough inspection,
even a 100% inspection, does not identify all errors. More
significantly perhaps, Q.C. is very expensive.

Quality Assurance (Q.A.) is not an inspection. Q.A.
looks at the processes used to control and produce products
or services and prevent errors. If a strong Q.A. system is in
place, errors are unlikely to occur. That confidence allows
companies to change their focus from inspections and to
focus on oversight to make sure processes remain under control.

AUDITOR/ASSESSOR AND EXAMINER/JUDGE

There is no difference between an auditor and an
assessor, although the term assessor sounds a little less
threatening than auditor. An *auditor* or an *assessor* is a qualified individual who conducts an audit. The individual's job is
to audit a quality system against a recognized standard.
According to the ISO Guideline 10011, auditors:

- Are familiar with the standard against which they
  conduct audits.
- Have quality auditing experience.
- Have relevant process (product or service) knowledge and experience.
- Can communicate effectively and interact successfully with auditees.

The Registrar Accreditation Board (RAB) has three

categories of assessors/auditors. They are:

- *Provisional Auditor:* This individual has completed an accredited auditor course but has minimal experience in quality auditing activities and is in a learning status under the direct control of a lead auditor. Once the individual obtains a specified number of days of auditing experience, he or she will be granted auditor status.

- *Auditor:* This individual has completed an accredited assessor course and has participated in an established number of audits.

- *Lead Auditor:* This individual is an experienced auditor who has participated in a number of audit days both as an auditor and as a team leader. The term *lead* is both a qualification level (training and experience) and a position description (leader of an audit team).

The Baldrige Board of Examiners evaluates award applications. Their categories are examiner, senior examiner, and judge. *Examiners* perform the same functions as ISO auditors. Their job is to assess the application of the quality system against the established standard. *Senior examiners* head teams of examiners to evaluate applications and, when appropriate, make site visits. They serve the same functions as the ISO lead auditor. *Judges* make the final determination of who will win the award.

Throughout this book the term *auditor* is used to refer to an individual who conducts ISO audits, *examiner* to an individual who evaluates Baldrige applications, and the term *assessor* to an individual who audits or evaluates training organizations. Further, the terms *assess* or *assessment* are used to refer to the process of auditing. Trainers do not need to adopt these conventions. They are used here as a matter of convenience. Nevertheless, trainers and procedure writers should adopt terms and use them consistently.

REGISTERED, ACCREDITED, CERTIFIED

According to ISO, a company's quality assurance process is *registered*, usually by a registrar who conducts third-party audits of quality assurance systems. An individual company is registered to an ISO 9000 Standard, listed in the list of registered companies published by the registrar, and then allowed to display a certificate of registration in its advertising, correspondence, and letterheads. A registration tells the customer (usually not the public or consumer, but another manufacturer or company) that the registered company's quality assurance system is in place.

Registrars are *accredited* by a accreditation body. The accreditation body accredits registrars to conduct audits, register companies, and issue certificates of registration.

Products are *certified*. That means they have been manufactured in accordance with some government or industry standard. The product certification is marked on the product itself and informs the final customer (usually the public) that the particular item has met a manufacturing criterion and will provide established performance. For example, a piece of SCUBA gear is certified to operate at a designated depth.

SYSTEMS AUDIT, COMPLIANCE AUDIT

A basic tenet of ISO registration is to Say What You Do, Do What You Say. The difference between systems and compliance audits reflects these two steps:

- A *systems audit* looks at documents to make sure systems and processes are established to meet the criteria. Usually a systems audit is a comparison between the quality manual or procedures and the standard.

- A *compliance audit* looks at application of procedures and work instructions. Usually auditors observe processes, interview personnel, and examine records to gain evidence employees are following company procedures.

REGISTRATION AUDIT, PRE-ASSESSMENT, SURVEILLANCE AUDITS

A *registration audit* is a formal audit conducted by an ISO registrar to register a company's quality assurance process. It is conducted in accordance with the ISO 10011 series guidelines and the registrar's accreditation body requirements. Registration audits are a combination of both systems (documentation) and compliance (application of procedures) audits. When a company passes a registration audit, it receives a certificate and registration number and is permitted to display the registrar's mark in its marketing and on its letterheads.

A *pre-assessment* is a mini-audit conducted before the registration audit. It is an opportunity for the registrar to visit the company and for both company and registrar to become comfortable that there are no major gaps in the quality assurance system. It is primarily a systems audit, focused on documentation, but also has some elements of a compliance audit. Passing a pre-assessment does not guarantee that a company will pass the registration audit. However, it is an opportunity to identify any major holes in the system.

Surveillance audits are mini-audits conducted, usually at six-month intervals, after the company has successfully registered its quality assurance system. These mini-audits are generally shorter, have fewer assessors on the team, and focus on only part of the quality assurance system. As a rule, the registrar will attempt to divide surveillances so the entire quality system is reviewed once every three years. As a matter of practice, registrars will look at prior non-conformances, management reviews, internal auditing, and corrective actions during every surveillance audit.

INTERNAL AUDITS, EXTERNAL AUDITS, EXTRINSIC AUDITS

There are three kinds of audits, each with several names.

26

- An *internal (first-party) audit* is something an organization does for itself.
- An *external (second-party) audit* is usually by a customer who audits his supplier.
- An *extrinsic (third-party) audit* is conducted by a disinterested third party such as an ISO registrar or MBNQA Award Team.

Two elements of the ISO standard require companies to conduct internal audits and perform corrective actions to ensure they are living up to their quality system. There is also a difference between assessment and compliance audits. The *compliance audit* is conducted under rigid procedure rules established by the registrar and ISO Guideline 10011. An *assessment audit* is an informal look to ensure the company has all its bases covered. Compliance and assessment audits can be internal, external, or extrinsic.

MAJOR AND MINOR AUDIT FINDING AND OBSERVATIONS

Typically auditors categorize findings into three types.

- *Major nonconformances* usually reflect a significant hole in a system. That is, an element is not addressed, and there is no process to address the issue. Major nonconformances frequently show up in a systems audit.
- A *minor nonconformance* usually means there is a procedure in place, but that for some reason, individuals are not following it. Frequently, a minor nonconformance will show up in a compliance audit. Note, however, that several minors nonconformances in different areas (not the same mistake repeated several times) may cause an auditor to consolidate them into a major nonconformance.
- The final category, an *observation*, has two purposes. First, an observation is a note from auditors to themselves to do some more investigation. Also, it

is an informal way for an experienced SME auditor to alert the company that it ought to look at something. Usually an observation is a warning of potential trouble. On subsequent visits, auditors will always follow up on previous observations.

OBJECTIVE EVIDENCE

Audits are, at best, a flawed activity. Auditors cannot look at everything, and, even if they could, without first-hand, daily experience in a process, they are hard-pressed to make judgments about processes. They must rely on comparing a procedure or standard with some physical record or evidence. Although no auditor can be completely sure the assessment is accurate, auditors look for a sample of objective evidence to support findings. Essentially, *objective evidence* is records, observations, or statements of fact that can be located or verified.

CHECKLIST

A *checklist* or auditors' guide helps auditors be organized and efficient during an audit. It is a road map or list of questions auditors are prepared to ask. Before the audit begins, auditors will review relevant procedures and standards and select items to include in the list. Generally, checklists are laid out in landscape format with several columns. The first column lists the procedure or standard number and paragraph from which the question is drawn. The second column is a list of questions, usually restating a requirement in question format. The next column provides space to record objective evidence. Remaining columns might include a check of yes/no that the item is in or not in conformance, an additional notes column, and finally a checkoff that they wrote and the Management Representative accepted a non-conformance.

QUALITY PLAN/QUALITY ACTIVITY

The *quality plan* is part of the project plan for an ongoing process. It identifies the stop points where a Q.A. activity needs to take place. The quality plan neither needs to be a separate document nor a complex undertaking. Rather, it identifies stop points where a quality activity is necessary to ensure the next step can be done. A *quality activity* is necessary whenever failure at a particular point would affect the next step. Some points do not require a stop or may have less rigorous inspections. The challenge in drawing a good quality plan is to identify all pertinent stop points while eliminating unnecessary ones. A quality activity may require compliance to regulations or standards and probably requires using test or measuring devices.

CHAPTER 4

How to Organize a Training Quality Project and Prepare for a Registration Audit or Award Visit

Organizing a Training Q-Project

Transforming a training organization to meet the Malcolm Baldrige National Quality Award Criteria or the ISO 9000 Standard is like starting on a long journey. There is high enthusiasm at the beginning, but time, inevitable difficulties, and roadblocks weaken resolve and slow progress. Trainers interested in transforming their processes to meet either the ISO 9000 Standards or Malcolm Baldrige National Quality Award Criteria will discover these are major change projects. Therefore, before undertaking such a major change project, they should focus on some basics that will help to sustain their work. Every successful project reflects at least four general characteristics:

- It is extremely well organized.
- It employs knowledgeable and committed participants.

■ Participants obtain needed information and support.

■ Participants are politically astute at publicizing their project's goals and outcomes to gain support.

An ISO 9000 or Baldrige Quality Training Project will need, as a minimum, these four characteristics. These dozen practical ideas reflect the four general characteristics that will help the training quality implementation team, or Q-Project Team, undertake a training quality implementation project.

GATHER COMMITTED AND KNOWLEDGEABLE PARTICIPANTS

Knowledgeable and committed members should come from every level and from every department within the organization. As part of building ownership in the training quality assurance program, participation from across the organization will give members an opportunity to work and create together. Besides developing understanding of each other's daily tasks and problems, this tactic helps members see each other as customers and thus to align tasks and outcomes to meet each other's needs. Most importantly, assignment to the Q-project should be formalized and time commitments established. Q-project members need authorized time away from their daily tasks to participate. This requires commitments of support from management and coworkers.

Each member of the Q-team will need his or her individual copy of the standard or criteria. As the team works through the implementation process, members will use them frequently. Single copies of the Baldrige criteria are available without charge from the National Institute of Standards and Technology (NIST), and multiple copies may be purchased from the American Society for Quality Control (ASQC). ISO 9000 Standards and guidelines are also available for purchase from the American Society for Quality Control.

RECRUIT TOP MANAGEMENT SUPPORT

A Training Quality Team (TQT) should oversee the entire project. Members of this team should represent the

31

organization's major line and administrative departments and should be relatively high in their department hierarchies. Their primary jobs are to knock down interdepartmental barriers, commit resources from their own areas, communicate Q-project objectives and accomplishments within their own areas, and support upper management's quality commitment.

CHOOSE A MANAGEMENT REPRESENTATIVE AND PROJECT LEADERS

ISO 9001 sub-paragraph 4.1.2.3 requires organizations to appoint a Management Representative (M.R.) to oversee the ISO 9000 process. The training manager may assume this role; however, in many organizations training managers must often be master political operatives focused on budget and resource issues. The M.R. job is primarily an administrative leadership role. Therefore, a good approach is to have a senior trainer assume this role, freeing the training manager to focus on strategies and tactics. Finally, behind every great project there is one unsung hero—the person who keeps every detail under control and the entire project on track. The Q-project needs a crackerjack administrative person empowered to push and pull to get tasks accomplished. Again, this job is not a full-time position, but ought to be filled by the best person available.

IDENTIFY AND TRAIN TEAM MEMBER SKAS

Q-team members should be knowledgeable about both team membership and quality, and they should be trained to support the project. Necessary team member SKAs include team dynamics, the ability to be a good team member, and meeting participation skills. These skills will help team members contribute to project objectives and be able to do group work and function as a team.

IDENTIFY AND TRAIN PROBLEM SOLVING SKAS

Quality project skills include problem investigation and solving tools such as flowcharting, Isakawa diagrams,

32

and root-cause analysis. This training does not need to be separate or come before the start of the Q-project. These quality topics can be introduced in short learning sessions as part of the ongoing project and meetings. The team should keep minutes of these meetings and take credit for this training as part of ISO 9001, Element 4.18, Training.

IDENTIFY AND TRAIN QUALITY SKAS

Q-project members should be trained in the ISO standards or Baldrige criteria, development of documentation, including work instructions and procedures, and internal auditing skills. An introduction to the ISO standards or Baldrige criteria—what they are all about and why the organization is pursuing the Q-project—needs to be presented throughout the organization.

TRAIN AN INTERNAL AUDITING GROUP

Depending on the size of the organization, one successful tactic is to train a few internal audit teams consisting of members from various departments. As soon as possible, these teams should develop an annual audit schedule and begin conducting internal audits. See Chapters 22 and 36 for more information.

APPLY TECHNOLOGY

Project management software helps develop a logical approach to the myriad of details and scheduling deadlines in any major project. It is nearly impossible to run a successful, large, multi-person, multi-layered Q-project without a good computerized project management program. Several good ones are on the market, and time invested in obtaining, learning, and setting up such software to organize the project will pay handsome dividends and save time and frustration. The software will force Q-teams to flowchart their own processes and develop steps and timelines to keep projects moving. It will also show the interrelationship and interdependence of individual members' contributions to the effort. Equally importantly, it is a communication medium to help all members understand their assignments and deadlines. Moreover, publishing schedules will help eliminate delays and show progress to management.

EMPLOY DOCUMENTATION FLYING SQUADS

A few documentation writing teams should be established. Organizations attempting to train everyone to write their own documentation will struggle and experience delays as individuals try to find time to write. A flying squad of procedure and work instruction writers can schedule time to go into an area and work with department members. In this team setting they can develop process flowcharts, identifying responsibilities and authorities, and gathering other needed information. An investment in flowcharting software will greatly aid this team. The flying squad can then work by itself with a standard template and quickly produce a useful procedure and pass it to responsible departments for approval. Because department members have worked with the writing team on the material, they should easily recognize their ownership in the accuracy and usefulness of the document. This approval process should be scheduled to take only a few days.

TAP EXTERNAL QUALITY SUPPORT

Connect into the quality literature and quality support organizations. Consider professional help, at least in the beginning. Seek out free help and sources to contribute to the Q-project. Membership in the American Society for Quality Control (ASQC) establishes a primary source for general information about ISO and Baldrige and the quality community. Membership will provide access to most resources and every mailing list connected to quality.

There are several consultants and professional associations that can, at a minimum, conduct a gap analysis for an

34

organization. A gap analysis is an excellent way to begin identifying tasks and structuring a Q-project. In a few days a consultant can assess the status of the quality assurance program and develop a list of improvements needed to achieve registration. Professional associations also offer lead assessor courses, ISO implementation, and internal auditing seminars. Reputable consultants and professional associations encourage their clients to limit expenditures on these services and to do as much work in-house as possible. They know that when organizations do most of their own work, they take ownership in their quality assurance program which in turn helps them create added value from their ISO or Baldrige project.

Free or low-cost information sources for Q-projects include local junior college business and industry outreach efforts. Several around the country sponsor ISO or Baldrige support groups. Members include businesses and industries working to set up an ISO or Baldrige project. These support groups conduct self-help meetings, invite speakers, conduct training, and share ideas. The members decide what they need to know and design meetings to provide information to their membership. An alternative is to establish an interest group within a local chapter of a professional training organization. Finally, it is possible for several trainers from individual companies to benchmark ideas and mutually support each other's ISO or Baldrige projects.

PUBLICIZE AND CREATE OWNERSHIP

Politically astute Q-project leaders employ several tactics to create ownership and publicize their goals and outcomes. Drawing Training Quality Team members, internal audit teams, and documentation flying squads from throughout the organization helps establish ownership. Posting Q-project flowcharts in conspicuous areas and publishing newsletters help keep progress visible and connect these efforts to all members in the organization. Additionally, sending participants individual schedules and task assignments, outputs from the project management computer program, and meeting and project minutes will help keep them informed and motivated, and just as important, help them remember and meet deadlines.

Keep Upper Management Informed

Short progress reports to upper management will help keep them and the team focused and on schedule. Project management software can produce timelines and milestones on one page and quickly and easily show progress to both the TQT and upper management. Concurrently, it can identify barriers and bottlenecks and, if necessary, identify resources, tactics, or motivation to break through and keep the project on schedule.

Preparing for an Audit or Award Visit

Preparing for a registration or an award visit requires several steps. First, learn the standards and thoughtfully evaluate them against corporate needs and strategies and decide if the standards will help the company reach its strategic goals. Trainers ought to evaluate the value of aligning their activities to the MBNQA criteria or ISO standards before beginning.

Second, organize a project team to conduct a self-evaluation. This requires evaluating the current situation against the standards and then organizing efforts to meet the standards. The initial analysis may take several weeks, and it is generally a good idea to allow 18 months to conduct a complete Q-project.

Third, find a registrar. Because companies establish long-term relationships with their registrars, they should do considerable basic investigatory work to find a registrar they and their customers will accept, one who has expertise in their product(s) and service(s), and whose philosophy and approach are consistent with their own.

Fourth, start a dialogue with the selected registrar. It is a good idea to ask the selected registrar to identify one individual to serve as a point-of-contact. This individual will be a source for information and an administrative coordinator to schedule the audit visit.

The last step is the audit or visit, which may take several days. There is usually a brief opening meeting during which everyone is introduced, welcome statements are made, and the company gives the audit team a brief orientation, including specific house rules such as safety or security arrangements. A room is reserved for the team to work in during their visit. Telephones, fax, office supplies, facility map, work surfaces, and chairs are provided in this room. The team also requires several guides to take members to various locations in the company so they can interview employees. The audit team's primary objective during the visit is to see routine, everyday operations. The best way for the team to do this is to observe operations and talk to employees. At the end of the visit there is usually a closing meeting to exchange thanks and resolve last minute administrative issues.

Before the audit or award team leaves, the team leader will put together a draft report and present it to the M.R. The formal report from the registrar will follow shortly afterward. Audit teams do not have authority to grant registration. Rather, team leaders assemble the information gathered by the team members into a final report and make a recommendation based on their findings. The registrar has a board that grants registration. The Baldrige team will write and submit a report that then goes to judges, who make the final award.

The final step is not final. Registration implies an ongoing requirement and relationship with the registrar.

Usually ISO registrars establish a three-year contract, during which they conduct visits to make sure the company's system continues to maintain the standards. Usually these mini-audits are done semiannually or quarterly and are short looks at only part of the system. Over the three-year period the registrar will have had an opportunity to review the entire system. Baldrige winners also find themselves involved in benchmarking activities and helping NIST and the Department of Commerce promote and support future award applicants.

Part Two

The ISO 9001 Standard and the Z-1.11, Education and Training Guideline

These chapters address each of the ISO 9000 elements, identify items an ISO auditor might look for, and provide practical ideas to facilitate ISO implementation.

CHAPTER 5

Introductory Material in the ISO 9001 Standard and the Z-1.11, Education and Training Guideline

This chapter contains an overview of the introductory material to the ISO 9001 Standard and the Z-1.11, Education and Training Guideline. Because the clearly presented material in both requires little interpretation, the discussion in this chapter moves quickly to develop a framework for examining the 20 ISO 9001 elements. The purpose of this chapter is to present a model showing how the 20 elements support each other and how users can interpret them.

Introduction to ISO 9001

This ISO 9001 Standard is the most comprehensive of the three international standards. It contains 20 elements for quality assurance in "design, development, production, installation and servicing." The original purpose of the standards was to harmonize quality assurance standards throughout the European Community member-nations as they prepared to cooperate as the European Union. They were intended to give suppliers a way to assure customers that their quality system would enable them to meet a buyer's contract requirements. The assumption underlying the standards is that if a well-designed quality assurance system is functioning, then the product or service will conform to contract requirements.

The introduction to the 9001 standard makes a strong argument against seeing the standards as a way to enforce uniformity among quality assurance systems. The 20 criteria are generic, so any organization can tailor and apply them to its quality assurance process. The generic nature of the standard has both positive and negative results. It recognizes there are important differences among organizations. On the other hand, new users often complain the standards are so general that they do not provide sufficient guidance. In the end, organizations must address each of the 20 elements and structure their quality assurance processes individually. The standards identify issues to address. Each organization must respond to the issues in ways that meet its own particular needs.

Finally, the introduction provides some flexibility. It says companies may tailor standards by adding or deleting individual requirements. This means an organization may choose not to address a particular element. Companies should use caution, however, when electing not to address a particular element since auditors will usually challenge the line of reasoning used to reach such a decision. Industries also may add elements to the standards, as the automotive and chemical industries have done. For example, U.S. auto makers have published their QS-9000 which contains the ISO standard plus several requirements directly supporting automotive manufacturing quality assurance needs.

Besides giving suppliers and customers a shared basis against which to assess quality assurance processes, the ISO standard is being used in other ways as well. Many organizations which do not intend to seek ISO registration use the standard as a foundation for structuring their quality assurance systems. Other companies are using the Malcolm Baldrige National Quality Award criteria as an in-house quality program.

Introduction to Z-1.11, Education and Training Guideline

The guideline, like the standard, represents a generic set of quality assurance elements. There is no attempt to describe best practices. Each organization must consider its own needs. The introduction identifies five principles for applying the standard to training and education. The five principles paraphrased here are recurring themes throughout the guideline.

- Successful training programs require more than good curricula and good trainers. Well-organized training processes are evidence of efforts that contribute to the organization's success.
- Each company must structure its own quality assurance process within its unique constraints. The ISO Guideline provides underlying principles of quality assurance. There is no one or right way to do ISO.
- The best quality assurance system is the simplest one that works well. A frequently heard complaint is ISO is too complex or relies too much on written procedures. Although its implementation can be complex, it is important to remember that well-defined processes are simple. Useful procedures are short.
- There are two separate results or products in a training interaction. One product is training materials and systems used to design and deliver the

instruction. The second product represents an outcome, the changes in trainees and organizations resulting from training.

■ Training and educational institutions must conduct ongoing internal quality audits, just like manufacturing and service organizations. Audits verify that training is achieving its objectives and providing high quality, effective, and efficient training to support trainees' job needs.

The 20 Elements

The 20 brief and generic elements take up just nine pages in the standard. However, volumes (including this book) have been written in an attempt to explain and interpret them. One way to look at the 20 elements is to visualize them as a three-level pyramid comprised of strategies, tactics, and operations. Each of the 20 ISO elements can be assigned to one of the three levels in the pyramid. While Q-Project Team members may elect to adopt or adapt this categorization scheme, the basic approach provides a useful overview of how the 20 elements fit together in each of the categories:

Strategy: The big picture, the overall goals, and mission; why the organization is in business; and what its members hope to accomplish.

Tactics: Policies and practices across many departments or activities, including the internal structure supporting these activities.

Operations: The day-to-day steps and processes used to accomplish the work.

Strategy Level Elements

4.1 MANAGEMENT RESPONSIBILITY

Management provides the overall vision and direction

44

for the organization. Any quality assurance system will fail if there is inadequate strategic commitment from top management.

4.2 QUALITY SYSTEM

A quality system is a pervasive connecting thread or theme in an organization. The quality system directly affects all of the organization and influences its success in achieving its mission.

4.14 CORRECTIVE AND PREVENTIVE ACTION

This element could fit into the tactics category. However, corrective and preventive action is so critical to an organization's quality assurance success that it should be a strategic issue. Many auditors will argue the proof of a successful quality assurance system is in management's handling of its corrective and preventive action program.

4.18 TRAINING

Including this element in the strategy category reflects my conviction that effective and efficient training is critical to an organization's strategic success. I hope readers of this book agree.

Tactical Level Elements

Tactical elements permeate the organization, influencing several departments or functions at the same time. They are connecting points between functions. Each organization may structure and adjust this list to its own needs. Elements related to tactics include:

4.4	Design Control
4.5	Document and Data Control
4.9	Process Control
4.16	Control of Quality Records
4.17	Internal Quality Audits
4.20	Statistical Techniques.

Operations Level Elements

The remaining elements fall into the operations category. These elements are day-to-day processes and operations performed by the various individuals, departments, and work groups to produce and deliver products or services.

Alternative Structures

Besides the pyramid, there are several other ways to visualize the interwoven nature of the relationships among the 20 elements.

ELEMENTS 4.1 AND 4.2: MANAGEMENT RESPONSIBILITY AND QUALITY SYSTEM

The relationship between management responsibility and the success and effectiveness of its quality system is fundamental. An effective quality system cannot be started or sustained without management involvement and support.

ELEMENTS 4.14 AND 4.17: CORRECTIVE AND PREVENTIVE ACTION AND INTERNAL QUALITY AUDITS

The corrective and preventive action element is often associated with internal quality audits. Audits result in nonconformance reports, and corrective action fixes the problems. Some organizations see these two functions as mutually supporting. In contrast, some organizations have created a firewall between the two elements either to prevent quality personnel from becoming involved in operational decisions or to prevent line personnel from relying on quality organizations to fix problems. There are valid arguments for both approaches.

ELEMENTS 4.5 AND 4.16: DOCUMENT AND DATA CONTROL AND CONTROL OF QUALITY RECORDS

Document and Data Control and Control of Quality Records fit together naturally since the outcomes of documents and data are quality records. Organizations should ensure these two procedures are mutually supporting.

ELEMENTS 4.3 AND 4.6: CONTRACT REVIEW AND PURCHASING

Contract Review and Purchasing essentially ask the same questions. In one, ISO evaluates the supplier's relationship to its customers, in the other the supplier's relationship with its subcontractors. The two primary questions are: do the parties understand what the other needs and do they have the capability to meet the needs?

ELEMENTS 4.10, 4.11, 4.12, AND 4.13: INSPECTIONS

Inspection is a major tool of any quality control process and quality assurance process. These elements therefore fit together logically: Inspection and Testing; Control of Inspection, Measuring and Test Equipment; Inspection and Test Status; and Control of Nonconforming Product. It is also possible to include 4.7, Control of Customer-Supplied Product, and 4.8, Product Identification and Traceability, in this category.

ELEMENTS 4.4. AND 4.9: DESIGN CONTROL AND PROCESS CONTROL

Design Control and Process Control each are logical outcomes of the other. One advantage of the ISO standard is that it forces the marketing department, engineers, and production staff to establish strong communication links and to treat each other as internal customers based on these connections.

Reality Check

Although the ISO guidelines at first may appear disjointed, there is an interrelated and mutually supporting structure to the elements. The pyramid structure and alternative structures presented in this chapter are two ways to look at the elements. Trainers need to see the elements as a coherent whole. Q-Project Team members must work hard to ensure their procedures and processes are connected, are not contradictory, and adequately meet the ISO requirements.

A final note is in order about the differences among the ISO standards, especially as they apply to training and education institutions. ISO 9001 is the most comprehensive and complex of the three (ISO 9001, 9002, and 9003) contractual standards. Standards 9001 and 9002 are similar; in the new 1994 version, the only difference between them is Element 4.4, Design Control. Although few training organizations in the U.S. have registered their programs against the ISO 9000 series, many training organizations in Great Britain have registered against the 9002 standard. Training and education institutions electing to structure and evaluate their training programs under ISO 9002 should skip the discussion of Design Control in Chapter 9.

Training and education organizations that design their own materials and activities should consider using ISO 9001 because Element 4.4 provides a structure for a design process. If the in-house training staff revises purchased materials or develops materials in-house, then ISO 9001 is probably the better choice. Organizations that either contract with consultants to provide training or buy off-the-shelf materials for presentation might consider using ISO 9002.

ISO 9000 is a guideline on how to select from among and use the three contractual standards. It is important to remember, however, that it is a guideline and therefore open to interpretation. Nothing requires organizations to select a particular standard. Some organizations with significant research and development, engineering, and/or other design functions elect to use ISO 9002. Their rationale is that their certificate specifies the scope of their organization's registration. Organizations that contract with ISO-registered companies should understand these differences. Registration to ISO 9002 simply means the organization's design function is not included in their registration.

CHAPTER 6

Element 4.1

Management Responsibility

There are wizards in every organization—management folks on the fast track, the rising stars of the organization. They are wizards because they see opportunities rather than problems, and they get things done. They believe in their coworkers and trust them to help move the organization toward its objectives. Importantly, they generally appreciate the need for employee development and training.

Wizards are not magicians, however. They need help from trainers to support their efforts. Training must succeed and show value in return for resources spent. The relationship is reciprocal; in return, wizards will support training because it helps them move the organization forward. Devising a structured, controlled training process according to the ISO 9001 Standard and Education and Training Guideline gives trainers a basis for achieving and demonstrating positive results to support the organization's wizards.

Progressive, highly competitive and successful companies promote their wizards to executive management positions. These executives understand the value of ISO 9000 and quality assurance. Element 4.1, Management Responsibility, establishes requirements for management to support an ISO quality assurance program, provide vision and leadership, and break down barriers to success. It helps managers understand their role in a quality assurance program.

What the ISO 9001 Standard Says

This element lays down two basic management responsibilities.

- First, management must define and document the company's *quality policy* to meet the organization's specific needs. The quality policy has two parts: objectives and commitment. Objectives reflect the organization's goals in terms of customers' needs and expectations. Management proves commitment by providing oversight of quality programs and resources to support them.

- Second, as part of commitment, management must ensure everyone in the organization understands the quality policy and actively follows it. This reflects ISO's basic tenet: Say What You Do, Do What You Say.

A foundation concept in quality management is that every employee contributes to the quality program because every job affects quality. Although ISO does not use the term *employee empowerment*, this element clearly specifies that employees whose work affects quality should be empowered to take actions, identify and prevent quality problems, and find solutions and fix problems. If every job affects quality, then the element language referring to those "who manage, perform and verify work affecting quality" essentially means all employees.

The element requires executive management to

appoint a Management Representative (M.R.) who has responsibility to establish, implement, and maintain the ISO quality assurance program. The M.R. does not need to be a full-time position. However, this person must have a direct reporting link to executive management. To be credible and effective, the M.R. must be relatively high in the company hierarchy. The management representative provides information to executive managers, who in turn routinely review quality results. Management uses this information link and these reviews to determine whether their quality assurance process is effective and whether it is continuing to meet the company's stated quality policy and objectives. Simple bean counting will not satisfy this requirement. Managers must assess trends and progress toward achieving goals. Managers also must ask: "Does the quality assurance system itself meet the company's needs?"

What ISO Auditors Look For

Auditors know a quality system will fail without top management support. When auditors want to know if the company truly believes in and supports its quality assurance system, they will look at the company's Corrective and Preventive Action Process (Element 4.14) and Management Responsibility (4.1). Element 4.1 is so critical to quality assurance success that a nonconformance written against it is usually considered a major nonconformance.

To evaluate Management Responsibility, auditors will interview both top management and the Management Representative to assess the communication link between the two. Auditors will look at the quality manual and evaluate the quality policy and its objectives. In addition, auditors will review records, usually meeting minutes or M.R. reports, of management reviews of the quality assurance program. These reports must show management is working to assess "suitability and effectiveness in satisfying the requirements of this International Standard and the supplier's stated quality policy and objectives." Auditors are looking for more than a summary of facts and figures. They should have evidence that management is conducting trend analyses and using statistical tools to predict and make sure they are on the right track to reach their objectives and goals. For this reason, quality goals should be written in measurable terms. Management also should monitor the Q.A. system's costs as part of their analyses.

Auditors do not limit their assessment of this element to talking only with top management. A favorite auditor tactic is to find and interview employees far down the corporate hierarchy, such as an average worker on the shop floor or a first-level administrator. A very telling question they often ask is: "Tell me what the corporate quality policy is, and what specific, practical things you do in your job to support the quality policy?" Some companies believe it is enough to conspicuously post the policy and give employees copies on wallet cards to memorize. However, it is important to note that the element says the quality policy will be "understood, implemented and maintained at all levels of the organization." Therefore, auditors will seek to learn if the quality policy has meaning in employees' everyday work lives or if it is just lip-service.

What the Education and Training Guideline Says

Besides reflecting the standard, this element begins to establish a need to structure training to analyze, design, develop, deliver, and evaluate training. The guideline repeats the standard by saying:

- The training quality policy should be consistent with and support corporate quality policy.
- All members of the training organization con-

52

tribute to training quality. They should understand how their jobs contribute to and affect training success.

■ Training organization members should be empowered to identify and fix problems and potential problems.

■ One person, a management representative, should provide advice to management and ensure the training quality policy meets the Education and Training Guideline on an ongoing basis.

■ Management should review the effectiveness of the training quality system and instructional and support systems to assure they satisfy customers' needs and requirements.

■ Records of these reviews should be kept.

The guideline, like the standard, talks about resources. However, the guideline expands and focuses the discussion to begin to tie in verification and assessment activities. In this element, and throughout the guideline, there is a consistent thread and emphasis on assessment of results and review of training outcomes.

What Training Assessors Look For

The training assessor has the same concerns and would employ the same tactics as the ISO auditor to assess this element. The assessor wants to know:

■ There is a training quality policy in place and members of the training organization base their daily work activities on it.

■ The training organization has its own quality objectives, and all members help to reach those objectives.

■ Top-level management supports the training quality policy and provides necessary resources.

- Top managers and trainers routinely and consistently focus on reviewing the effectiveness of training results and outcomes.

Because training is a function within the organization and the training quality policy is a subset of the organization's quality policy, assessors would expect to see a direct link between corporate policy and training policy. This link should include close communication between the corporate management representative and the training management representative.

Q-Project Action Items

FIND THE WIZARDS

Find and court the company wizards. These rising stars need trainers' support. Establish formal and informal liaisons with these individuals and decide how best to help them. The wizards will lead to all the people in the organization for whom quality makes sense. The Q-Project Team wants to create a critical mass of interested individuals to help encourage and sustain the project. The payback is enormous.

TIE INTO QUALITY POLICY

Write a training organization quality policy supporting the corporate quality policy. Develop training quality objectives directly tied into and supporting corporate quality objectives. Get management's agreement on both. Post policy and objectives conspicuously in training office areas, classrooms, and meeting rooms. Keep the objectives visible and find daily ways to live up to them.

TIE INTO M.R. REPORTS

Ensure training topics are included in the corporate Management Representative's reports. Establish routine and frequent communication with the corporate M.R. and find ways for the training organization to support the M.R.'s effort.

USE TQTs

Establish a Training Quality Team (TQT) consisting of as many department heads as possible. Include the corporate M.R. The TQT should serve as an advisory group to the training organization and help them tie training to corporate strategic plans. The TQT is particularly useful for obtaining funds and recommending how resources will be spent on training.

IDENTIFY MEASURABLE OUTCOMES

Find measurable ways to display training outcomes. Wizards need ammunition. Trainers must find measurable ways to show value for training resources. It isn't enough to simply report numbers such as total days in training or total numbers of trainees. That is bean counting and an easy trap to fall into. Find ways to show trends and establish a routine, simple way to sell effective results. Chapter 25, Statistical Techniques, contains more details on this topic. Managers find a few charts on a one-page report more useful than a 25-page narrative.

Reality Check

Trainers are sometimes frustrated because they think management does not value their efforts to contribute to corporate strategic goals. Regrettably, like quality, training receives only lip-service in some organizations. It is important to remember that managers are not training experts. They do not understand the jargon or process necessary to design, develop, deliver, and evaluate a good training program. They should not be expected to—that is the trainer's job.

Management will appreciate training's contribution

when trainers finds ways to demonstrate their contributions. It is important for trainers to know and support management's overall objectives. A successful training organization knows and courts company wizards, finds ways to support their activities, and involves them in the training process. The rewards for such a strategy can be as simple as trainers keeping their jobs and as wide-reaching as keeping their companies competitive and in business.

CHAPTER 7

Element 4.2

Quality System

Models are representations or ways to think about how to organize a process. ISO 9000 is a model for a quality system; its parts include the 20 elements in the standard, the introductory materials, and supporting guidelines that help interpret the elements. Another model, Instructional Systems Design, or ISD, is a five-step process to analyze, design, develop, deliver, and evaluate training. At least two members, including the chair, of the writing group for the Education and Training Guideline have instructional systems backgrounds. Throughout the guideline, and in this element in particular, the influence of instructional design methodology is evident.

ISD, one of several instructional models, became popular in military settings and has been adopted in various technical settings including airlines, utilities, and apprenticeship programs. The idea is that if the training process is organized within such a model, then it is possible to have a structured process in which all participants understand what must be done. Essentially, the model brings order to the process. In fact, the guideline provides a flowchart for an ISD-like model.

What the ISO 9001 Standard Says

This element, very simply, says that a quality model or process must be in place to make sure the company can provide products which meet customer requirements. Companies planning to become registered to ISO must produce a *quality manual* explaining how they address each element in the standard. The manual must be tied directly to the company's procedures showing application of the quality process.

Besides a quality manual, the company needs to develop *procedures* explaining how they support the company's quality assurance needs while complying with each element in the ISO standard. These procedures need to tell how each of the 20 ISO quality elements is used routinely in the company. A strong caveat here is that companies should write as few procedures as possible and make them useful by keeping them as simple as possible. The standard says "the range and detail of the procedures . . . shall be dependent upon the complexity of the work, the methods used, and the skills and training needed by personnel involved in carrying out the activity." So companies should think carefully about what procedures are appropriate. Additional information on procedures is available in Chapter 10.

Besides procedures, the company must have a *quality plan.* The idea behind a quality plan is simple: it identifies routine stop points throughout processes to check that all requirements are being met. Quality plans should not dictate how the company goes about doing its business. Rather, plans should reflect the quality system and be formatted according to the company's own way of doing business. The element lists eight items for companies to consider when devising quality plans. The challenge in drawing a good quality plan is to identify all pertinent stop points while eliminating unnecessary ones. In simple terms, this element asks the company to "Say What You Do, Do What You Say."

What ISO Auditors Look For

Auditors will conduct a systems audit of the quality manual to confirm that each element in the standard is covered in the manual. Some companies go as far as using the ISO numbering system to format their quality manual. This is useful but not required. Providing a matrix of ISO elements to topics in the manual is helpful so auditors can find where and how an element is covered. Auditors will also appreciate, and the company should consider devising, a matrix of quality procedures to ISO elements in their quality manual. Procedures in turn should list related work instructions.

Auditors also will conduct a compliance audit of the quality plans. That is, auditors will review quality plans while assessing all elements during an audit and look to see if the company is following the procedures and quality plans it has established.

An important warning: When auditors write a nonconformance against this paragraph, it means the company has failed to address one or more of the elements in the ISO 9000 Standard, or if they have put procedures in place, personnel are routinely ignoring them. Either way, an NCR against Element 4.2 is usually a major nonconformance.

What the Education and Training Guideline Says

The guideline element mirrors the standard element. It requires organized quality processes for training activities that include all individuals involved in the training processes and procedures and a quality manual which controls these processes. The guideline then specifies that control of quality can be exercised in a six-step ISD quality training model:

- *Instructional needs assessment:* analysis of what training is needed and how best to meet those needs.
- *Instructional design:* selecting instructional strategies and training activities to structure needed information for delivery to trainees.
- *Instructional development:* writing and producing all training materials, including lesson plans and their objectives, performance tests, job aids, and instructional aids such as overhead transparencies.
- *Delivery of instruction:* transmitting information to trainees through job talks, classroom instruction, on-the-job training, and all other delivery strategies, including such approaches as computer-based instruction.
- *Operation of:* libraries, workshops, and laboratories to support training.
- *Evaluation:* evaluating success trainees have in learning materials plus evaluation of training, including trainers and lesson materials.

Finally, the element, like the standard, calls for quality planning and refers users to the standard. This is the first of several places in the guideline that refers directly back to the standard.

What Training Assessors Look For

In addition to the items looked at by ISO auditors:

- Assessors will look for a training quality manual supporting the corporate quality manual as well as all elements in the ISO standard and guideline.
- Although not specifically required, the assessor will expect to see an ISD-like model around which the instructional process has been organized. The

guideline lists a five-step process. Assessors will expect to see each step addressed.

■ While assessing all other elements, the auditor will regularly refer to this element to ensure the training quality process is a coherent structure supporting instruction to meet corporate needs.

Q-Project Action Items

WRITE A Q-MANUAL AND PROCEDURES

Trainers need to decide how they are going to get their procedure writing process under control and what procedures they need. The standard refers to ISO Guideline 10013 for help on how to design a quality manual. Many books also are available on this topic. Additionally, several computer programs are available to help procedure writers meet the requirement. Also, Chapter 10, Document and Data Control, has more on this topic.

USE AN ISD MODEL

Make use of the flowchart "Design of Instruction Within a Quality System" in the guideline. It is a modified ISD model and can be tailored to meet the training organization's needs. Chapter 9 on Design Control contains more information about this flowchart.

AVOID COMPLEXITY

Training organizations and their companies are more efficient and flexible when they adopt strategies to reduce the number and detail of required procedures. Personnel skill and training are inversely proportional to the number and complexity of procedures. That is, better trained and knowledgeable employees need fewer and less detailed procedures. Availability of work instructions and job aids reduces the need for formal training because individuals have the information nearby, on the job, when they need it.

Do Not Paraphrase the Standard

Avoid the temptation to paraphrase the ISO guideline when writing the quality manual. The Q-manual should present the overall training policy and how it complies with the standard and supports the company's vision. It should serve as a foundation to describe training processes and explain how procedures fit together to support a quality training process. There is more detail on this in Chapter 10 on Document and Data Control.

Commit to ISO

Put a general statement in the quality manual that commits the training organization to follow any changes in the international standards or guidelines and that the Q-manual and procedures will be updated to reflect these changes.

Reality Check

The only thing management and employees see is the actual training being conducted. They have no reason to be interested in processes necessary to produce high quality training activities. That is the trainers' job. Regrettably, in the rush to do training there frequently is little time to worry about an ISD process; the analysis and evaluation steps particularly may get short shrift. ISO does not require an ISD process, but it does require training processes to be well structured and clearly supporting the corporate strategic mission. Several elements in the guideline refer to analysis, design, development, delivery, and evaluation. Although the guideline does not term these steps ISD, they are an ISD model. In the end, the training organization, like the company, must "Say What You Do, Do What You Say." An ISD model is one appropriate way to structure an in-control, effective, and efficient training process that "Says What You Do."

The training organization's *Q-Manual* is a very powerful marketing tool. It tells management and employees how training supports the company's strategic goals. In addition, it serves to help justify resources spent on training.

CHAPTER 8

Element 4.3

Contract Review

A contract is an agreement between two or more parties. Each party in a business transaction has expectations of the others. Typically, one party will provide a service or produce a product in return for compensation, reward, or action from the other party. Usually the agreement is written, but sometimes it remains verbal. In either case, each party may have poorly understood or unexpressed expectations. Applying principles of contract review to routine training processes may help eliminate some poor communication and misunderstandings.

Three contracts are inferred in any training transaction.

■ First, trainees expect training will help them. In most situations, trainees need to obtain something from training to help them improve their job performance.

■ Second, the trainer has expectations both for financial reward (a salary) and personal satisfaction when trainees succeed. Also, as a payoff for good, effective training, trainers expect both trainees and management to see them as credible and competent.

■ Third, management has a set of expectations. Management expects some payback, some positive exchange, for resources spent on training. The training department budget, including salaries of both trainers and trainees, is one portion of these costs. Another is the less obvious cost of employee time while they are away from work to attend training. Expected paybacks might include improved employee productivity, improved processes, reduced costs and waste, improved safety, or a better operating record. Because management deals with measurable outcomes in most aspects of their jobs, they readily understand and are drawn to measurable outcomes. A good contract review process will help provide measurable results and establish a clear understanding of expectations among management, trainers, and trainees.

The primary tangible elements in a training contract are program descriptions and course and lesson objectives. Clear and thoughtful course descriptions and objectives are the foundation of a well-defined contract between trainers and management and between trainers and trainees. Such documents can improve communication and satisfaction by clarifying unexpressed or assumed expectations.

What the ISO 9001 Standard Says

This element is concerned with practical aspects of contractual relationships between suppliers and customers. This relationship affects several departments: marketing wants to obtain orders for products or services; and operations and engineering departments are concerned with physical properties of products, that is, how to produce the product. Usually purchasing and legal departments are concerned with factual and legal aspects of contracts. Management wants to make a profit on the transaction. The purpose of this element is to help the organization address these concerns. A well-designed and efficient contract review process helps all parties understand the others' expectations. Here is what the element requires:

- Besides a procedure to control contract review, ISO requires proof (records) the review has taken place.
- Suppliers must ensure they have the capacity and capability to satisfy the contract, that is, the supplier organization has the necessary resources to do the job.
- There must be a process to resolve any difference between what customers require and what a supplier delivers. It asks the supplier to verify that customers get what they expect.

The unspoken requirement in this element is that the supplier must attempt to find out what the customer wants, needs, and expects. The connection between this effort and customer satisfaction is direct. In a simple transaction the supplier may only verify that the desired item is in stock and can be shipped. In more complex situations, such as when original engineering designs and manufacturing specifications are the products, understanding customers' needs may be a long and arduous process requiring significant resources throughout the planning stages.

There is an additional note in this element that encourages the organization to establish communication and interfaces with the customer's organization. These links should be structured and formalized to discuss contract matters and ensure mutual understanding.

What ISO Auditors Look For

Auditors would expect to see a contract review procedure. This procedure might include a flowchart showing the contract review and approval steps. The procedure should describe how to conduct a review and identify who is responsible for conducting it. The procedure should specify whether responsible individual(s) both conduct the review and approve the contract. Several departments might be involved in a contract review. For example, the operations department would ensure that resources are available to produce the product when needed, and the legal department would make sure that the organization does not create liabilities because of wording in the contract.

An important part of the contract review procedure is an explanation of how the organization understands its customer's needs. Steps required to identify and meet customer needs should be listed in the procedure. Thus, in complex situations, the procedure would describe such things as how the organization holds meetings to resolve and record issues, draws detailed specifications, conducts product tests, and devises acceptance points to ensure that the final product meets customer needs.

Review documentation might be as simple as an approval signature (or series of signatures) on a cover sheet included on the contract. Other documentation might include monthly reports to management describing contracts and identifying who conducted reviews. If this requirement is written into the contract review procedure, it is a good idea to avoid creating additional management reports. Contract review statistics can be a one- or two-line addition to an existing monthly operations report.

What the Education and Training Guideline Says

The guideline equates training proposals to purchase

contracts. A training proposal (purchase order) is a request made to the training organization by a department or group within the organization. The guideline discusses a variety of transactions between trainees (customers) and trainers (suppliers) beginning with a need for written descriptions of training programs, including administrative details such as credits offered and diplomas awarded. The supplier, the training organization in this case, should review contracts at the proposal stage. The guideline implies that the training department should make sure it is able to meet customers' needs.

The element also says proposals should be reviewed annually to make sure requirements still are being met. The element does not suggest who should do this review. However, both training management and corporate management should probably conduct this adequacy review. The training guideline is similar to the standard in saying there should be a way to resolve differences between proposals and training offered. Changes between proposal or request and product delivered must be mutually agreed to by the supplier (the training organization) and the customer (the group who requested the training), and that agreement must be recorded. An easy and effective way to generate such a record is to include the agreement in meeting minutes.

The guideline implies that trainers should have a method to find out if trainee needs are understood and met. Trainers ensure this through needs assessment and job-task analysis. A job-task analysis is usually conducted as part of an Instructional Systems Design (ISD) model. Although the guideline does not require organizations to use ISD, an organization that uses it or an alternative model is well positioned to satisfy the guideline requirements. One good contract review strategy is to structure needs analysis as part of the ISO Contract Review process, then document and structure the job-task analysis as part of Design Control, Element 4.4. This strategy would cleanly distinguish the two and eliminate redundancy caused by talking about both needs analysis and job-task analysis in each procedure.

A final note: the guideline refers to both written and oral and also actual and implied contractual obligations. The guideline recognizes there are often unspoken and frequently unspecified expectations on both sides of the training equation. Expectations exist between trainer and trainee, between trainee and management, and between trainer and management. This element helps trainers address these expectations in an orderly contract review process. As a result, each party in the contract will have a clear understanding of desired training outcomes. Understanding and agreement lead to satisfied trainers, trainees, and management.

What Training Assessors Look For

In addition to the items ISO auditors look at, training assessors would expect to find the following:

- A training procedure must describe how requests for training and proposal review processes work, and there should be documented evidence that required reviews have taken place.
- There must be a way to show that trainers have established ways to help them understand customer's needs (perhaps a needs analysis) and that the training process meets identified needs (usually a post-training evaluation).
- The training organization must show it has expertise and resources to satisfy trainee needs and prove they can do the job.

Q-Project Action Items

Do Needs Assessment

A procedure should specify that a needs assessment will be conducted as part of the contract review process before the training organization accepts a training assignment. Trainers and the requestor should conduct needs assessment together to clearly identify desired job performance. Needs assessment should identify differences between desired performance and what jobholders can do currently. As a first step, this needs analysis will force the customer, in this case management, to clearly define their needs. The needs assessment will also serve as a foundation for a job-task analysis. Job-task analyses are conducted as part of the design stage to identify skills, knowledges, and attitudes (SKAs) job incumbents must have to do their work.

A needs assessment gives trainers a real advantage. Sometimes customers request training to correct a problem or satisfy a need that cannot be met by training. For example, employees cannot do a job successfully if organizational processes are working against them. A job flowchart, developed as part of the needs assessment, can reveal situations training cannot correct.

If the needs assessment shows a good training program actually can improve job performance, the assessment provides a basis for a job-task analysis. That analysis will serve as a foundation during the design stage that follows. Taken together as part of the contract review process, these efforts provide a road map of what needs to be done. They give trainers a start on design and development of a focused program to meet needs and expectations of management and trainees.

PUBLISH COURSE DESCRIPTIONS

The training organization should prepare detailed descriptions of programs, courses, and lessons. Besides routine administrative details, such as time and location of these activities, program content should be defined clearly so potential trainees and their management will understand what specific job skills the training program is designed to improve. Detailed descriptions should tell potential trainees both what they are going to learn and how that learning will be useful in their work. A course catalogue should be up-to-date, and there should be an established way to ensure that it is available to all individuals in the organization.

SPECIFY LESSON OBJECTIVES

Lesson objectives should specify skills, knowledges, and attitudes (SKAs) trainees will gain by participating in training. Trainers should provide trainees with a list of lesson objectives immediately before the course. These objectives are an outline of what they can expect to achieve by completing the program successfully. Lesson objectives are a primary method to show what to expect and what performance requirements are going to be. Giving trainees a copy of objectives before the course provides them an opportunity to focus on the subject matter contained in the course.

PUBLISH PREREQUISITES

Every training program should have established prerequisites. Trainees and their supervisors should know what specific experience(s) and expertise level a trainee must have before entering the course. Publish prerequisites as a part of the course catalogue.

REVIEW PRIOR BACKGROUND

Trainers and the trainees' supervisors should review background experience of all trainees before they attend training. Management can review trainees' training records. A survey can ask trainees specific questions about their knowledge and experience. Also, trainers should survey trainees' immediate supervisors routinely for ideas on their needs and trainee readiness to attend.

ESTABLISH A TRAINING QUALITY TEAM

A great way to obtain customer needs information is to establish a Training Quality Team (TQT). Team members should review all proposed training programs, training requests, needs analyses, and job-task analyses. These people know the job requirements trainees need to learn. They know practical job aspects and what SKAs are necessary for incumbents to work successfully. TQT members should review all lessons for technical accuracy and relevance to trainee needs. A Training Quality Team is an excellent way to structure training processes to meet the guideline requirements for a contract review, particularly the note in the standard encouraging channels of communication and interfaces with the customer. It is also possible to take credit for TQT activities to satisfy requirements for management review.

ASK VENDORS FOR DELIVERABLES

If training is purchased, vendors should provide detailed outlines of their training programs. Outcomes and deliverables from vendor training programs should be specified. Also, because outsiders are not as informed as in-house trainers are about needs, culture, and personalities of attendees, a special effort should be made to send vendors an audience analysis.

DEMONSTRATE TRAINING CAPABILITY

The training organization must show it can provide the training. The most obvious part of this requirement is that instructors must have experience and knowledge to provide the training. Element 4.18, Training, will help trainers document that instructional staff can conduct training. Also, a structured approach to the entire training process, as outlined in a training department quality manual, will help show that the function is organized to meet trainee needs. Finally, the training organization must have financial resources, including time, to be able to produce and conduct training. This is a budgeting issue. The training organization must acquire resources and track their expenditures to show they have both the capacity and capability to provide the service.

EVALUATE OUTCOMES

An evaluation process should always be in place to follow up and ensure that trainees received what was needed and training delivered what was promised. Follow-up evaluations are discussed in various elements throughout the guideline, especially as part of Management Review, Design Control, and Process Control, which underscores their importance to the overall quality process.

Reality Check

The guideline requirement for contract review provides trainers with an excellent opportunity to structure a needs analysis process to support successful development and delivery of effective and efficient training programs. Unhappily, trainers sometimes take one of two unproductive approaches to needs analysis. At one end of the complexity continuum, enormous resources are spent developing extremely detailed and convoluted needs analyses and job-task analyses. This minutia-filled approach becomes so encumbered and complex that the entire process collapses under its own weight and no one has time to do any training. At the other extreme is the shotgun approach that takes a fly-by-the-seat-of-your-pants-and-hope-for-the-best approach. Neither is reasonable nor useful, and neither is very successful.

Needs assessment can be a hard sell because some managers and supervisors do not understand the value of the process. They are pressed for time to do their own work and cannot devote resources to help trainers figure out what is needed. Sometimes supervisors simply do not know what they need or what they want.

Needs analyses and job-task analyses get short shrift in many organizations. Although the rush to get training underway makes finding time to do these two important steps seem difficult, skipping them is false economy. Trainers who skip the analyses steps will get bogged down in the design and development steps. Thoughtful analyses pay dividends during design and development because they clearly focus development efforts. In terms of this ISO element, conscientious contract review (needs analysis) ensures customers' (trainees') needs are understood and met.

CHAPTER 9

Element 4.4

Design Control

The design step is the connecting point between what customers want and what companies produce. Design translates need into product or service. In ISO companies, design follows contract review, which in turn articulates customer needs. Contract Review and Design Control are closely related and logically follow one another. Trainers do Contract Review as part of the ISD analysis step and use Design Control as part of the design step to translate trainee needs into training activities. The design step of ISD includes gathering information and selecting effective instructional strategies.

Trainers who purchase off-the-shelf materials, send employees to public seminars and workshops, or hire external consultants to conduct training might try to avoid this element and rely on Element 4.6, Purchasing, to address these issues. That approach is counterproductive for most of them, however, because it short-circuits the ISD design step and reduces opportunities to connect SMEs and line personnel contributions to the design process.

What the ISO 9001 Standard Says

This element requires a procedure to control design activities so that companies focus their design and engineering efforts to ensure customer needs are met. The 1994 version of this element has been strengthened in several ways to help companies make connections to customer requirements. The element lays out several clauses to address each step in the design process. Identifying customer requirements and planning are recurring themes within each clause.

First, the company needs an overall plan for its design activities. Plans may be simple or complex, depending upon the complexity and detail of the design process. Some companies have a generic design plan which they tailor for individual projects. The element does not require flowcharting or computer project management software; however, both tools would be useful for complex design projects. The plan needs to show each step in the process, and the plan should be updated as designs evolve.

Qualified personnel and adequate resources must be assigned to design activities. Also, communication links between individuals and groups must be defined and documented. Throughout design projects there should be ongoing assessments of the effectiveness of these communication links.

This element distinguishes two activities: *design inputs* and *design outputs.* The *design input* represents the data gathering stage. Besides information from contract review to identify customer needs, data gathering includes any kinds of information that help design teams produce an acceptable design. Existing designs, current research, product and sub-component specifications, and data sheets are some kinds of data to be gathered. Additionally, the standard refers to statutory and regulatory requirements. The authors wisely point out that sometimes regulatory requirements conflict with one another. Nevertheless, the authors forbid finger-pointing or excuses and require the ISO company to address any such conflicts and to decide how to proceed. All design inputs must be documented and readily available for use by the design team.

The designs themselves, termed *design output*, are usually in the form of blueprints, specifications, data sheets, drawings, task or project lists, and the like. Whatever their form, the language used in the design outputs must reflect the language in the design inputs. An auditor familiar with the products or industry ought to be able to see these visible links among language and terms in the customer's contract and design inputs reflected in design outputs.

The design output clause has three criteria:

- Meet input requirements.
- Contain or refer to acceptance criteria.
- Identify critical characteristics related to safety or factors affecting products, such as operating instructions, maintenance requirements, and disposal issues.

Auditors ought to be able to see these three criteria in design outputs. Unless auditors are intimately familiar with the products or industry, they probably will have a difficult time assessing the adequacy of these criteria. They will rely on documentation from design review, design verification, and design validation to judge the usefulness of design outputs.

Finally, design outputs must be reviewed before they are released to the production or operations groups. This statement under design output may appear redundant with the next clause on design review, but it is not. Here the requirement is to check outputs for completeness and correctness. This is a proofreading step. In fact, creating an accurately documented but faulty design is possible. The faulty design issue is handled under the clauses on design review, verification, and validation.

The next three clauses in this element address efficacy, requiring companies to make sure their designs meet their customer's needs, can be fabricated, will function as required, and are not faulty. Formal reviews must be built into the design plan and conducted throughout the design process. They must include all functions, departments, or affected individuals within the company in these reviews, which must be documented. The company may consider using personnel who are specialists in the product or industry to help in these reviews.

The structure of the next two clauses—*design verification* and *design validation*—is new to the 1994 version, although the ideas were contained in the 1987 version. The new, restructured clauses help ISO companies see the distinction. *Design verification* is a requirement to link inputs to outputs. The authors suggest several ways to conduct verification, including performing alternate calculations, comparing the design with proven designs, and doing tests or demonstrations. Essentially this step allows the design team to make sure that they are meeting their customer's requirements and that the product can be fabricated.

The next step, *design validation*, requires the team to make sure the product will work under operating conditions. Sometimes companies build a prototype and test it before starting a production run. Other times the company may elect to construct and test parts and subassemblies. Validation usually follows verification, and if the product has several intended uses, running validation tests under different conditions may be appropriate.

The final clause in this element says everyone in the design process ought to be kept informed about changes and modifications, that changes and modifications ought to be reviewed and approved by affected personnel, and that these reviews ought to be documented.

What ISO Auditors Look For

This element may be the most complicated and difficult of all elements for auditors to assess. Every registrar audit team is required to have at least one subject matter expert on the audit team. Usually, this SME auditor assesses Design Control. Even knowledgeable SMEs may struggle, however, because they must rely on a good, documented paper-trail rather than first-hand knowledge of the design team's work. Moreover, the design process is so intimately interwoven with Contract Review and Process Control and pivotal between the two that it is difficult for auditors to develop a simple list of questions to ask. Auditors must try to follow the design process completely through its iterations and changes. Here is a start on a list of items auditors might look at while assessing this element:

- There is a design control procedure.
- Personnel are qualified to do the work.
- Design personnel have adequate resources, i.e., time and access to needed information.
- Management routinely assess communication links to make sure everyone is in the loop. There is documentation of these assessments.
- The communication links are documented, by memos and reports for example, so there is a detailed trail to allow someone to see how the project was undertaken.
- There is a library of design inputs available for reference. Applicable statutory and regulatory documents are readily available.
- The language in design outputs is consistent with and reflects language and information contained in design inputs.
- The design inputs contain acceptance criteria and critical characteristics such as safety issues and fac-

79

tors that might affect proper functioning of the product.

■ There are good communication links among and across departments, and relevant personnel are included in the design review process.

■ A design verification process is included in the process, and records are available showing these verifications are accomplished.

■ The company conducts validation of its designs. Validation is adequate and well documented.

■ There is a process in place to make sure everyone is informed about changes and modifications.

■ Affected personnel are consulted about and have opportunities to review and approve changes and modifications. They are following this process. There are records showing that these notifications, reviews, and approvals are taking place.

What the Education and Training Guideline Says

Design Control is the longest of the 20 elements in the guideline, and it reflects the authors' ISD orientation. They emphasize the critical connection between identifying customers' requirements, needs analysis, and a solid design process to produce effective and efficient training. The "Design of Instruction Within a Quality System" flowchart, provided at this point, strengthens their emphasis on this element.

The authors provide a short introduction to this element and identify several applications of Design Control, including its use by accreditation bodies to evaluate training and educational bodies that award credits, degrees, or certificates. The authors adopt verbatim the general section from the standard that requires a documented and controlled design process to ensure that specified customer requirements are met. Then the guideline specifies a need for two reports: an *assessment report* and a *design report*.

They identify ISD needs analysis as a way to identify customer requirements. A needs analysis identifies two things. First, it determines what SKAs are needed to do a job or task. Then it identifies the difference between what SKAs employees currently possess and what they need. There are several possible ways to conduct a needs assessment, and the guideline authors provide a general flowchart of such a process. The design process presents an opportunity to determine how and whether they can provide needed SKAs. Trainers and customers should work together to produce the needs analysis.

The outcome of a needs assessment is a *needs assessment report*. The design control procedure should identify responsibilities and authority of individuals who will review the report. Trainers and customers should review the report to reach a consensus on desired goals and possible revisions. When this review is completed, the report will then serve as the basic *design report*.

Besides summarizing results of needs analysis and goals of the proposed training program, both the needs analysis report and the design report should identify expected trainee performance standards, characteristics of trainee populations, and the means by which instruction will satisfy those needs. Additionally, these reports may identify a variety of issues, including potential employee quality failures, contributions or changes customers must make before instruction takes place in order to ensure its effectiveness, and any relevant safety or regulatory or statutory requirements. The authors make an interesting observation on this last point. They identify trainers as responsible for safety and regulatory requirements even if the customer does not identify their relevance or importance.

The authors also strengthen their focus on training evaluation in this element. They connect needs assessments directly to the evaluation step in the ISD model because it is

81

in the design step that trainers begin to identify how they will assess trainee performance after participating in training activities. The connections are obviously interrelated: assess what is needed, assess what is currently available, and assess whether training satisfied the need.

Any external consultants the company uses should employ a recognized assessment process and provide a detailed description of how they are going to conduct the assessment. They should provide this report, along with evidence that they conducted the assessment, to the customer.

Like the standard, the guideline requires a planned approach to design activities. Additionally, the guideline specifies qualified persons to conduct the analysis, design, and development phases of an ISD process and refers to Element 4.18, Training, to emphasize the need for knowledgeable and experienced trainers to do these tasks. The guideline, like the standard, recognizes the need for good organizational and technical communications and interactions during design stages.

Once a needs analysis is completed and the report presented and approved, it is turned over to an instructional designer. The designer will use the report as the basis for designing instruction, using its information about customer needs, instructional goals, target populations, relevant standards, and any existing or potential quality failures. The instructional designer may do some additional analysis activities as the design process evolves.

The guideline specifies that designers use a documented design process. Design steps include gathering relevant content or subject matter information about the SKAs to be taught, determining instructional strategies appropriate for target populations, and deciding on locations where training will be done. Also necessary are assessment and evaluation activities to demonstrate trainee acquisition of needed SKAs and suitability of instruction provided. The designer will produce a *design report* before beginning to produce training materials. The design report includes SKAs to be taught, assessments and evaluations to be used, strategies and objectives, and media or delivery systems. Essentially, the design report is a map or outline of the training program. The guideline says knowledgeable persons affected by training should review and approve this design report.

The element addresses design verification and validation. Its discussion of verification is long and detailed, whereas validation is accepted verbatim from the standard. Before instructional materials are created, knowledgeable individuals, usually other trainers and most assuredly SMEs and line management, should review the design report and verify its adequacy. An established process should describe how this review and subsequent revisions will be handled.

Once the design report is approved, the work of preparing instructional materials begins. As development work progresses, the guideline authors expect designers to continue to review and analyze the design report based on their experience with this and other projects and also with experience and information gained as the project proceeds. If a subcontractor or outside agency designs the instruction, they should have a copy of the needs analysis report and provide a design report and evidence of a design review for the customer.

The design process describes established ways to produce instructional materials. These ways may be described in a flowchart or a checklist format and depend on the nature of instructional content and the instructional delivery strategy selected. The design process procedure will include the sequence of steps, including personnel involved, review process, and appropriate criteria for each step. As instructional materials are developed, an ongoing evaluation should assure that they are meeting design specifications. A *development* or *progress report* usually satisfies this.

The guideline specifies that instructional developers should conduct formative evaluations during the development phase. *Formative evaluation* is a continuing in-process evaluation throughout the development process. It compares needs analysis, job-task analysis, lesson plan or course plan objectives, instructional and support materials, delivery strategies, and trainee performance measures. The basic question it should answer is: what SKAs do trainees need and will this instruction meet those needs? There should be established acceptance criteria and ongoing reviews by SMEs for content and technical accuracy, approval of graphs, drawings, and illustrations, and editorial and proofreading accuracy. Small organizations may use line supervisors as SMEs to evaluate instructional materials under development. In larger organizations, an important part of formative evaluation is a test or pilot of materials using samples of target trainee populations in the intended instructional setting. The ongoing formative evaluations will allow instructional developers to revise the design report as well as their development processes.

If a subcontractor or external agency completes the development work, the same development processes should be used, and they should conduct formative evaluations and provide reports to the customer. Finally, the guideline authors accept verbatim the standard's requirements for design validation and design changes. Design validation is the part of pilot or test programs in which instruction is presented to a sample of trainees from target populations in intended instructional settings.

What Training Assessors Look For

Like ISO auditors, training assessors will have a difficult time evaluating the design process. However, instructional design processes are probably more generic and easier to track than are manufacturing or research and development design processes. Training assessors will need to rely on well-structured and documented procedures and processes rather than instructional SME knowledge to assess the training design function. In addition to the same kinds of concerns and questions raised by ISO auditors, here is a list of items training assessors might look at.

- There are planned and documented processes to do instructional design and connect the analysis phase to the development phase of ISD. There is a process flowchart similar to the "Design of Instruction Within a Quality System" that connects customer requirements to instruction design and development.

- SKAs are identified in needs analyses, job-task analyses, design reports, instructional objectives, instructional materials, and trainee performance measures.

- Needs assessment reports and design reports are formalized, reviewed, approved, and used to develop training materials.

- Design reports identify and link trainee population characteristics and required performance standards to instructional strategies.

- If the company uses external consultants, there are established, controlled steps and requirements linking the external provider to the customer. There is a distinct link between procedures controlling purchasing when external consultants are used.

- There is a validation process to pilot training to sample target populations in proposed instructional settings.

- There is an ongoing formative evaluation process that continuously reviews and revises instructional materials under design and development in order to tie customer needs directly to instructional activities and produce the most effective and efficient training possible.

Q-Project Action Items

PLAN THE DESIGN IN DETAIL

Write a detailed procedure describing the design process. Make good use of flowcharts to show these processes. Identify responsible individuals who will participate. Assign authority to these knowledgeable participants to conduct design reviews.

INVOLVE LINE PERSONNEL

Get line personnel and SMEs as well as the TQT involved in needs analysis and design stages. They should also participate in design validation activities, such as running a pilot of the training program. This participation will help ensure that training is on target, effective, and efficient. Their buy-in and approval afford the training program and trainers substantial credibility.

GET HELP

Consider the possibility of using external consultants or individuals from other divisions within the company to conduct needs assessments. They have little political stake in the process and as disinterested third parties have credibility with management who must approve training expenditures. They can also help trainers see issues and needs they are too close to recognize themselves.

CONDUCT PILOT PROGRAMS

Schedule and conduct practical applications of portions of training in real world settings to pilot programs before rolling them out to the general population. Set up these pilots to get valuable feedback from participants. Make sure SMEs participate and get their help to find out what works, what needs more elaboration, and what should be eliminated, refined, or added.

86

USE REPORTS

The guideline specifies needs for two reports: an assessment report and a design report. Devise quick and easy formats for reports. Fill-in-the-blank reports and checklists will help control information and provide both reviewers and instructional designers easy access to information they need to make reasonable judgments and work with the information.

CONDUCT FORMATIVE EVALUATIONS

Formative evaluations sound like a scary undertaking. They are neither scary nor difficult. Formative evaluations are simply ongoing adjustments and revisions as new information becomes available and as instruction begins to take shape. Formative evaluations are part of the creative process while producing instruction. Trainers routinely do these evaluations almost subconsciously as they design, develop, and deliver training. In fact, the only time they do not do formative evaluations is when they do summative evaluations. At that point they hand trainees performance measures and must step back, watch, and hope.

Reality Check

Training does not happen magically. Moreover, neither does training design. A flowchart and checklists of tasks provide excellent ways to control resource expenditures and keep everyone on schedule. They also limit last-minute panic situations requiring trainers to do miracles to prepare training programs in time.

No registrar or auditor is as smart and as knowledgeable as are company trainers about their own training. Unless auditors are subject matter experts or specialists in the particular areas, they will have difficulty assessing the validity of the training designs. Therefore, the auditors must rely on good documentation to assess how well trainers are doing in this area.

The guideline authors have placed considerable emphasis on this element, making very strong connections between analysis, design, and evaluation steps of the ISD model. The element may be somewhat easier to apply within technical and skills training programs than it is to apply within such soft-skill training as communication, diversity training, or leadership training. What is most important, trainers need to avoid monstrously convoluted and complicated processes when addressing the design element. Some carefully conceived, well-defined planning steps that draw line personnel into the design process will produce useful training.

As detailed and as elaborate as this element appears initially, in practice it is a simple matter to set up the analysis and design phases of an ISD process. The political problem is obtaining willing support from line personnel to participate and contribute to its success. Therefore, couching these contributions in terms line personnel understand is critical. Trainers must emphasize the payoffs to employees rather than payoffs to the training organization. In other words, emphasize WIIFM, What's In It For Me.

CHAPTER 10

Element 4.5

Document and Data Control

An ISO 9000 quality assurance system is based on documented procedures. In fact, a basic tenet of ISO is "Say What You Do." Companies say what they do by writing procedures covering each of the 20 ISO elements. Documentation also includes forms for recording data generated while using a quality assurance system. They are the second half of the ISO basic tenet: "Do What You Say." Records are *objective evidence* of compliance. As employees follow the system and complete documentation, they create records as evidence the work has been accomplished. Companies sometimes combine both Document and Data Control and Control of Quality Records together in one procedure. Although these elements may be addressed independently or together, it is a good idea to clearly tie together procedures addressing these two elements.

Documentation requirements for Elements 4.1, Management Responsibility, and 4.2, Quality System, are usually found in the company's quality manual rather than in separate procedures. However, the remaining 18 elements require procedures and records. In its first paragraph, each element usually says: "Shall establish and maintain documented procedures . . ." A few of the elements begin with "where appropriate," and then call for a procedure. Element 4.5, Document and Data Control, requires a procedure. Therefore, writing a procedure to describe how procedures will be written and controlled is required.

A new idea in the 1994 version of the standard shows the authors recognize that many companies are moving toward a paperless environment. In Note 15, they allow documents and data to be in any media form or type, including computer data.

What the ISO 9001 Standard Says

Organizations that use established procedures will recognize many basic requirements of a good procedure system in this element. A list of element requirements serves as an outline for what to include in a document and data procedure:

- A procedure to control all documents, including procedures, work instructions, forms and records, and any other kinds of data that serve as objective evidence employees are using the quality assurance system.
- Where specified, procedures to explain and document how the international standards are applied.
- When necessary, a means to control documents and data received from outside sources, such as technical manuals from equipment manufacturers. Not all external documents must be controlled; however, many should be. It is up to the company to have a method for deciding which is which.
- A system for authorized and knowledgeable per-

sons to review and approve all documents before they are used. That means persons affected by procedures should have an opportunity to comment on them.

■ A means for the same persons who wrote the procedure to review and approve any changes or revisions to it. These individuals should have any information they need to be able to assess changes before approving them.

■ Clear identification of changes to documents. Sometimes companies highlight or use strikeouts to identify changes. Another method is to have a change sheet as the first page of the revision.

■ A master list of all procedures. This master list must be constantly updated to show the current revision of each procedure on the list. This master list must be readily available.

■ A means whereby documents are available to employees who need them. That means copies of procedures and work instructions and also any necessary forms should be within easy reach.

■ A way to remove old revisions of documents from circulation so only new versions are used.

■ A system to mark outdated documents maintained for historical or legal purposes, so their status is obvious and their inadvertent use is prevented.

What ISO Auditors Look For

ISO auditors will look at documents and records to evaluate this element. Specifically, auditors will look to make sure up-to-date copies of relevant procedures and work instructions, as well as needed forms, are near all employees or are easily obtained for their use. Auditors will always ask employees if they use their procedures and work instructions and if procedures are correct and helpful. They will frequently ask employees to walk through a work instruction and show how they follow it. Auditors will usually ask employees what they do if they have a question that cannot be readily answered by consulting a procedure. An acceptable answer is to ask the supervisor.

Auditors will ask for a copy of the master list of controlled documents before going out to conduct an audit. They will remain alert to find outdated copies of documents in circulation. Where numbered copies of procedures or the quality manual are part of the system, auditors will ask individuals to produce their copy of the document and check the controlled circulation list to make sure it is accurate. Auditors might look at obsolete copies of documents maintained for legal or historical purposes to see clear and obvious marks of their status.

What the ISO Education and Training Guideline Says

This element of the guideline elaborates on the standard element in several important ways. First, the guideline reiterates a basic intent and need for procedures to control documentation and, like the standard, requires procedures to be reviewed for adequacy. *Adequacy* means they clearly have to help trainers do their jobs and must help control and improve quality in education and training. Then it emphasizes the need for procedures to control "important activities within education and training institutions" and refers to Element 4.9, Process Control, which emphasizes an ISD model of analysis, design, development, delivery, and evaluation. It is a good idea to have a procedure for each of these major steps in the model of instruction.

The guideline identifies three specific areas education and training organizations must address.

■ Revisions of trainee materials such as textbooks or

92

handouts must be controlled, and there must be a direct link from each revision back to the design process. This means when such materials are changed, updated, or revised, trainers must return to the design step to evaluate whether the new edition meets trainee needs.

■ Documents such as lesson plans should follow consistent formats. Data gathering forms such as course evaluations or job-task analysis forms should have a consistent format. Additionally, routine administrative forms such as grade reports and course registration forms should be standardized.

■ There should be a review process to approve documents, including procedures and forms. Trainers should review originals and revisions to help decide if these documents will help them do their jobs and support the training organization's quality assurance process.

Like the standard, the guideline identifies the need to control external documents and changes to documents.

What Training Assessors Look For

To assess the document system according to the ISO element, training assessors will follow essentially the same steps outlined above. Knowledgeable training assessors have two concerns. The first relates directly to the ISO standard, and the second relates specifically to the needs of training organizations.

■ Training assessors will be particularly interested in finding clear links between revisions to lesson materials and the design process. Assessors will want to see trainers use the design step to control changes and enhancements to lesson materials.

■ Assessors will want to see evidence of reviews of both administrative forms and lesson materials to ensure all involved or affected individuals have an opportunity to evaluate changes to help them do their trainer tasks and to support the quality assurance process.

Q-Project Action Items

CORRAL DOCUMENTS

Get document and data issues under control. Write and live with a useable procedure to control documentation. To do this, keep both procedures and documents, particularly administrative documents, as simple as possible. Exert organizational discipline and make sure everyone follows procedures. Corral renegades. At the same time, make the procedure change process quick and painless, and encourage everyone to contribute to making procedures more useful.

USE PROCEDURES AND FLOWCHARTS

Procedures are supposed to help people do their jobs. Use a flowchart method to structure procedures and initiate changes. Often everyone thinks they understand not only what others are doing but also how their actions fit into the overall process. A team-based procedure writing process will uncover many discrepancies between what folks think ought to be happening and what is really going on.

PRODUCE A RESPONSIBILITIES MATRIX

Each procedure should have a section specifying who has responsibility and authority over duties described. Consider constructing a matrix showing the relationship of procedures to persons affected by them. Such a procedure-to-person matrix will give responsible individuals a convenient list of their tasks. There is nothing worse than having an auditor ask individuals about their responsibilities and have someone deny knowledge they were supposed to be doing something.

CROSS-REFERENCE DOCUMENTS

Procedure writers frequently refer to other procedures or work instructions in their procedures. Just as each element in the quality manual should refer to specific, relevant procedures, a procedure on document control may include reference to work instructions on how to fill out a form. This tactic is useful, but it is easy to make it too complex by including too many references. Additional problems arise when a document referencing others is changed. Consider developing a matrix to track references contained in procedures and work instructions. Most importantly, avoid referring to any document the organization does not control or have readily available. Any referenced document is fair game for an auditor to review. A procedure or work instruction referring to a document or book, for example, leads the auditor to believe the organization follows all ideas contained in the book. A story making the rounds among auditors recently concerns an organization that referred to a famous book on quality then discovered—much to its horror—the auditors wanted to see how the company was applying all of the many ideas in this major reference tome.

CREATE A MASTER LIST

The requirement for a master list showing current revisions of all procedures to be readily available so no one inadvertently uses an outdated procedure can easily turn into a major headache. Some companies elect to include their master list as an appendix to their documentation procedure and routinely update this appendix as documents are changed. This is a significantly complex approach to satisfying this element. Carefully consider how many official copies of the master list are really needed and what constitutes *readily available*. A few master lists posted in a few conspicuous places may be sufficient.

BECOME PAPERLESS

Consider the idea of a paperless office or at least a less-paper office. Several excellent computer programs allow training organizations to maintain all their procedures in a computer-based format. For the ISO requirements, the only caveats connected to computer use are that the computer software must prohibit unauthorized changes to procedures and that the company must maintain records of changes made. Definitely consider any one of many computer programs for trainee registration and record keeping. These programs represent a moderate investment, but they will save significant resources once they are in place.

WRITE THE QUALITY MANUAL LAST

Most definitely, do not start a quality improvement project by attempting to write the quality manual. Organizations attempting to write their quality manual first often create a major political problem for themselves because the organization perceives the project as a large, unknown, and scary change process. To move into it in manageable increments, the team should begin by writing all necessary and required procedures and work instructions. Once these are completed, it is a simple matter to summarize the main ideas into a quality manual. At this point, the quality manual should take no more than four or five hours to write and two or three days to approve. For example, one Baldrige winner claims they wrote the application in a weekend. The same is possible for an ISO Quality Manual.

USE QUALITY PLANS

The 1994 revision of the ISO standard changed quality plans from a guideline to a requirement. As such, quality plans are now part of documentation and record-keeping processes. Quality plans may be a separate level of documentation or a generic procedure quality plan with specific documentation for each project. Whatever method is chosen, the documentation control issue will be an auditor concern. Quality plans are important and are discussed in several elements in the standard and guideline, particularly in Quality Systems and in Design Control.

Reality Check

When organizations begin to build a documentation system, they face two significant dangers. First is a temptation to pencil-whip the process, that is, to write a procedure for every detail and task. This weighs down not only the writers but also the people who are to use these documents. The philosopher Pascal, in Provincial Letters XVI, said, "I make this letter longer than usual because I lack the time to make it shorter." It is a difficult and time-consuming challenge to write short, focused, useful procedures and to limit procedures to the absolute minimum. The payoff from spending energy to write such procedures is a useable quality assurance system which helps people do their work.

The opposite is also true. Teams should avoid trying to minimize this task by not writing procedures on the theory that if they do not write a procedure then auditors cannot write nonconformances. That tactic is ineffective because the guideline and the standard require there be adequate procedures to control all processes affecting quality. There most definitely must be procedures to address each of the 20 elements in the standard. Within each element, especially Design Control and Process Control, several procedures will be needed to cover various activities. The guideline does not ask for more procedures than the standard; trainers, however, will need several procedures to support an ISD process in their organizations.

The second significant trap some teams fall into is attempting to write procedures based on an idealized and fictitious way of doing things. Their notion is to write procedures first and then change behaviors to fit procedures. Beyond creating chaos, this approach is guaranteed to cause hate, discontent, and resistance from anyone affected by the imposed changes. A much wiser approach is to flowchart the current process. Then write procedures reflecting how things are actually done. Once that first step is completed, then draw affected individuals into a continuous improvement process. Use the guideline elements as a goal to direct continuous improvement processes. The flowchart describing the current process will have credibility with users and will quickly reveal areas for improvement. Then involved personnel can work together to find better ways to accomplish their tasks.

CHAPTER 11

Element 4.6

Purchasing

This element is the second of two that establish a relationship between an ISO company and external companies. The first half, Element 4.3, Contract Review, establishes the relationship between the ISO company and its customers. Here it establishes a relationship between the ISO company and its subcontractors. Both elements reflect the same concerns and ask the same questions: "Does the provider of the product or service understand what the customer needs, and can they satisfy that need?"

What the ISO 9001 Standard Says

Besides the requirement for a procedure, records, and a list of approved subcontractors, this element has three broad requirements.

- First there must be a method to select subcontractors.
- Second, the process must establish techniques to identify product specification data and include that

data in purchase contracts or orders. This data should describe the product and help the supplier understand what the customer needs.

■ Third, where agreed to in a contract, there must be a way for either the ISO company or the ISO company's customer to inspect products or services at the subcontractor's location.

First, companies must have a way to select subcontractors. Generally, an ISO company is interested to know if subcontractors can meet their needs. To judge capacity, the company can look at a subcontractor's quality assurance system. One way some subcontractors demonstrate their quality assurance capability is to become registered to the ISO 9000 Standard. Therefore, the ISO Purchasing element provides a hook to encourage companies to become ISO registered. At a minimum, this element provides some vertical integration among and between customers, suppliers, and subcontractors. ISO registration provides all three with confidence and a mutual basis upon which to build a business relationship.

The language in this element specifically allows a degree of flexibility to exclude some purchases and therefore some subcontractors from the process. Some purchases simply do not affect quality. For example, office supply products may not need to be made from approved suppliers. Nevertheless, a good purchasing procedure will help the company, and sometimes including all suppliers is simply easier. Also, the language allows grandfathering of long-term subcontractors who have shown their capability to provide quality products. Despite these two types of exceptions, the standard does not allow a company to slough this issue. There must be a documented method supporting decisions to invoke either of these two alternatives.

The second requirement concerns purchasing data and documentation. There must be some way to identify product, i.e., by class, grade, or another positive identification to ensure that delivered product will meet specification needs. As in Contract Review, the company must have a method to review and approve purchase orders to make sure information contained in them is adequate to meet their needs.

The third requirement applies in those contractual situations in which suppliers or suppliers' customers wish to verify product or service at the subcontractor's premises before the product is shipped to the supplier. A very interesting idea applied here and again in Element 4.7, Control of Customer-Supplied Product, focuses ultimate responsibility for quality on the ISO company. This element says whether or not the customer has inspected the component at the subcontractor's premises, the ISO company remains responsible for the quality of the subcontractor's component. Even though the customer approves the subcontractor or the subcontractor's sub-component, that approval does not relieve the ISO company from doing its own verification. Additionally, even if the customer has approved the subcontractor's component, the customer may subsequently reject the ISO company's finished product if the subcontractor's component proves defective.

What ISO Auditors Look For

ISO auditors will concentrate primarily on the first two issues and address the third concern only when it is applicable. In addition to a procedure and purchase order records, auditors will want to see a list of approved suppliers or subcontractors. They might select a sample of purchase orders looking for purchases made from subcontractors who are not on the approved list. Also, auditors will review these purchase orders to ensure there is sufficient data to identify the product. If a design function is included in the purchase package, auditors will sometimes try to trace back to design specifications to ensure that they are reflected in the purchase order. Finally, auditors will look for a release authorization on purchase orders to make sure the company reviews and approves purchase orders for adequacy according to its own procedures, and to meet the ISO standard, before releasing them.

If the customer is involved in approving or inspecting subcontractors, auditors will generally interview purchasing and quality assurance personnel to ensure they are following the third part of the element. In such situations, auditors might look for evidence of customer complaints or product or shipment rejects to learn how the company deals with such situations.

Finally, a really sharp ISO auditor might be interested in reviewing the process used to select and hire an ISO registrar.

What the Education and Training Guideline Says

The guideline relies heavily on the standard and begins by identifying typical products purchased by training or education organizations. These include items such as books, computers and software, course-ware, vendor training and consulting services, and reproduction services. Additionally, personnel services such as food and housing are sometimes purchased for trainees in residence. A method for evaluating all purchased products needs to be established.

Trainers use the third element, verification at the subcontractor's site, to cover such items as training provided to company employees away from the company. For example, the company might send a trainee to a public seminar or an educational institution. In these cases, the purchase contract might include provisions to assess materials and services at the instruction delivery site.

What Training Assessors Look For

Knowledgeable training assessors look at the same things ISO auditors will review. This includes a list of approved suppliers and a procedure explaining how subcontractors and suppliers are selected. Similarly, assessors would look at purchase orders and attempt to tie them back to training design specifications. Assessors will be particularly interested in several items directly related to training processes:

- They want to ensure off-the-shelf or generic training materials, particularly such formula programs as introduction to supervision or basic maintenance, are carefully selected to meet trainee needs. Auditors will attempt to see a connection between trainee needs analyses and purchased products.
- Off-site or public seminars and workshops are another subject for attention. Some companies typically budget time and money for staff to attend these functions and then do not oversee the usefulness of these activities to meet identified job needs.
- There needs to be a specific tie between instruction presented in programs brought into the company and conducted by external consultants or seminar leaders and trainee job needs. Assessors want to know how the company helps the consultants or seminar leaders prepare to present in their company. For example, assessors would look for audience analyses provided by the company to the external trainer. Additionally, assessors would look for reviews of supplier objectives and course descriptions.

Q-Project Action Items

CONTROL PURCHASING

Get the routine administrative purchasing process under control. That includes working directly with the purchasing department to handle purchase orders and process invoices effectively and efficiently. Make sure detailed identification data are included in the purchase orders and make sure appropriate review and approval is conducted before releasing the order.

DEVELOP TRAINING SOURCES

Have in place a good research process and information sources to help trainers find learning materials. There are many obvious suppliers, but a little digging will help identify the less obvious. For example, the "International Directory of Professional Organizations" lists several thousand groups that can lead to seminars and learning opportunities.

EVALUATE MATERIALS

Promotional materials are an insufficient source from which to make a reasoned judgment about usefulness or quality of training materials. Obtain detailed descriptions and learning objectives before hiring external trainers. Carefully review all received materials for suitability. The review must be timely so that if the materials are not adequate, they can be returned. Trainers, trainees, and SMEs should routinely review purchased products to make sure they obtained not only what was ordered, but also what was needed.

EVALUATE OFF-SITE TRAINING

Get details about off-site training, seminars, workshops, and conferences before sending employees. There are many excellent outside training opportunities, so do not limit selections to the most obvious. Always do a follow-up evaluation anytime anyone returns from a conference and include that adequacy review as part of the Management Review under Element 4.1.3.

ANALYZE AUDIENCES

Spend some extra time and funds to help vendors and

consultants understand employees' needs when they conduct seminars and workshops on-site. These external providers want their programs to succeed because they want to be invited to return and because they want the company as a future reference. Take the time necessary to fill out audience profile questionnaires provided by consultants. If appropriate, fund necessary tailoring of programs to trainees' specific needs.

USE H.R. TO HIRE NEW TRAINERS

Work closely with the Human Resources Department or other hiring authorities when bringing new people into the training organization. This issue is directly addressed in several areas in the guideline, most definitely in Training, Element 4.18, Design Control, Element 4.4, and in Quality System, Element 4.2. However, under the guideline requirements, hiring processes might be considered a part of purchasing, also.

Reality Check

Too frequently, companies bring in consultants or training programs or send people out to seminars and conferences with only a vague idea of what they are buying. Many such decisions are based on a good salesperson's efforts to build a relationship with a buyer. Sometimes that buyer is a department supervisor or upper level management person, and the buying decision does not include the training organization. The ISO standard should, at a minimum, give trainers a stronger role in the purchase of training-related materials. Trainers need to be involved in purchasing processes, and these processes should be tight enough to ensure purchases will always deliver what is needed while adding credibility to the training organization.

CHAPTER 12

Element 4.7

Control of
Customer-Supplied Product

This important element is frequently used in manufacturing settings and might have some relevance to training
organizations. Trainers should scan through this chapter for
information and make reference to it in their quality manual
as either applicable or not applicable to their needs. ISO auditors expect organizations to address each element specifically even if it is not applicable to them.

The element is concerned with a relationship among
three parties: the supplier (the ISO company), the supplier's
customer, and the supplier's subcontractor. Sometimes a customer will order a product from a supplier and provide a
component, materials, or a subassembly to the supplier to be
incorporated into the product. Other times the customer will
order a product from a supplier and require the supplier to
purchase some components, materials, or subassemblies
from a particular subcontractor. At these times, this element

comes into play. Essentially, this element is founded on the idea that companies (suppliers) seeking ISO 9000 registration are responsible for the quality of all components and materials used in their manufacturing process regardless of where they come from.

For example, an automobile manufacturer is a customer when it orders parts, materials, or subassemblies from an ISO supplier. Sometimes the automobile manufacturer will send a part or some materials to the ISO supplier for incorporation in a product. Other times the automobile manufacturer may tell the ISO supplier that as part of the contract, the ISO supplier must use a particular part, material, or component from a certain subcontractor. It does not matter where parts or materials come from, the ISO supplier is responsible for the quality of the product. Also, the standard says the customer (in this case the automobile manufacturer) is responsible for providing acceptable products to the ISO supplier. Even if the customer does not follow ISO standards, the ISO company remains responsible. The basic message for trainers is that they are responsible for training outcomes regardless of the source of any lesson materials or any part of the instruction.

What the ISO 9001 Standard Says

Element 4.7 continues the ideas in Element 4.6, Purchasing. Besides requiring a procedure, this element requires ISO suppliers to verify, store, and maintain any product, material, or sub-component that customers provide for incorporation into manufactured products. If there is a problem, such as if customer-supplied products are damaged, lost, or unsuitable for use, then the ISO supplier must notify the customer. The fact that the ISO supplier has notified the customer, however, does not absolve the ISO supplier from responsibility for solving the problem or relieve the customer from having to provide acceptable products.

What ISO Auditors Look For

For any company, ISO auditors would look for a statement in the quality manual that says whether this element is used for the company's quality program. It would be included if the company used customer-supplied products or services in making its own products. If no customer-supplied products or services are used, the company should indicate that and note that this element is excluded. They should include an additional sentence saying if they do accept them in the future, then they will follow this element. If the element is included, auditors will review procedures covering this activity and would look for evidence that the procedure is being followed. If there is no evidence the company has ever had such problems, the auditor would be limited to asking employees, probably quality control personnel who do incoming inspections, what they would do if such a problem were to occur.

What the Education and Training Guideline Says

The guideline element refers to items trainees are required to bring to class such as texts and workbooks, computers and software, test equipment, and other supplies. These items may have been provided by the employees' department or they may be manuals or equipment purchased through another contract. Most of these items should be adequately covered in Element 4.6, Purchasing; however, trainers remain responsible for ensuring such items are suitable for trainees' use in the training program.

What Training Assessors Look For

Whether or not trainers use this guideline element, assessors will expect to see a statement in their quality manual addressing it. A one-line statement such as "This element is not applicable to our organization; all quality issues are adequately addressed in Element 4.6, Purchasing" is sufficient. Such a statement must be in the quality manual to satisfy requirements of Element 4.2, Quality System, which says companies must address all elements in the international standard. If the training organization does use this element, assessors will review the procedure and talk with trainers and trainees to decide if it is effective.

Q-Project Action Items

CONSIDER APPLICABILITY

Carefully consider applicability of this element. In some situations, including it can be useful such as when a trainee's department purchases and provides equipment to their members for use in training. Such items may include commercially produced job aids, technical product manuals, or computers and software. Regardless of who provides these materials, trainers are responsible for their suitability for use in the training program. Note also that such manuals might be just as easily controlled under requirements of Element 4.5, Document and Data Control. Small and medium-sized training organizations should, if possible, try to cover the spirit and intent of this element under 4.6, Purchasing. Large training organizations that frequently need to address this issue may find it less complicated to address these situations under Element 4.7, Control of Customer-Supplied Product.

Reality Check

There is an important philosophical basis for this element. Finger-pointing and other shifting of responsibility are not in the spirit of the quality movement or of the ISO standards. If there is a problem with anything related to the quality system, the supplier—in this case the training organization—needs to take responsibility and make sure the problem is fixed.

CHAPTER 13

Element 4.8

Product Identification and Traceability

One major difference between quality in training and quality in other organizations is the dual nature of the training product. One product of training is program materials—including lesson plans, job aids, overhead transparencies, and all other produced materials. It is equally the case, however, that the training product is changes in trainees' knowledges, skills, and attitudes (SKAs) resulting from training. This dual nature of the training product has important implications for procedure writers. It also is an issue during compliance audits. In particular, if auditors consider training materials to be training products but find instances in procedures where the company talks about products as changes in individuals' SKAs, there may be confusion.

Fortunately, this guideline element concerns only training materials as the product. Nevertheless, the procedure writing team needs to keep their assumptions clearly in mind. Explaining their assumptions in each procedure is neither necessary nor recommended, but the writers must maintain consistency and not shift perspective in mid-procedure.

What the ISO 9001 Standard Says

Product identification and traceability mean the company must have an identification system in place that identifies both finished products and their components. Numbering systems usually work well, but it is also possible, especially when handling products in process, to use an alphabetic or color code system to identify status. Manufacturers are familiar with this kind of system, but some service and training organizations find this element slippery.

A superficial approach to this short and seemingly innocuous element can lead to administrative disaster. First, the element waffles the requirement by saying a procedure and documentation are needed *where appropriate*. This statement is guaranteed to create disagreement and confusion. Companies must decide what is appropriate. Unfortunately, the phrase does not provide much guidance to interpret the requirement nor is it much protection in discussions with auditors during compliance audits.

It is important also to understand that this element does not refer to general product labeling found in inventory and accounting systems. Instead, it concerns identification and traceability of individual finished products and their constituent parts. For example, in producing such things as medical devices, electronic gear, and industrial machinery, manufacturers must exert good quality control over their finished product. Because their product is the sum of its parts, they must exert good quality control over the parts as well. This is complicated because many manufacturers frequently buy parts from other suppliers rather than fabricate them themselves. ISO requires manufacturers to identify and trace each component because if there is a product failure, they must find its cause. Tracing and identifying the component that failed are one way to diagnose causes of product failure.

What ISO Auditors Look For

Auditors would look for a procedure and documentation to identify and trace both products and their components through the manufacturing process. Typically, auditors might select a finished product and follow its paperwork back through design specifications and drawings to the original purchase contract. Alternatively, auditors might start with a purchase order and trace the process through to product shipment.

What the Education and Training Guideline Says

This element is as short and seemingly innocuous as the standard element. The guideline recognizes only training materials as the product. Identification and traceability of trainees are covered in Element 4.18, Training. The guideline focuses on identification of seven items and suggests a data system to number and identify each to satisfy the element. Two items refer to course records and relevant prerequisites usually dealt with under Element 4.18, Training. The remaining five items to handle under this element are syllabus, schedule, lesson materials, instructor(s), and textbooks.

Even though the standard establishes rigid requirements to track and control product and constituent parts throughout manufacturing processes, the guideline does not convey the same stringent intent. However, trainers must carefully track the paths of many constituent parts of their training materials, from lesson objectives to performance tests and on-the-job tasks. It should always be possible to identify any task done by an employee and trace its training though task analysis, lesson objectives, lesson materials, and, finally, the examination or performance tests. Other materials often identified and tracked include such things as overhead transparencies as part of lesson materials and job-aids as part of performance qualifications. Because so much of the training product is documentation, meeting Element 4.5, Document and Data Control, may satisfy these identifications.

What Training Assessors Look For

- A procedure and documentation system to satisfy this element need to be in place. These must not conflict with procedures and documentation for Elements 4.5 and 4.16 because assessors are sure to look for inconsistencies between this procedure and documentation and record-keeping procedures. They will also be interested in traceability throughout the documentation system.

- A numbering system is needed for the five items specifically identified in the element: syllabus, schedule, lesson materials, instructor(s), and textbooks.

- Correct and consistent use of the identification scheme on lesson materials, textbooks, and other written products is needed. Assessors would also review the organization's procedure for this element and ensure all items required to be identified are correctly marked.

- Assessors would be particularly interested in how examinations and performance tests are identified and protected from compromise. Control needs to be in place from the time a question is written, through its review and approval for use, during its use in the program, during grading, and finally in its protection for future use.

- Assessors would review trainee records to ensure that the record system is used consistently and that employee records accurately reflect the training individuals have completed.

Q-Project Action Items

CONTROL MATERIALS

It is critical for trainers to gain control over all materials used for training. Control means deciding what parts of their products to identify and setting up a master identification scheme. Usually a numbering scheme works well. Using color codes for such things as draft copies of examination questions also is possible. Also, master copies of documents must be maintained and protected.

DEVISE NUMBERING SCHEMES

Depending upon the complexity of the training program, trainers should consider a numbering system for, among other things, drawings, flowcharts, job-aids, statements of objectives, and exercises. The numbering system for these items should be structured so the base document— usually a lesson plan—is the anchor number for the numbering scheme. Regardless of the scheme used, trainers should keep it simple and useful.

CONTROL REVISIONS

A revision numbering system to update lesson materials needs to be in place. Trainers need to decide how to handle lesson material revisions. For example, what happens when an overhead within the lesson plan is revised? Is the entire lesson plan revised, or just the identification for the overhead transparency? Either system might be satisfactory when applied consistently. Also, there must be a method to remove old materials from circulation as training materials are revised.

IDENTIFY FOR TRAINING USE ONLY MATERIALS

The company needs to decide if trainees may use training materials on their jobs. Some companies, particularly in technical manufacturing or operations environments, allow employees to use only approved manufacturing or operations procedures. If training materials are not allowed on the job, they should be labeled carefully. For example, some organizations mark every page of a training document *For Training Use Only.*

PROTECT CONFIDENTIALITY

An issue related to training materials concerns confidentiality. Product designs and company procedures might be considered confidential for business reasons such as competition. In such instances, training materials must be marked and safeguarded appropriately.

Reality Check

This guideline element covers an administrative function, which may be the least interesting type of requirement. However, auditors perceive a well-structured administrative process as proving organizational credibility. Good administrative systems always impress auditors because good systems convey the message that the organization knows what it is doing and has its processes in control. A messy administrative process is confusing and frustrating for everyone who uses it. Of all the work trainers accomplish, administrative process is what assessors can see. It is evidence trainers can offer that their programs are in control. The most effective training program in the world cannot be audited without good administrative paperwork.

CHAPTER 14

Element 4.9

Process Control

This element should help eliminate the black-box syndrome typical of many processes, particularly training processes. The *black-box syndrome* reflects the insufficient understanding some individuals have of processes, that is, how work is done and what it takes to produce products or services. In the end, customers do not care what it takes to provide a product or service. They want their needs satisfied, and how ISO suppliers achieve that goal is immaterial. What is important to customers is that the product or service is right the first time. A basic tenet of quality assurance and ISO 9000 is that if processes are in control, then products or services will meet customer requirements.

The people who most care, however, about processes are those who must work within the system to implement them. Too frequently, people doing work do not understand either what they are doing or how their tasks affect the finished product. The net result is islands of knowledge where each individual may understand only a small part of the process. This is the antithesis of learning organizations and continuous improvement processes, because in this situation no one can help the organization learn from its errors or make improvements. Element 4.9, Process Control, addresses these issues.

What the ISO 9001 Standard Says

This element of the standard requires the company "to identify and plan the production, installation and servicing processes which directly affect quality and ... ensure these processes are carried out under controlled conditions." This one sentence may be the most powerful of the entire standard. It says companies have to figure out what they are doing now and how and what they should be doing. Companies state what they should be doing in their quality policy, objectives, and goals. In this element companies articulate what they are doing. Several tactics can help companies figure out what they are doing. Flowcharts of major processes and individual jobs and tasks can help the company tie together all the knowledge about what the organization is doing. More information and detail should be contained in procedures which serve as excellent communication devices within and among various departments to help employees know what they are doing.

The element lists seven areas companies should address. The company needs:

■ Documented procedures to tell how work is done.

The element says "where the absence of such procedures could adversely affect quality." The simple truth is any process could adversely affect quality, and there is little practical reason for any company to use this criteria to judge whether to develop a procedure to cover a process. The company must prepare and use a procedure for each element in the ISO standard and should prepare and use a procedure for

117

each major or primary process in their operation. Language in Element 4.2.2, Quality System Procedures, provides more reasonable criteria to decide what procedures are needed when it says this decision is "dependent upon the complexity of the work, the methods used, and the skills and training needed by personnel involved in carrying out the activity." The more complex a process or the less well trained the employees, the more detailed procedures need to be. Simple processes and experienced employees do not require detailed procedures.

- Suitable production equipment and working environment.

This requirement is reflected in several areas throughout the standard, including control of inspection processes and also handling and storage requirements. When auditors address the working environment issue, they are concerned about the safety and well-being of both people and machinery.

- Compliance with regulatory/statutory codes and the company's own procedures.

This requirement is directly tied to and strengthens the clauses on Quality Planning, Element 4.2.3, and also Design Input, Element 4.4.4.

- To monitor and control *process parameters* and *product characteristics*.

This requirement supports elements related to inspection and testing, measuring devices, and control of customer-supplied and nonconforming products.

- To approve use of processes and equipment.

Management must approve process procedures and the use of equipment. This requirement should be tied into and support company efforts to satisfy Element 4.1.3, Management Review, and 4.2.3, Quality Planning.

- Established workmanship criteria.

Workmanship criteria refer to product physical characteristics and how well the product is fabricated. Acceptance criteria are mentioned several places in the standard including Design Control, Purchasing, the elements related to inspection and testing, and perhaps most importantly 4.1.1, Quality Policy. Established workmanship criteria are reflected in product specifications and customer expectations of how the product will work. They are directly related to the company's commitment to quality.

■ Equipment maintenance.

This requirement is related to several activities, including process capability. Configuration management and preventive maintenance programs are also related to this item.

Finally, the element talks about special processes such as welding or painting. A special process (see Note 16) is one where subsequent inspections will not reveal nonconformances. For example, painting an airplane wing covers hairline cracks that may ultimately lead to structural failures. Once the wing is painted, inspections will not reveal defects. Any such special process requires either continuous monitoring or should be done only by qualified personnel. Both equipment and personnel requirements for special processes need to be clearly specified and records for both maintained.

What ISO Auditors Look For

Auditors enjoy assessing this area. After all, process control is the heart of the operation and where real work gets done. Additionally, there are lots of documents in use for auditors to look at. They include flowcharts, task lists, checklists, travelers, routing cards, posted notices, test/inspection routines, shop tickets, work instructions, and many other documents showing sequences of activities.

Auditors will talk to line personnel and evaluate their training and experience to do the work as a way to judge adequacy of process control documentation. Better trained and more experienced personnel need fewer or less detailed procedures. When documents are required, auditors will look to see if they are readily available in the workplace. There is a hidden dilemma here, however. Documents must be controlled. At the same time they must be readily available for use. Auditors will tie availability of documents back to Document and Data Control, Element 4.5, as they assess process control.

Auditors will interview operations personnel and ask about workmanship criteria, look at specifications, and then tie them to records of operating parameters or run-charts. However, unless the assessors are production experts in the particular process, they really cannot judge the adequacy of workmanship criteria. They are only able to assess that the criteria are available and used.

Beyond these obvious items, auditors will also try to tie process control back to design control and quality plans to ensure that design and plans support production. The auditors ought to be able to find obvious connections such as product specifications, inspection points, product characteristics, and production steps in all three: process control, design control, and quality planning. Finally, they will look at preventive maintenance records and records of equipment failures. Auditors will expect to see trend analyses of such events and their effects on process capability. It is at this point that auditors will tie process control into Statistical Techniques, Element 4.20, and Management Review, Element 4.1.3.

What the Education and Training Guideline Says

The element begins by supporting the standard's concept that processes need to be controlled to ensure that desired outcomes are achieved. This control includes identifying important activities, ways to measure these activities, and criteria of acceptable performance. The major activities outlined are essentially the five steps in an ISD model. The element identifies these as "needs assessment, instructional design, development, delivery, and outcomes measurements." The guideline authors also require trainers to control the seven major support processes identified in the standard. All these processes should be documented and controlled. Management should review their efficacy. Changes should be documented and evaluated.

The guideline authors consider all education and training activities to be special processes as defined by the standard. They are correct. Education and training outcomes cannot be, in the language of the standard, "fully verified by subsequent inspection and testing." It could be argued that if the trainee can demonstrate proficiency on a performance evaluation, then the training process was effective. Unfortunately, that argument cannot be relied upon because, first, some trainees will not succeed, and, second, sometimes some trainees succeed in spite of the training.

The standard offers two ways to address a special process. The first is to perform continuous monitoring of the process. Obviously, education and training activities cannot be continuously monitored. Therefore, as a practical matter, trainers will need to use the second alternative and use qualified personnel to conduct training activities. Additionally, qualified educators and trainers must structure their processes to ensure that they achieve desired outcomes. Or more simply, controlled processes support desired quality outcomes.

Interestingly enough, the guideline authors suggest a way for trainers to choose not to use the ISO guideline. They suggest trainers could use an Instructional Plan rather than ISO. However, the guideline description of what should be included in an Instructional Plan is a neat summary of a five-step ISD model and in effect brings together all of the ideas contained in the ISO Education and Training Guideline. In fact, an Instructional Plan would meet, if not the letter of the guideline, then its entire spirit. The authors say *Instructional Plans* include prerequisites, lesson objectives, assessment standards, instructional strategies, controls of any kind, post-course assessments and follow-up of learning, and the role of materials selected for use. It should also include a needs assessment and results analysis report.

Trainers who use the guideline should use an Instructional Unit Plan. This plan is often called a Training Map or Instructor's Guide. It details roles of trainers and trainees, activities of both, and assessment of both. The plan for trainee-led activities will be different from the plan for instructor-led activities. Regardless, evaluation of training activities and trainees is required in both.

Finally, the authors make a strong tie between this element and Element 4.18, Training. They require that personnel who are responsible for instruction need to demonstrate and document their capabilities through employment records, operations and trainer experience, observations of trainers by supervisors, and formal education and training. There is a detailed requirement for vendors to provide evidence of instructor qualifications and detailed information about the content of instruction to be delivered.

What Training Assessors Look For

Training assessors, like ISO auditors, enjoy assessing this element. After all, process control is where the entire quality and production efforts come together. It is visible evidence of all of the work. Like ISO auditors, they will look at the seven items specifically mentioned in the standard and then look at the five items of the ISD model mentioned in the guideline. As part of this element and Element 4.18, assessors will judge experience levels of trainers and observe training in progress to judge how well instructors are delivering instruction. Finally, training assessors will tie all processes and procedures together to form a judgment about how well the training organization is meeting its own goals and supporting its company's corporate goals.

Q-Project Action Items

PUBLISH A MASTER FLOWCHART

Devise a training process flowchart and try to limit it to 20 or so items. The master flowchart is supposed to show the primary steps and be easy to understand. Do not make this flowchart too detailed. Make sure each of the five steps in an ISD model, 20 elements in the guideline, and seven items in this element of the guideline are reflected in the master process flowchart. Include this flowchart as part of the Training Quality Manual and post a large version in a conspicuous place in the training offices. This flowchart will help dispel the common black-box syndrome and give management and employees a visual picture of what is going on.

FLOWCHART PROCESSES

Devise more detailed process flowcharts for each element in the standard and each step in the ISD model. Include these flowcharts in their respective procedures. As a starting point, before writing procedures, these flowcharts will help trainers understand each of the individual processes and, when seen with the overall flowchart, will clarify how individual processes fit into the overall process.

DEVELOP INSTRUCTIONAL UNIT PLANS

Training Maps or Instructor's Guides are excellent devices to help trainers stay on track. As lesson materials are designed and developed, it is a simple process to produce Instructional Unit Plans. However, do not fall into the trap of merely copying lesson plans and calling them Instructor's Guides. Instructor's Guides need to tell trainers what their activities are and what trainees are supposed to be doing. For example, they should include notes on when to show overheads, how to conduct exercises, and what questions to ask to sample trainee understanding. Do not fall into the other trap of writing extremely detailed Instructor's Guides. Guides are supposed to help instructors, not handcuff them. A good Instructor's Guide will allow an experienced and knowledgeable trainer to spend a relatively short amount of time preparing to deliver a training activity.

QUALIFY INSTRUCTORS

This element requires trainers to demonstrate the capability to deliver effective and efficient instruction. That means trainers must be both subject matter qualified and trainer qualified. There needs to be an ongoing program for trainers to stay current and improve in both topics. This is essential if they are going to remain credible and satisfy their customers' needs.

Reality Check

This is either the easiest or most difficult element of the ISO guideline to assess. On a superficial level it is difficult because there is so much to look at. There are so many hooks into every other element of the guideline that stepping back and seeing how everything fits together is difficult. For the same reason it is easiest to assess because looking at process control gives assessors an opportunity to step back and see how all elements fit together into the whole.

Assessors need objective evidence when they assess quality assurance programs. Much documentation is required in this element, and there is plenty of objective evidence to be gathered. Objective evidence allows assessors to judge if training processes do what they say they do and if they support the organization's strategic goals.

Some trainers might attempt to avoid writing process procedures on the grounds that subsequent tests and inspections will find problems. This tactic would rely on quality control, i.e., inspections, to catch errors. This tactic is fundamentally flawed because the entire ISO 9000 concept rests on quality assurance to control processes so products or services are right the first time, rather than on quality control/inspections that attempt to fix problems after they happen.

One final note: The guideline authors raise the issue that some individuals may see process control as an infringement on *academic freedom*. The argument that ISO will infringe on academic freedom is at best a non-issue and at worst, a red herring. Capable and experienced trainers who know both the standard and guideline know process control has nothing to do with academic freedom. It has everything to do with being capable, well organized, and prepared.

CHAPTER 15

Element 4.10

Inspection and Testing

This element establishes the need to establish quality assurance checks at appropriate points in a process and include them in a quality plan. The questions to ask when deciding which points in a process need a quality check are:

- If there is a problem at this point, will it adversely affect the next step?
- Is it possible the next step will correct the problem?
- Is a quality check at this point important?

The element identifies three obvious places in any process where a checkpoint might be appropriate: the start (receiving materials), in process, and the end (final). Inspection records are necessary at each step as evidence that inspections were completed. Quality plans can be structured to handle inspection points concurrently with Element 4.9, Process Control, which identifies what inspection will be done. This element allows the company flexibility to identify checkpoints in its processes and quality plan where inspections should occur.

Element 4.10 helps training organizations in several ways. First, plans specifying process and outcomes help structure training processes. Second, plans identifying process and outcomes within an ISD model help eliminate the black-box syndrome in which non-trainers fail to appreciate the effort required to produce a training program. Trainers know that about 75% of the total work takes place before and after delivering training; delivery is only one of the five steps in an ISD model. Third, Inspection and Testing gives trainers an opportunity to invite management and supervision to participate in designing and developing training as part of the review and approval process. By participating in these processes, they gain an appreciation for resources needed to produce effective and efficient training programs.

What the ISO 9001 Standard Says

There are five clauses in this element. Two require an overall procedure (or a quality plan) for inspection and testing activities and records as evidence of completed inspections. Records must clearly show that inspected items either passed or failed according to the criteria established by the plan. If they fail, then Element 4.13, Control of Nonconforming Product, must cover subsequent actions. Element 4.10 also requires the plan or procedure to identify who has inspection authority and responsibility for releasing the product.

The remaining three clauses address inspections at receiving, during the process, and at completion. All three require plans to identify stop or inspection points and descriptions of how inspections are conducted. Each of the three clauses discusses:

- Specifications, acceptance criteria, and work instructions detailing how to conduct inspections.
- Descriptions of inspection documentation and

identification of who conducts inspections and who is responsible for ensuring they are conducted correctly.

What ISO Auditors Look For

Auditors evaluating inspection and testing would:

- Review inspection procedure(s) and completed records.
- Look for work instructions and see if blank inspection forms are available at inspection points.
- Try to learn if acceptance criteria are defined clearly.
- Assess the physical layout of receiving areas to see if they are segregated from other areas to prevent inadvertent use of incoming materials before they are inspected.
- Compare a sample of purchase orders with their receiving inspection records.
- Observe in-process inspections to ensure required inspections are adequate and conducted before items are sent forward.
- Ensure nonconforming products are marked, segregated, and not used.
- Review final inspection checklists for evidence that all required inspections are conducted before the product is released.

What the Education and Training Guideline Says

The guideline has six clauses, in contrast to the standard's five. The first clause in the guideline and standard similarly requires a documented process for inspection and testing activities. The additional guideline clause refers to trainee transcripts and, like Element 4.18, Training, requires specific record keeping.

The guideline equates entrance or diagnostic examinations to receiving inspections. Trainers should assess the ability, aptitude, and prior work experience of trainees entering a program to confirm that the pace and level of instruction are appropriate for their needs. Training organizations should establish and publish prerequisites in course catalogues and promotional materials. If there are no prerequisites, the instructor should plan an activity at the start of the program to assess trainees' needs. This activity will help the instructor adjust the pace and content. However, this is a last minute change tactic and, in practice, might not work effectively.

The element also addresses inspection of audiovisual equipment and training supplies, such as software or videotapes, to verify that they meet acceptance criteria specified in purchase orders. The element specifically mentions services supplied, such as training programs provided by a vendor, in this context. It should be routine practice to specify criteria and then inspect these materials on arrival to verify that they meet specifications.

The three guideline clauses connected to in-process inspection or evaluation activities relate to the following information:

- Inspections of the trainees, i.e., formative evaluations, are spaced throughout the training to ensure trainees are learning the material.
- Inspections are held to discover whether materials are adequate to meet trainees' needs.
- Inspections of instructors' performance are conducted.
- Instructors following the course plan are doing a good job meeting trainee needs during instruction.

The guideline equates end-of-course performance examinations to final inspection and tests. These are summative evaluations at the conclusion of the instruction.

129

There are three parts to final inspections:

- Assessment of trainees' final performance.
- Confirmation that trainees passed all required examinations before they are certified.
- Assessment of the effectiveness of training and trainees' ability to perform on the job.

Management should document their reviews of these assessments. Finally, an additional clause in the guideline calls for post-training evaluations to identify incorrect or omitted information and ways to improve the program. It includes a process to notify former trainees of incorrect or omitted information.

What Training Assessors Look For

Knowledgeable training assessors would take the same approach as ISO auditors, looking at the following items:

- An assessment plan.

Assessors would expect to see a plan to conduct appropriate inspections throughout training and would review records to see they were conducted.

- Pre-training assessment of trainees and their needs.

Assessors would be interested in seeing techniques used to evaluate incoming trainees' abilities. Some trainees may be ill-prepared to profit from training, either because of inadequate prior training or job experience. Other trainees may believe the activities are a waste of time because they already possess the SKAs.

- Assessments during training to ensure trainees are making good progress in the training and the instructor is doing a good job.

Assessors would look for evidence that trainees are mastering the material through such things as written examinations and performance demonstrations. To see if the instructor is effective, assessors would be interested in reviewing examinations and lesson plans and, if possible, watching training activities in progress. During observations, they might be particularly interested in how instructors get feedback that participants understand the material. Questions the instructor asks during presentations provide one indication of feedback.

- Reviews of final examinations to ensure trainees complete all requirements before certification.

Assessors would look at final examination records as part of the review of Element 4.18, Training.

- Recommended revisions to improve training.

Assessors would review the procedure controlling recommended revisions. Recommendations may come from trainees, trainees' management or supervision, and from instructors. Assessors might try to follow a submitted recommendation through its review and resolution; for example, its incorporation into the next revision of lesson materials.

- Post-training assessments.

Again, assessors would review records and the procedure for handling corrections and omissions. They might interview former trainees and ask them if they were contacted about the training and if they had made any suggestions for corrections or improvements. Assessors would attempt to find examples of how this process worked by following a recommendation through to its incorporation into lesson revisions or other appropriate resolution.

- Records of all inspections and tests.

This is a review of training department documentation of events within the training organization. Although the guideline specifically refers to trainee transcripts, some reviews, such as in-process evaluations of instructors, are not maintained in trainee transcripts. These kinds of reviews require a separate record-keeping process. These data will support Element 4.20, Statistical Techniques.

■ Inspections of purchased materials and supplies.

Assessors would probably cover most of these under Element 4.6, Purchasing. However, they might review incoming materials against purchase orders as part of Element 4.10.1, Receiving Inspection and Testing.

Q-Project Action Items

SPECIFY PREREQUISITES

Ensure that all publicity materials and course catalogues clearly specify trainee prerequisites. Frequently, a section entitled "Who Should Attend" lists job positions of those who would benefit from training. That level of detail is satisfactory for many general or information-type programs. However, when a trainee needs specific prior training and/or job experience, curriculum materials (for training staff) and publicity materials (for potential attenders) should describe these requirements specifically and in careful detail.

USE PRETESTS/SURVEYS

Give a pretest or conduct a survey of individuals who have signed up for training before they attend. A pretest (a formal, controlled activity) would measure specific, required SKAs. A survey is a form of a needs analysis. It should solicit ideas from trainees on their job needs and what they expect to gain from training to satisfy those needs. The survey should also ask about previous training and job experience.

CONDUCT EXPECTATIONS EXERCISES

A useful instructor exercise at the beginning of training is to conduct an expectations discussion. The instructor asks: "What do you expect from this training?" As trainees respond, the instructor writes ideas on a flip chart. The instructor should post the list where it is easily accessible. As the class meets the objectives, the instructor checks off or adds items as appropriate. During multiple-day classes, the list can be used each morning to review past ideas and focus on upcoming activities.

CONNECT EXAMINATION QUESTIONS

Examination questions and performance assessments should be developed concurrently with training materials and approved before instruction begins. These training assessments should be based on performance objectives established during the design phase. This approach ensures that training activities and examinations are mutually supporting.

INCLUDE FEEDBACK QUESTIONS

Feedback questions instructors plan to ask during instruction should be written into lesson plans at appropriate points. Ongoing assessment of trainee progress is critical to success. Too frequently, instructors attempt to ask questions on-the-fly to see whether trainees are understanding material. As a result, they get little useful information from feedback questions, or they confuse trainees. Effective oral questioning techniques help trainees assess their progress and prove to them they are succeeding. This immeasurably enhances trainees' self-confidence and success. Including carefully prepared questions in lesson plans is an excellent training technique and an excellent in-process inspection device.

SCHEDULE VISITS/OBSERVATIONS

Schedule trainers' and attenders' supervisors to attend portions of training to assess the quality of instruction. Besides providing in-process assessments, these visits demonstrate management's support for training and send a clear message that training is an important activity.

Reality Check

Too frequently, management has a black-box perception of training activities. They see trainees go to training and magically emerge trained. They do not appreciate the resources needed to prepare and execute effective and efficient training programs. Moreover, many managers fail to understand the value of good follow-up, post-training evaluations.

Element 4.9, Process Control, and Element 4.10, Inspection and Testing, are powerful tools to correct these perceptions. Essentially, these two elements make sure training processes are in place and are in control. They help trainers establish plans that draw management and supervision into the process. This has at least three outcomes. First, because management is involved, trainees receive the clear message that training is important. Second, the element helps prove training is effective in meeting trainees' and supervisors' needs, so trainers gain credibility. Third, because they see the process and product of training more clearly, management can associate strategic results with resources spent on training.

CHAPTER 16

Element 4.11

Control of Inspection, Measuring and Test Equipment

Element 4.11, Inspection, Measuring and Test Equipment, may be the most difficult of the 20 elements in the ISO 9001 Standard to apply to training. Although calibrating test and measurement equipment is a priority in high-technology, regulated, and environmentally sensitive arenas, in many other settings it is not a major concern. Whereas the ISO 9001 Standard element is lengthy, the Education and Training Guideline element is very short, limited to calibrating laboratory equipment. Training programs in health physics, engineering, drafting, surveying, or any training using measuring instruments should address this element.

Ironically, by limiting this element to laboratory equipment, the guideline authors have sidestepped an extremely important issue. Examinations, whether written or performance-based, are measurement instruments, and this element can help show training's effectiveness. Training is demonstrably effective when performance standards require trainees to show proficiency as an outcome of training. Based on this philosophy, instruments (tests) must effectively measure what they say they measure. That is, tests must be valid. A test is valid if it is calibrated or validated in some way. The easiest way to validate a test is to show connections between examination questions, lesson objectives, and the SKAs needed on the job. Therefore, the best tests are ones in which trainees actually perform tasks they do on their jobs. Without demonstrating that trainees can use training, results are at best guesswork. Validating examinations also will help trainers meet requirements in Element 4.20, Statistical Techniques.

This chapter is organized around two separate issues because this element addresses two divergent areas (laboratory equipment, if used) and examinations (neither a requirement nor suggested in the guideline). Readers who do not have laboratory equipment or who elect not to address the examination issue should briefly review the standard and guideline.

What the ISO 9001 Standard Says

This element requires control, calibration, and maintenance of measuring devices used to verify that products meet specified requirements. This element includes test software. Companies meet these requirements when they ensure test equipment:

- Is calibrated properly against a known standard.
- Is appropriate and can produce required measurements.
- Measures consistently (so environmental variables such as heat do not affect calibration).
- Is used correctly and consistently.
- Is not adjusted by unauthorized persons.

Procedure(s) should address each applicable item

from the nine listed in the element. Besides a procedure to control test and measurement devices, a statement in the quality manual should commit the company to calibrate and control measurement equipment. Procedure(s) and/or work instructions should explain:

- Who is responsible for policy implementation and use.
- How to calibrate each piece of equipment.
- What are calibration frequency and calibration standards.
- The required placement of visible tags or identifications on calibrated instruments including when the next calibration is due.
- How control (traceability) and maintenance of records are handled.
- Use of a system of warning labels not to use equipment exempt from the calibration program.

What ISO Auditors Look For

This element is a record-keeping function and easy to audit. However, questions may arise when the company seeks to exempt a piece of equipment, such as employee-owned equipment, from calibration. The 1994 version of the standard eliminates this point of contention. It requires companies to identify and control "all inspection, measuring and test equipment that can affect product quality" no matter who owns a particular instrument. From a practical standpoint, avoiding philosophical discussions and differences of opinion by simply including all measurement equipment in the calibration program is easier. Auditors might review these items:

- The general procedure describing the test and measurement equipment control program.
- A list of all measurement equipment by serial number and type.

137

- Work instructions describing how to calibrate each piece of equipment.
- Calibration records to show completed calibrations and next calibration due dates.
- Instruments used in production and test areas to ensure only correctly marked instruments are available and used.

To check application of the procedures auditors might:

- Select a sample from the list of instruments and go into production areas and find those instruments.
- Work backward by selecting several instruments in production areas and look up their records.
- Talk with personnel or ask them to show how they use a work instruction to calibrate a piece of equipment.
- Discuss adequacy of test equipment with both production and design personnel.

What the Education and Training Guideline Says

The guideline adds little to the standard. The guideline contains a parenthetical note in the title that it refers to laboratory equipment. It also mentions that test and measurement equipment used in routine production might be used to support a training program. Where that occurs, this equipment should be covered in the company's quality assurance program, and the training program would refer to the company's Q.A. program, thereby eliminating the need for trainers to have their own test equipment program.

What Training Assessors Look For

Training assessors should decide on their approach to this element based on how the training organization structured its test equipment program.

■ If the training organization has no laboratory or test equipment, assessors will not address this issue.

■ If the training organization uses its own measurement equipment, assessors would rely on the standard rather than the guideline. Because the standard focuses primarily on the quality of production output, training organizations should decide if their instruments need to meet the same rigorous standards as production measurement devices.

■ If the training program uses production instrumentation, assessors would expect to see a quality manual statement (a single sentence is sufficient) that the training program relies on the company's quality assurance methods to ensure test and measurement equipment accuracy.

■ When the training organization owns test equipment, a simple solution is to agree with the production organization to include training equipment in their calibration program.

Q-Project Action Items

Trainers may legitimately elect not to define performance tests and written examinations as measurement devices and remain within the ISO guidelines. The remaining discussion and suggestions in this chapter will help trainers who see value in addressing examinations in this way.

CORRELATE LEARNING OBJECTIVES AND EXAM QUESTIONS

The test or examination should adequately reflect mastery of all materials taught in the lesson. A simple matrix of lesson objectives to test items will help visualize this correlation between learning objectives and examination questions. From a practical standpoint, such a matrix of examination items to objectives is adequate to see how well the examination samples desired outcomes.

CONNECT OBJECTIVES AND SKAS

Generally, training should change trainees' skills, knowledges, and attitudes appropriate to the objective. A shortcoming in both academic and corporate examinations is that objectives are identified at one level and examinations are evaluated at a different level. An examination question asking pilot trainees to list three procedures to use in case of engine shut-down will not adequately show that pilots can successfully apply those procedures. A firefighter's skills objective might be to chop through a burning roof with an ax. An examination question asking firefighters to state the weight of an ax does not prove they can chop a hole. A clear connection between objectives and resulting skills, knowledges, and attitudes is critical. A matrix of examination items to objectives, with a subcategory identifying SKAs and their levels, will show the examination accurately tests desired training outcomes.

USE WORK INSTRUCTIONS AS A CALIBRATION

Demonstration of a work instruction or procedure steps may be used as a performance test. A work instruction or procedure is, by definition, calibrated. If doing the task in a work setting is not possible, a work instruction may be seen as calibrated if it accurately represents the steps in the task.

USE ITEM ANALYSES

It is wise to use item analyses in settings where many individuals must be trained and pass a written proficiency examination. An item analysis is a statistical technique showing that a given examination question can distinguish between those trainees who know the material and those who are simply guessing. It associates correct answers on particular target items with high overall scores and/or with low overall scores. In general, individuals who earn high scores on the examination will answer the question correctly while individuals who earn low scores on the examination will answer the question incorrectly. An item analysis thereby identifies the value of individual questions in determining if trainees have learned the material and are not just guessing. In some situations, particularly in highly regulated or environmentally sensitive arenas, item analyses are a way to show examinations are calibrated to desired training outcomes.

PROTECT EXAMINATION MATERIALS

One important guideline point requires protecting measuring devices from "adjustments that would invalidate the calibration setting." Defining examinations as measuring instruments means every training organization must be prepared to protect examinations from compromise. Training assessors will challenge both procedures and their application to protect examinations either under this or another element. Protection must be practiced throughout the life of the examination and its individual questions. This includes all phases: writing, review and approval, administration to trainees, scoring, and storage for future use.

Reality Check

The reality is that if the training program does not have laboratory equipment, trainers do not need to address this element. If the program does have laboratory equipment, including its calibration under corporate procedures for measurement and calibration of instruments is practical.

It is important for trainers to consider including examinations under this element. Doing so sends a clear signal they are focused on outcomes to help employees develop tools needed to meet their objectives and the company's. Examinations are both extensively used and frequently misused to demonstrate training outcomes in academic and corporate settings. Test validation is difficult and sometimes esoteric. Statistically challenged trainers may struggle through the process. The severely left-brained may bog down in minutia and complexity. As a result, unfortunately, many training organizations fail to capitalize on how examinations can show that training programs are helping people improve their job performance. Including examinations in this element and as part of the ISO process can demonstrate positive outcomes from training.

CHAPTER 17

Element 4.12

Inspection and Test Status

Element 4.12, Inspection and Test Status, probably is the ISO element least applicable to training. However, that does not mean it is irrelevant. Some ideas in the guideline deserve attention. Essentially, this element requires clearly marking all items, whether they are components or finished products, so their test status (awaiting testing, passed, or failed) is clearly visible.

Making status visible has several advantages. First, it is evidence of work in progress. Also, it shows that the process is under control. For training organizations, the entire process of training (other than presenting material) frequently is invisible. Applying this element can draw attention to the many processes involved in training programs and help non-trainers track and participate in training activities.

What the ISO 9001 Standard Says

The Inspection and Test Status element builds on Element 4.10, Inspection and Testing. Its focus is the final step in the inspection process, requiring labels, or some marking, on components and products to make inspection status apparent. Status categories include nonconforming items, items waiting inspection, and passed or O.K. products and components.

There is no requirement in this element for records. However, inspection signatures on work orders or other inspection documentation prove achievement.

What ISO Auditors Look For

ISO auditors would look at the written procedure and then go into production or service areas to look for appropriate labels on components and finished products. The element requires identification throughout all stages of the process, so auditors would look in the receiving (incoming) area, shipping (outgoing) area, and all areas in between. Auditors would look at products, inspection labels, and records. As a subset of this element, nonconforming products must be, if possible, physically separated so they are not used inadvertently.

What the Education and Training Guideline Says

The guideline relies on trainee records to satisfy this element. However, it also refers to two training elements that should be inspected: facilities and materials. Facilities include classrooms, meeting areas, laboratories, or any area where training is conducted. Facilities might also include equipment such as videotape machines, computers, and overhead projectors. One benefit of having use and inspection records of facilities is that they help establish training resource needs.

Materials include all curriculum materials such as lesson plans, trainee handouts, overhead transparencies, and examinations. Documented procedures should describe how

144

and when training materials are inspected and reviewed as they move through the development and approval process. Training materials should be inspected at the end of the development process and before use.

Finally, a pilot or demonstration of all or part of a training package before it is presented to the general population would help satisfy the requirements of this element. The idea of piloting portions of training materials is covered at length in Design Control, Element 4.4.

What Training Assessors Look For

A training assessor would look to see:

- If review of lesson materials is addressed in a procedure or in the quality manual.
- Whether inspection or review points are identified and lesson materials and examinations in development are marked or labeled appropriately.
- Whether supplies and materials, including purchased training materials, are inspected according to requirements in purchasing contracts and if these inspections are noted on incoming materials.

Q-Project Action Items

PUBLICIZE PROJECT STATUS

Flowcharts and progress reports are excellent ways to publicize what trainers are doing and how they are using their resources. Establish a facilities and materials inspection review process that includes ways to identify the inspection status of all products. Flowchart processes and make a public display (on bulletin boards or in monthly reports) of training projects under development.

MARK MATERIALS IN DEVELOPMENT

Mark draft copies of lesson materials and use a revision number system for training materials under development. A simple system will help ensure materials under development are under control.

SCHEDULE SME REVIEWS

As training materials are produced, use non-training supervisors and subject matter experts to review lesson materials as part of the quality plan. These line personnel understand the purpose of inspection points. Couch the review in terms they understand, that is, as quality assurance inspections. Use SME language to stress suitability of materials to satisfy trainees' needs. Asking subject matter experts to inspect materials helps them appreciate their own contribution and makes their time and energy appear worthwhile.

Reality Check

Besides having practical outcomes of helping trainers manage their business, applying quality plans and making inspection status known have some political advantages. What gets measured gets attention. What gets marked gets noticed. Training teams who know their corporate culture or who recognize this tendency—to value visible, measured data over other types—in their corporation can turn this element into a strategic advantage.

The team should use this element to promote their activities and obtain support for needed resources. Project plans for obtaining or producing lesson materials should have approval or inspection points from both training and corporate supervision built into the process. A visible indicator such as a large, conspicuously located flowchart helps personnel outside the training organization understand "something is happening here." Establishing a visible process builds support for training activities.

CHAPTER 18

Element 4.13

Control of
Nonconforming Product

A reality of the world is that things do not always go as planned. Element 4.13, Control of Nonconforming Product, addresses the status of products or services anywhere in the system that are not in conformance, that is, not as they ought to be. Nonconformances can exist in relation to government regulations, quality standards, customer contracts and specifications, or company procedures or policies. Element 4.13 is the capstone of five ISO 9001 inspection-related elements beginning with 4.8, Product Identification and Traceability, through 4.12, Inspection and Test Status. This element requires a quality assurance system to identify how to handle products or services properly that do not meet established or required standards. Because of its scope, it also provides an opportunity to look at overall performance of manufacturing or service processes.

Element 4.13 addresses nonconformances in the system. There are two levels of nonconformances, major and minor, and two categories of nonconformances, systems and compliance. A systems nonconformance would usually be classified as a major nonconformance. A systems nonconformance means:

- There is no process in place to address an element of the standard, or
- If there is a system, it is not documented adequately in a procedure or work instruction, or
- If it is documented, there is significant failure by employees to follow the procedure, i.e., personnel are ignoring the procedure.

When a nonconformance is labeled as minor, it usually means the system and procedures are in place, but individuals are not following the procedures adequately. These nonconformances are usually found in compliance audits and can occur because:

- Individuals do not know or understand the procedure, or
- Management is not providing adequate oversight to ensure that personnel follow procedures, or
- The procedure is inadequate or incorrect, or
- Individuals have found a better way to do a task.

In a training situation there are at least four possible kinds of nonconformances. They occur when:

- Training materials or programs do not meet trainees' needs.

For example, a program may not provide information trainees need on their jobs. Additionally, lesson materials may not be user-friendly or reach the trainees' experience level.

- The instructor is not doing a good job.

The instructor may be new to the material or not have practical subject experience or instructor skills. Another possibility is that, for some reason, the instructor is distracted and not giving full attention to either the presentation or trainee needs.

■ Trainees are not doing a good job.

Trainees may not see the training as important to their jobs. Concerns about what is happening at their job while they are attending training may distract them from the program. They may already know or believe they know the material.

■ There may be an administrative support failure.

Examples of administrative support failure include unavailable handouts, a poorly planned schedule, substandard facilities (for example, too hot, too noisy, or poorly lit), or inoperative audiovisual equipment.

What the ISO 9001 Standard Says

The element requires a process be in place to ensure that nonconforming product does not continue through the process. Although the element does not directly say all uninspected products are nonconforming, it is a wise idea to treat all materials (from initial receipt all the way through to shipment) as nonconforming until they have been inspected. The previous elements of the standard, particularly 4.10, Inspection and Testing, and 4.12, Inspection and Test Status, require that all components and finished products be labeled with their correct inspection status. Element 4.13 carries this process into nonconforming products, which also must be identified (labeled) and segregated so they are not used.

This element provides several possible ways to correct nonconforming products. These include:

■ Fix the defect so products meet the standard.
■ Ask the customer to accept products that do not meet specifications.
■ Use the product for another suitable application.
■ Turn the product into scrap.

149

There are two additional requirements in this element. First, if the company decides to fix the defect, reworked products must be reinspected before they are accepted. Second, if the company decides to ask the customer to accept nonconforming products, they must provide a description of the nonconformity and/or the repairs.

What ISO Auditors Look For

Usually registrars organize audits so the auditor who looks at Inspection and Testing (4.10) and Inspection and Test Status (4.12) also looks at Control of Nonconforming Product (4.13). The thinking is that if a company does a good job with inspection elements, it will generally do a good job with Element 4.13. That is, the natural outcome of addressing inspection is control of product or service that does not pass inspection, i.e., Control of Nonconforming Product.

Additionally, auditors would ensure there is a procedure in place to meet the requirements of the standard. There might also be work orders showing repairs and re-inspections for auditors to review. Auditors might review records of discussions with customers concerning acceptance of nonconforming products.

What the Education and Training Guideline Says

The guideline identifies four kinds of potential nonconformances. These nonconformances may occur during:

- Needs assessment.
- Instructional design, development, and delivery.
- Outcomes measurement.

Regardless of when they occur, the nonconformance is that either the trainee fails the instruction or the instruction fails the trainee, i.e., does not give the trainee what is needed. Potential nonconformance areas might include:

- *Instruction specification:* The training does not meet

150

the need originally identified by the customer.

■ *Instructor and/or trainee performance:* Instructor evaluations and trainee feedback do not meet expectations, or trainee performances on tests and on their jobs do not meet requirements.

■ *Materials:* Materials used in the instruction process are inadequate, confusing, not user-friendly, and they do not help trainees gain the SKAs they need.

■ *Services purchased for instruction:* Purchased lesson materials delivered by in-house trainers or instruction presented by consultants or individuals external to the organization do not meet contractual or need requirements.

Also, like the ISO element, the guideline provides options to correct nonconformances. They are:

■ Provide additional instruction and retest (rework).

■ Continue at the discretion of the trainer (hoping improvement will follow).

■ Transfer trainees to another program of study (alternate application).

■ Request to leave. The guideline equates this to scrap. The guideline refers to allowing the trainee to leave (scrap the course); however, any area of the instruction which is nonconforming, including the instructor, might be scrapped.

What Training Assessors Look For

Knowledgeable training assessors, like ISO auditors, would probably review three inspection elements simultaneously because they fit together. If the training organization is doing a good job with Inspection and Testing and Inspection and Test Status, it is likely it is doing a good job with Control of Nonconforming Product. No matter how well the training organization is doing with the first two inspection elements, however, it needs to address separately concerns and issues identified in this element. Some specific things assessors might look for include:

- A procedure that covers requirements of this element.
- Instruction specifications and interviews of supervisors after completion of training to see if training met trainees' job needs.
- Observation or evaluations of instructors by training supervisors and trainee evaluations of instructors.
- Trainee records of performance tests.
- Interviews with supervisors for ideas on trainee performance on-the-job after training.
- All lesson materials, including instructor guides, trainee handouts, and audiovisual materials.
- All support documents, such as procedures, technical drawings, and manuals used for instruction.
- Controls of purchased instruction, seminars, and workshops provided by outside consultants to ensure that these purchased services meet trainee needs.
- Reviews of seminars, meetings, and conferences attended away from the organization.
- Records of trainees who have not met requirements of the training program.

Q-Project Action Items

AVOID INCONSISTENCIES

This element is a capstone for all the inspection-related elements. Because it is always easy to become inconsistent and/or redundant in two or more areas, make sure procedures written for all other inspection elements do not conflict with procedures written for this element. Potential inconsistencies include where purchasing procedures may contradict process control procedures, or where inspection and testing procedures may conflict with inspection and test status procedures.

CONSIDER HUMAN RESOURCE AND LEGAL ISSUES

Carefully establish authority and responsibility for all participants involved in controlling nonconforming product. When nonconforming product is a trainee, human resource concerns and legal issues come into play. Make sure training management, trainee supervision, human resource management, and top level management agree about what happens when a trainee is unable to meet performance requirements.

Reality Check

Organizational upheaval happens when individuals fail training. It is demoralizing to the trainee and frustrating to management since they must decide what to do for or with the individual. If a good Instructional Systems Development process is in place, it is likely training will provide the skills, knowledges, and attitudes individuals need to do their jobs. Trainees will be motivated to do well when they see training as useful to their jobs and their future success in their company.

Good training delivery and evaluation processes increase the likelihood that most trainees can succeed. However, it is always possible that someone will not make it. Rather than wait for such a situation to arise, the training organization, in conjunction with management, should develop a process to handle failures, the training function's nonconforming products.

CHAPTER 19

Element 4.14

Corrective and Preventive Action

This element is closely tied to Element 4.17, Internal Quality Audits. Internal audits generate nonconformances (NCRs), and Corrective and Preventive Action requires companies to correct problems. The 1994 version of this element contains a major enhancement from the 1987 standard which was criticized by practitioners working with Baldrige criteria and other quality management processes. Criticism centered on the mistaken interpretation that ISO only requires companies to ensure that they are following established procedures. The 1987 standard was not particularly clear that improvements to the system are expected. In fact, Element 4.1.3, Management Review, requires management to ensure that their quality assurance system is meeting company and customers' needs. And Element 4.17, Internal Quality Audits, requires the internal audit process to determine the effectiveness of the quality system. These two elements suggest the Q.A. system should support improvements to processes. Although Element 4.14 does not use the term *continuous improvement*, there is a strong implication in the corrective and preventive action clauses that continuous improvement is at the heart of the ISO standards.

To strengthen the emphasis on continuous improvement, the 1994 element was divided into a general section and two parts, one on corrective action and the other on preventive action. Taken together, along with elements on internal audits and management review, corrective and preventive action helps companies focus on customer needs, assess the effectiveness of their quality assurance system, and take steps to improve their processes.

What the ISO 9001 Standard Says

Besides the requirement for a procedure, the general clause requires two things. First, are documentation changes. If the company changes a process because of a corrective or preventive action, it must update any affected procedures. Companies may deal with this requirement either in their procedure on corrective and preventive action or in their procedure on documentation and data control.

Second, language in this clause helps companies focus on addressing important concerns first. The clause refers to taking action "appropriate to the magnitude of problems and commensurate with the risks encountered." More simply, companies should address big problems or fix things that may cause big problems. This language is very similar to the idea in Element 4.17, Internal Quality Audits, that directs companies to schedule audits and focus on "status and importance of the activity to be audited." This wording in both clauses helps companies focus on what is important so quality assurance can focus on customers' needs rather than attempting to achieve perfection in minutia. Do the big stuff first. Once that is under control, then start attacking second- and third-level concerns. Continuous improvement means always finding ways to do things better. This element says take care of the big problems first.

The corrective action clause requires four issues to be addressed:

- First, in keeping with most quality programs, there must be an effective process to handle customer complaints.
- Second, there must be a process to handle product nonconformances effectively. Customers may identify these product nonconformances, or the company's own internal audit or inspection and quality control processes may identify them.
- Third, the procedure must explain how causes of nonconformances are investigated. Although the element does not require root-cause analysis, there is a strong suggestion that companies need to structure ways to investigate problems and correct causes, rather than just applying a Band-Aid or eliminating a symptom.
- Fourth, the company must determine corrective action to eliminate cause(s) of the nonconformity and put controls in place to make sure that both the solution is effective and the problem does not reappear. In other words, the element requires the company to fix the problem and make sure it stays fixed. Usually, as part of internal quality audits, auditors will schedule a follow-up to revisit prior nonconformances and corrective actions to make sure the solution worked and the problem has not reoccurred.

The final clause concerns preventive action. It requires the procedure to show four steps explaining how the company:

- Gathers data from all relevant information sources.
- Figures out steps needed to deal with problems

(again, the standard does not require a problem-resolution process per se; however, this second requirement is probably best satisfied by establishing a problem-solving process).

- Fixes the problem and makes sure the fix is the right fix (again, the standard is pushing companies to get at root causes rather than Band-Aid solutions for symptoms).

- Informs management about action taken through corrective action. Element 4.20, Statistical Techniques, and Element 4.1.3, Management Review, are related directly to this requirement.

What ISO Auditors Look For

This element reflects a dramatic departure from the old style of dot the "i's" and cross the "t's" quality-control auditing and, therefore, is probably the most challenging for auditors to assess. Essentially, auditors have a few basic concerns related directly to this element. However, when assessing other elements, auditors will always keep corrective and preventive processes in mind and may attempt to relate issues found in other areas back to this element.

First, several areas in the standard require companies to focus on customer needs. Therefore, auditors generally become cranky when they perceive a company is sloughing customer concerns. Similarly, auditors will want to see how quality control and inspection nonconformances are handled. These customer concerns and quality control inspection results will be relevant issues while assessors are looking at such things as quality plans, contract review, purchasing, and—within the design element—verification and validation. Second, auditors will expect to see a direct, documented link so upper level management is informed about results of corrective and preventive action processes.

157

This information should be a routine part of Element 4.1.3, Management Review.

Beyond that, auditors will review company procedures and want to know that there are established ways to identify and fix problems, whether these are identified by customers, through internal audit process, by quality control, or by suggestions or reports from line personnel. Auditors are primarily concerned that the company is getting to fundamental causes of problems and fixing causes. Just as importantly, auditors want to be assured the same problems are not recurring, i.e., the right cause is identified and the right fix is applied so that fixes stay fixed.

Finally, auditors will look at corrective and preventive action and/or documentation procedures to see how they are changed when corrective actions change processes. Frequently, this step is included in the corrective and preventive action procedure, and auditors will include a question or two in their interview checklist to gather feedback from line personnel concerning how these changes are handled.

What the Education and Training Guideline Says

Like the standard, the guideline has three sections. The first section describes potential sources for corrective action, including customers complaints, student comments, and quality audit results. Unlike the standard, the guideline directly ties statistical techniques to corrective and preventive action. Specifically, it cites use of trainee retention and success rates as ways of identifying the need for corrective and preventive action.

In keeping with the ISD model, the guideline specifies corrective and preventive action as part of the analysis, design, development, delivery, and evaluation processes. The guideline, unlike the standard, directly calls for root-cause analysis before taking corrective action. Specifying a need for identifying root causes strengthens the guideline's emphasis on avoiding quick and superficial fixes.

The clause on corrective action identifies both instructors and training activities as potential sources for corrective action. Among possible corrective actions are revising or canceling training and retraining or replacing instructors. It also requires a way to help trainees who did not succeed in training activities and a record showing how they were helped.

The clause requires an instruction record that focuses on trainees and results of instruction and contains data/results of objective trainee assessments such as tests or job-performance measures. It also establishes a need to conduct and document reviews of instruction. Particularly, there is a need to specify who is responsible for reviews, how reviews are conducted, and how these review results are used to improve instruction. The clause identifies several areas to review, including concerns reported by trainees about any aspect of instruction, concerns reported by instructors about materials or instructional strategy, and comments from subject matter experts about the content or delivery. The clause also requires that evaluations go beyond instruction, and, although it does not talk about job performance assessments, it does identify the need to tie initial job analysis and evaluations together to judge adequacy of training and training materials to meet trainee job SKAs.

The final clause in this element addresses preventive action. The clause distinguishes between preventive and corrective action. Preventive action is taken early, during development steps, and corrective action is characteristically taken later, during evaluation processes.

This clause also ties Statistical Techniques, Element 4.20, to Corrective and Preventive Action and suggests that good statistical techniques throughout all instructional steps will help eliminate potential problems, identify and correct problems, and enhance training outcomes. There is more discussion on this topic in Chapter 25.

What Training Assessors Look For

The element in the standard does a good job of connecting corrective action to continuous improvement. The element in the guideline also does that, and it ties corrective and preventive action to use of good statistics. In addition to ISO auditor concerns, training assessors have several concerns.

- The primary concern for any training assessor is whether instruction helps trainees do their jobs. The element allows knowledgeable training assessors to look at available statistical records to see that an evaluation process is applied throughout instructional processes and to tie statistics and evaluation to corrective and preventive action.

- Like ISO auditors, training assessors want to arrive at an overall conclusion about how well training is meeting corporate goals and satisfying its customers' needs. The element lists several criteria and kinds of information to help generate data and conclusions about effectiveness and efficiency of training. The guideline uses the Corrective and Preventive Action element to emphasize a need for a strong training evaluation process based on good statistical techniques.

- Training assessors are particularly interested in how companies respond to trainees who do not succeed. This can be a messy human resources issue if not adequately provided for before the situation arises. A decision not to conduct a trainee assessment is an inadequate resolution to this dilemma.

160

■ Training assessors, unlike ISO auditors, will expect to see a root-cause analysis or similar process in place that specifies how problem causes are identified. Similarly, assessors will expect to see a problem-solving process in place that defines how solutions to identified problems are developed, evaluated, and carried out.

Q-Project Action Items

TIE ELEMENTS 4.14 AND 4.17 TOGETHER

Tie together corrective and preventive action process with internal quality audit process. Make sure the documentation and data control procedure, particularly how changes are initiated and carried out, agrees with changes initiated because of corrective and preventive action.

IDENTIFY RESPONSIBILITIES AND AUTHORITIES

Identify responsibilities for internal audits, corrective and preventive action, training evaluation, and, finally, reporting of results to management. Make sure all are structured to work together. Develop flowcharts to show both individual processes and how they fit together.

ANALYZE PROBLEM SOLVING

Develop a carefully defined root-cause analysis and problem-solving process. These two have separate outcomes: the first identifies cause(s) of problems and the second develops solutions. They are separate tasks even if the company elects to structure them into one continuous process. In any case, a good process will help avoid a rush to solution before the problem is defined or its causes are known.

IMPROVE CONTINUOUSLY

Develop a user-friendly, team-based, consultive, and consensus-building process to do training evaluations. Label the process continuous improvement and emphasize benefits that will help everyone, i.e., good instruction helps trainees do their jobs well. Continuous improvement is a positive term and helps avoid the potential of assigning blame that often plagues corrective action.

CONNECT WITH HUMAN RESOURCES

Trainee assessments are a vital part of evaluation. Establish clear communication with relevant Human Resources personnel and include them on the TQT committee to do assessment of training. If H.R. persons are involved as members of TQT, they will have a buy-in and want training and trainees to succeed.

MANAGE STATISTICAL INFORMATION

Do good numbers. Make a clear tie between management review, statistics, internal quality audits, and corrective and preventive action. Good numbers justify resources spent on these activities. Management understands statistics, and good statistics and training evaluations help management understand value for resources spent on training.

Reality Check

This element of the guideline does some things much better than the standard. First, it makes a very strong tie to Element 4.20, Statistical Techniques. The use of statistics will strengthen evaluation processes and in turn make training results and outcomes understandable and valuable to non-training management.

The standard and guideline make a point of focusing concerns on those areas that are most important and most affect quality outcomes. The language of focusing and taking action "appropriate to the magnitude of the problems" will help keep everyone focused on what is important.

Assessment of performance in training, either on

written tests or via practical, performance tests, can be a tricky human resources question when trainees do not succeed. Some organizations have elected to avoid this potentially explosive issue by simply conducting training and not having any post-training assessments. This approach side-steps the guideline requirement, and ISO training assessors probably will not accept it. Also, like internal quality audits, training assessments can be sticky political issues and can develop into territorial warfare. Carefully structured and clearly communicated responsibilities and processes, along with emphasis on mutual benefit to all concerned, will help everyone accept and work together smoothly within the requirements of this element to support an effective and efficient training process.

CHAPTER 20

Element 4.15

Handling, Storage, Packaging, Preservation and Delivery

This element focuses on routine but pervasive administrative details in five areas, and it can play havoc with any quality assurance system. Too frequently, because they are separate from development and production tasks that often consume management energy, handling, storage, packaging, preservation and delivery tasks are taken for granted. Lack of specific attention to any one of these five can easily derail a process or lead to unrealized waste and other problems.

Like every other element, this one affects training quality because inattention to administrative details can result in delays and poor training design, development, and delivery. Other guideline elements adequately address several concerns raised in this element; however, some specific items need separate attention.

What the ISO 9001 Standard Says

Generally, the standard requirements are designed to protect the physical well-being of manufactured products. This protection includes both finished products and products in process, as they are fabricated or assembled. The 1994 version of the standard strengthens requirements that products be protected throughout production processes by adding the term *preservation* to this element. The element requires procedures and documentation. The Education and Training Guideline uses the plural term *procedures*, which suggests either five procedures, one for each of the five activities, or one procedure to collectively but separately address each of the five activities: handling, storage, packaging, preservation, and delivery.

Handling: There must be an established method to make sure all materials—both finished goods and work in progress—are protected from damage or deterioration. Besides specific instructions on how to treat these materials, handling procedures might include specifications for and training in the use of forklifts, pallets, and various containers. A strong safety concern is associated with handling any materials to protect the materials as well as employees.

Storage: The system must make sure storage areas are secure and separate from other areas. The organization should have systems to receive and issue items from stock and also to check the condition of the stock periodically. Storage is concerned with items received and awaiting inclusion in manufacturing processes as well as finished goods ready for shipment to the customer.

Packaging: Before shipment, products must be packed and marked to meet contract specifications and/or protect them until customers receive and accept them. This includes specifications about kinds of packaging materials used and training to ensure that employees know how to package products according to work instructions.

165

Preservation: This is a new term added to the 1994 standard. Although the intent of the requirement has not been changed, this addition strengthens the idea that products must be protected from damage and deterioration throughout production.

Delivery: This item requires product protection after final inspection and packaging and, if specified by the customer, until delivery to its destination.

What ISO Auditors Look For

Auditors would look to see if the company has organized its processes to address these five concerns and if employees are following work instructions in each of the five areas. Auditors are particularly interested in the use of safety-related items, such as transporting equipment, cranes, forklifts, and dollies. For small, delicate, or clean items, auditors look to see that there are special and fully defined processes for handling and they are followed carefully.

Auditors can usually find a fault in a storage process. Unauthorized individuals entering storage areas or individuals taking items out of storage without permission or proper paperwork are evidence that storage processes are not controlled. Another frequent failure is mixing finished goods with partially finished goods. From an auditor's perspective, it is an audit finding to have waste mixed in with or near finished products. Waste must be clearly labeled and separated from in-process and finished goods.

Additionally, auditors want to see a designated, secure (if possible) storage area for finished goods. A documented and controlled system needs to be in place to receive items into and issue items from the storage areas. Finally, auditors would review procedures and records looking for routine stock assessment or inventory control.

When reviewing packaging processes, auditors would review work instructions and then watch employees pack the product for shipment according to those instructions.

What the Education and Training Guideline Says

The guideline says application of these requirements to training organizations may be limited. Because most visible training products consist of printed materials, handling and storage of lesson and support materials are covered in Element 4.5, Document and Data Control.

The element also implicitly recognizes that trainees might be considered the training product. From this perspective, therefore, it reflects concern for the well-being of individual trainees' needs and comfort. This refers to the condition of classrooms, access to break and food areas, lighting and ventilation, and any other physical facilities that could affect the training process. Additionally, when trainees are resident at the training facility, there may be a need for personnel and personal services such as adequate housing and meals, sanitation, health care, and recreation opportunities.

Audiovisual equipment and supplies and materials used for demonstrations, mockups, and models are considered materials that must be handled, stored, and protected. How examinations are protected from compromise is an interest area for auditors, especially if the examination is for licensing or certification. The 1994 addition of the word *preservation* has application for trainers to protect examinations from compromise.

What Training Assessors Look For

Training assessors will take a somewhat different approach than ISO auditors when looking at this element. They will look at the five items; however, much of their effort will be in the document and data area. Nevertheless, training assessors will look at several items against this element.

- Assessors would look to see how lesson materials are maintained or stored and would examine the

167

lesson storage facilities to ensure they adequately protect materials.

■ Assessors will be concerned about protection and security of examination materials. This would include handling individual questions during development and approval stages and before examination questions are assembled into completed documents.

■ If there is a library or collection of support materials, such as books, manuals, and videotapes, assessors would evaluate how those are maintained and handled and whether they are accessible and protected. Of particular interest is the availability of these materials and how they are checked out for use by trainees. Also, how the organization ensures that these items are returned when due would be reviewed.

■ Audiovisual support equipment, such as videotape recorders and overhead projectors, should be included as part of handling, storage, and delivery processes. The system needs to ensure they are available as needed. A subset of audiovisual materials includes spare projector bulbs, adequate flipchart paper, clean erase boards and erasers, chalk, markers, and the like.

■ The physical plant, classrooms, laboratories, workrooms, and, if trainees are residents, all health and welfare facilities (such as lodging and recreation activities) are open for evaluation under requirements of this element.

Q-Project Action Items

STORE LESSON MATERIALS

Get lesson material storage under control. Make sure only current revisions of lesson materials are available for trainer and trainee use. If there is a requirement for historical storage of outdated materials, older materials should be marked clearly.

CONTROL AUDIO-VISUAL SUPPORT

Have a good system in place to maintain, schedule, issue, and retrieve audiovisual support equipment and provide spare parts, such as bulbs, blank overhead transparencies, marking pens, chalk, and erasers.

STORE MOCK-UPS

Have orderly storage setups for any kind of materials used for demonstrations or mock-ups.

PROVIDE TRAINING MATERIAL SUPPORT

Develop an accessible system for trainees to obtain support materials, such as textbooks, manuals, and other learning aids. Ensure tracking and return processes are timely and accurate.

CONTROL EXAMINATION MATERIALS

Control examinations and examination questions. Always! That means from writing individual questions through approval of examinations, their use, and storage for future use.

Reality Check

On its surface, this element might appear easy. Superficial attention to detail in this area, however, can lead to problems. Wasted time and reduced training effectiveness can occur in what are essentially easy areas. Auditors always count neatness and orderliness as a virtue. If auditors want to see a copy of a particular piece of lesson material, it should be quickly available. When auditors visit training areas, it is important facilities appear well maintained, support materials, such as fresh markers and spare bulbs (usually inside the machine), are readily available, and trainers can get to needed materials and avoid even minimum disruption.

CHAPTER 21

Element 4.16

Control of Quality Records

Control of Quality Records is closely linked with Element 4.5, Documentation and Data Control. Company activities are described and controlled in procedures and documents. These activities generate records. Records are objective evidence proving procedures are followed. Documentation is the "Say What You Do" portion of the ISO philosophy, whereas records reflect "Do What You Say." Records are tangible proof for auditors to see that procedures have been followed.

For many people, paperwork is the bane of work. Too frequently, unnecessary paper is generated when either management or employees try to dot each "i" and cross every "t" and thereby protect an individual or department. Obviously, some records are necessary, however, a useful records system is one that is simple, effective, and efficient. A useful record system is the result of conscientious efforts to limit records to the absolute minimum necessary to support the operation.

Many of the ISO 9000 elements include a parenthetical note referring to this record-keeping element. In fact, only six of the 19 other elements do not specifically mention Element 4.16, Control of Quality Records. Those that *do not* refer to it are:

- Element 4.5, Document and Data Control. However, there needs to be a record that documents and data are reviewed and approved for adequacy.
- Element 4.12, Inspection and Test Status. However, usually labels are seen and other records related to status are generated.
- Element 4.15, Handling, Storage, Packaging, Preservation and Delivery. However, there is a requirement to assess stock in storage. That type of inventory activity will generate a record.
- Element 4.19, Servicing. However, routine records will be associated with this activity.
- Element 4.20, Statistical Techniques. Again, keeping statistics, such as run charts or corrective action trends, will generate records.

Obviously, records are at the heart both of any business and the ISO standard. Companies need to find a happy medium between too many records and too few.

What the ISO 9001 Standard Says

The element requires a procedure that specifies how the company deals with records. Records include both internal records and, as in Document and Data Control, records received from customers and subcontractors. Note: Element 4.16 identifies only records from subcontractors; however, there are sufficient requirements throughout the rest of the standard to require control of records received from customers. For example, Element 4.3, Contract Review, and Element 4.14.2.a, Handling Customer Complaints and Reports, will generate records from customers, also.

The element calls for eight specific record-keeping

activities: identification, collection, indexing, access, filing, storage, maintenance, and disposition of records. Those eight can be summarized into a need to control the flow of records throughout the system and to be able to retrieve them when needed. Additionally, the element requires that records:

- Be legible.
- Be stored and protected from damage, deterioration, or loss.
- Have specified retention times.
- If contractually agreed to, be available for evaluation by the customer.

The element does not specifically require records to be available for review by ISO auditors; however, no company will pass an ISO audit without that access. Second, as in Element 4.5, Document and Data Control, this element recognizes the possibility of a paperless system and allows use of any recording media including computer records.

What ISO Auditors Look For

ISO auditors usually look at record-keeping systems in the context of other activities associated with an ISO audit. That is, while reviewing other elements, auditors will naturally be looking at records. Their three primary concerns are:

- Are records being maintained according to procedures to satisfy the company's Q.A. system needs?
- Are the records usable, that is, are they legible?
- Can personnel get to records they need, that is, are they retrievable?

What the Education and Training Guideline Says

Besides requirements in the standard, the guideline identifies three kinds of training records requiring attention:

- Trainee records, such as attendance records and achievement (pass/fail) status. The guideline also stipulates requirements to maintain privacy of these records.
- Records of instruction activities, i.e., reviews of examinations, job and task analysis, and all activities associated with the Instructional Systems Design model.
- A list of 14 types of records specifically associated with training and educational activities. This list represents only some of the many possible training and education records that are part of a good record-keeping system.

What Training Assessors Look For

Like ISO auditors, knowledgeable training assessors would spend a limited amount of time specifically focused on record-keeping processes. Generally, they accomplish their evaluation of records while auditing other elements. Again, legibility, utility, and retrievability are high on assessors' lists of concerns about records.

Q-Project Action Items

KEEP IT SIMPLE

Write a simple procedure to control all records and forms. Use flowcharts to show how records are generated and flow through the system. Get advice from the company records guru on how to set up such a system. Proceed with caution and avoid overly complicating the process.

USE COMPUTER HELP

Find a good, commercial administrative record-keeping computer program and use it. With a minimum investment and short learning curve, these programs can help trainers get their administrative trainee record-keeping processes under control.

DEVELOP A DATABASE

If a commercial product will not satisfy the need, use one of the wonderfully easy and very powerful relational data base programs available. Find an interested computer person to help develop a computer system to drive these administrative processes. Two cautions: first, get everyone on the same computer program and, second, make sure the selected program is a relational data base. A relational data base will allow flexibility to add and change features and structures without having to rebuild the entire system.

DO SELF-AUDITS

Routinely include records as part of internal audits and corral individuals who fail to follow requirements.

Reality Check

All golf hackers in the world know their favorite wood is their pencil. Unfortunately, every organization has its fair share of hackers. Hackers treat Element 4.16, Control of Quality Records, just like Element 4.5, Document and Data Control. They think everything must have a detailed procedure and every activity must be recorded meticulously. At the other end of the spectrum are the well-meaning free spirits who routinely and conveniently forget all records, except their travel expense reports. They "magic" their score and keep what is at best inaccurate records. There is a happy medium, and it is a medium worth seeking.

A well thought-out, carefully controlled quality record system represents objective evidence that trainers are following their procedures and succeeding in their mission. It is the visible result of all training activities. A system that simplifies easy flow and retrievable records always will impress auditors.

CHAPTER 22

Element 4.17

Internal Quality Audits

Internal Quality Audits logically fit with Element 4.14, Corrective and Preventive Action. Internal quality audits generate nonconformances (NCRs). These nonconformances are evaluated and resolved as part of corrective and preventive action. Therefore, both elements should be considered together when developing their respective procedures. Additionally, ISO Guideline 10011: Auditing Systems, will provide more information about how to structure and conduct internal audits (see Chapter 36).

There are practical and political questions to resolve when planning and conducting internal quality audits. From a practical perspective, procedures must clearly describe administrative processes, responsibilities, and paperwork flows. From a political perspective, most individuals do not like to be subjected to audits. At a minimum, they see audits as an intrusion into their work schedules. At worst, audits challenge their competence. Too frequently audits have been used as an excuse to place blame. Therefore, clearly defined roles and responsibilities for both auditors and auditees, as well as for management, will help avoid these traps and conflicts in this potentially explosive and emotional arena.

Underlying the notion of internal audits is the idea that employees who own a process probably have most to gain by making it effective and implementing it well. Internal audits are a powerful tool to help organizations determine what and how well they are actually doing. Another reality supporting the usefulness of internal audits is that most employees would prefer to identify and fix their own problems rather than having an external party point out needed improvements.

What the ISO 9001 Standard Says

This element has two goals: first, to make sure the company is doing what it says it is doing, and, second, to learn if it is doing what it ought to be doing to meet its quality objectives and its customers' requirements. One way to assess what and how well the company is doing is an internal quality audit process.

A couple of important structural issues are contained in this element:

- First, internal audits need to be conducted by people outside the process, rather than people who are responsible for it. There is some flexibility here; however, as a rule, persons directly responsible for a process or series of tasks should not conduct an internal audit of their own work. They probably cannot be objective, or they may be so close to the work they cannot see problems.
- Second, the audit should focus on important issues to ensure a quality product rather than investigate every detail of the process. The element specifically refers to status and importance of an activity. That means all activities important to quality need

to be assessed, but not every activity needs to be audited. Despite the loophole language in this element, auditors and companies routinely have difficulty deciding what is important and what is not.

■ Third, results, in the form of nonconformances, should be sent to line managers responsible for the area, and these managers should take timely action to resolve them. That does not mean line managers have to change the way they do business. It does require line managers to investigate NCRs and decide what to do and when to do it. The NCR may be a minor issue or not worth resources to correct. If line managers clearly gain upper management's agreement that the NCR is not worth the cost to correct, the NCR is effectively closed.

■ Finally, each audit schedule should include follow-up on past nonconformances to verify that resolutions have been completed and are effective.

A note attached to this clause says internal audit results should be part of the input to upper management as part of Element 4.1.3, Management Review. Notes, like guidelines, are not part of the standard and are not auditable. From a practical and political standpoint, internal audit and corrective action data must be an integral part of management's review of the quality system.

What ISO Auditors Look For

ISO auditors, like internal auditors, follow the guidelines in ISO 10011 and therefore have high expectations for excellence in this area. After all, they know how to conduct audits and expect internal auditors to do a good job, too.

■ Auditors will review the internal audit procedure. The procedure should closely reflect the ideas included in ISO Guideline 10011, Parts 1, 2, and 3 (see Chapter 36).

177

- There should be an annual schedule showing all areas of the company's operation and that each of the 20 elements is audited at least once a year. Many companies develop a matrix of areas-to-elements and schedule audits accordingly. Each audit should include time to follow up prior NCRs to make sure they have been resolved effectively.

- Auditors would prefer to see ongoing audit processes rather than one or two big audits a year. Ongoing audits show the company is routinely practicing its quality assurance system rather than making Q.A. and audits a special or occasional activity. This can be done with a small audit each month so at the end of a year everything has been audited.

- Auditors will talk to individuals who conduct audits and to individuals who have been audited. These interviews will help assure auditors that internal auditors are adequately trained and doing a thorough and effective job.

- Some auditors are particularly concerned about one key idea contained in the standard and reflected in the guideline on auditing. They want to know important areas are selected for review, as the standard requires. Too frequently, it is easy to choose trivial audit targets or to spread efforts so broadly as to miss high-risk items affecting quality. In particular, they will ask how the company decides what is important. Internal audits are supposed to help the organization improve its quality assurance system. Also, as part of this concern, auditors want to ensure that responsibility for corrective action is not shifted away from line management to the quality assurance group (see Guideline 10011-1, Element 4.1, Note 12).

- Auditors will review audit reports and corrective action follow-ups. They will assess how well management is supporting the internal audit process and if the process is supporting the quality assurance system.

What the Education and Training Guideline Says

The guideline neatly handles the issue of internal quality audits by saying the standard adequately covers the topic. That is, there is no difference between the standard and the training guideline.

What Training Assessors Look For

Training assessors will look for all the same things as ISO auditors. Additionally, because trainers are probably responsible for supporting the company's overall quality management process, assessors will pay particular attention to how well they conduct their own internal audits.

A caveat in the standard says persons responsible for a process should not be part of the audit team. That separation works for organizations with several departments from which they can draw internal auditors or for organizations that have their own Q.A. group. Because training organizations might not be large enough or have such an internal group, it may be necessary for trainers to audit training. It is possible, through creative job assignments, to use assessors from within the group. Assessors might expect to see this arrangement in small organizations and would find it acceptable, particularly if some members of the internal audit team were drawn from outside the training organization.

Q-Project Action Items

USE ISO GUIDELINES

Devise a good procedure based on ISO Auditing Guideline 10011-1, 2, and 3. All ISO registrars follow these guidelines, which were written to cover every kind of audit. These well-written guidelines offer a practical structure and good ideas on how to conduct internal audits (see Chapter 36).

AUDIT FREQUENTLY

Develop an ongoing monthly audit schedule rather than relying on one or two big audits each year. A matrix of procedures and activities to elements in the guideline is especially helpful. A well-conceived audit schedule will ensure that all areas are seen at least once a year and each individual audit takes only a few hours each month to plan, execute, and report. In fact, a reasonable expectation for a medium-sized training organization is one four-hour period per month for two or three people to conduct an audit.

ADOPT A GLOBAL PERSPECTIVE

Frequently, internal audits are structured to look at one department or one element of the standard. As a way to start, that tactic is useful. However, as the quality assurance system matures, learning how well the various functions simultaneously support all elements is important. One way to see cohesiveness and interconnection of functions is to structure audits to follow complete processes from initial request through analysis, design, development, delivery, to final evaluation. Tracking a project from start to finish will help reveal how well the entire organization and its quality assurance process support its quality goals and objectives.

USE CHECKLISTS

Design a good format for a checklist, framed around a series of questions auditors ask or questions needing answers. It is possible to purchase a generic checklist that restructures the standard's declarative sentences into questions. For example, the standard's requirement that "The supplier shall establish and maintain documented procedures for planning and implementing internal quality audits . . ." is rephrased to "Has the supplier established and maintained a documented procedure for . . . ?" Although this kind of rephrasing of the standard or company's procedures is one way to start, it is not adequate to meet either the practical needs of the organization or the requirements of the standard. Checklists should include questions that help internal auditors dig out objective evidence employees are using the Q.A. process. Simple rephrases of standard statements are inadequate to obtain this information. Checklists should also include plans on how objective evidence will be obtained. Generally, there are three ways to obtain objective evidence: personal observation of work being done, interviews with personnel doing the work, and review of records showing that work was completed. The checklist should also include space and format to record data and observations. These notations provide an audit trail record.

SIMPLIFY REPORTS

Design a good format for an internal audit report, something clean and simple. A fill-in-the-blank format with summaries of findings is a quick and easy way to handle audit reports. Long-winded, detailed descriptions bog down readers and hinder understanding. A good audit report is a one-page, fill-in-the-blank document with attachments, such as the audit schedule, NCRs, and opening and closing meeting agendas.

FLOWCHART I.A. AND C.A. PROCESSES

Flowchart the internal audit and corrective action processes so they can be seen together. Make sure they clearly spell out authorities and responsibilities in their respective procedures. Make sure these two procedures work together and, most importantly, that they do not conflict with each other. Some organizations elect to create a firewall between quality audits and corrective action, arguing that one group is responsible for one function and a separate group is responsible for the other. This structure helps to avoid some inherent tension and political issues. That is an acceptable and useful way to structure these processes. In any case, the two processes must mesh somewhere, and a single flowchart showing both will eliminate redundancies and conflicts.

PROMOTE WIIFM

Remember *WIIFM*: What is in it for me? For internal audits to succeed, participants need to see the process helping them do their work. Internal audits should identify areas and items for improvement. Management must support internal audits, taking an open approach to internal audits and expecting to receive NCRs. If personnel perceive management using the process as an excuse to fix blame or to mete out punishments, the internal audit process will fail. Companies will reap dividends by establishing a communication process to notify individuals of upcoming audits and spending time with auditees preparing them for the audit.

Reality Check

There is a distinction between efficiency and effectiveness. Efficiency means something is done well with minimum expenditures of resources and waste. Effectiveness means the right thing is done. It is possible to be very efficient but not very effective. The ISO standard correctly recognizes this issue and focuses on it in this element by requiring internal auditors to assess the effectiveness of the Q.A. system.

In the past, auditors were limited to making sure that procedures were followed. Once they found a couple of nonconformances, they could relax because they had proven they were doing their job. Now however, auditors are expected to broaden their perspective and assess how well procedures and quality assurance processes are helping the company meet the organization's goals and customers' needs. Auditors are going beyond quality control and inspection and are evaluating the effectiveness of the internal quality assurance process.

Also in the past, auditees operated in a defensive and protective way. They were afraid management would blame them for NCRs or see NCRs as proof that employees were not doing a good job. As a result they became jailhouse lawyers, focused on quoting the exact language of the requirement with no appreciation of its rationale or purpose. Rather than think about the spirit of the elements and how they could help improve their effectiveness, these folks spent time carefully trying to meet absolute minimum standard requirements. At that point, there was no advantage for anyone to be gained from an internal audit process. Auditees simply wanted to survive the process.

Knowledgeable auditors know the reality of any quality assurance program is evident in the way internal audit and corrective action processes are handled. It's still the case, however, that no one likes audits and no one enjoys someone from outside the organization identifying problems. There is a real political problem here. Prior experience with old style audits makes people wary. A carefully structured program, along with positive management support, will help overcome these inherent difficulties. A good internal quality process will help employees improve their work processes and be both effective and efficient.

CHAPTER 23

Element 4.18

Training

ISO training requirements give companies a system around which to structure effective and efficient training programs. In the process, training also helps management meet corporate needs. Management is interested in return on their investment, which includes resources spent on training. In focusing on outcomes and showing how training activities return value for expenditures, ISO 9000 provides a way to show the value training adds to an organization.

What the ISO 9001 Standard Says

Section 4.18 sets out three requirements:
- Companies must establish and maintain a procedure specifying necessary training for "all personnel performing activities affecting quality."
- Persons performing specifically assigned tasks must be qualified to do those tasks.
- Training records must be kept.

What ISO Auditors Look For

Auditors will interpret the key definition "all personnel performing activities affecting quality" from a practical standpoint. That is, they expect this element applies to everyone because from their perspective every employee contributes to quality. ISO says companies need to commit to quality throughout their organizations. Attempts to segregate some employees from quality processes would tarnish this idea and expose the company to substantial interpretation difficulties in an audit. Rather than open a philosophical debate on levels of degree, it is more practical to define training requirements for all employees.

Companies should define who does "specific assigned tasks." Again, auditors will interpret this to include everyone because every assigned task will ultimately affect quality. However, this wording gives companies opportunities and freedom to structure requirements according to specific job needs. The same training is not required for all employees, but individuals need appropriate training for their particular jobs.

Finally, ISO requires records of training. Element 4.16 specifies how to maintain records. Just like all other records, training records must be legible, identifiable, retrievable, and protected from deterioration, damage, or loss. Additionally, companies must specify retention times, and records need to be available for evaluation by auditors.

What the Education and Training Guideline Says

The guideline asks two questions. First, are trainers qualified to do their jobs? Second, are they meeting trainees' needs? The first requires companies to maintain information about each instructor, including academic degrees, employment history, certificates, special courses, and in-service training. The purpose is to ensure that they are qualified to perform assigned tasks. The guideline specifies records

185

should be reviewed periodically to ensure trainers can carry out tasks with minimal supervision.

In addition to a required procedure, a careful reading of this element suggests there is an implicit expectation that instructors will participate in training to maintain or improve their skills. Although it does not say so directly, training assessors would expect to see in-service training, including both technical topics and training to improve instructor SKAs. The guideline provides flexibility in establishing instructor qualifications. Besides formal instructor training, in-service training may be a communication procedure. The term *communication procedure* is not defined; the idea seems to allow various methods to provide information. For example, memoranda may be sent, there may be a required reading program, or informal discussions, meetings, or discussion groups may be held to satisfy this requirement.

The guideline also says records should show periodic reviews of needs. Because this sentence appears in the context of instructor training, it could be interpreted that these reviews are limited to instructor staff. This is not so, however. Periodic reviews of needs include all company employees. The section broadens the requirement to include trainer support staff and supervisors, besides instructors, as evident in the reference to those who verify instruction. The procedure should specify qualifications and training for these individuals as well.

The second point focuses on proving that training meets trainee needs. It calls for specifying ways to identify those who need help and implies that trainee needs and outcomes must be clearly defined. The curriculum must specify what a trainee is supposed to be able to do as an outcome of having participated in training.

What Training Assessors Look For

Training assessors will look at training requirements and records for both trainers and company employees. Some specific items include:

- There must be a procedure describing required qualifications for trainers, administration staff, and training supervisors. Qualifications include both subject matter or technical topics and instructor SKAs. Also, this procedure should describe in-service training to ensure trainers maintain and enhance both their technical SKAs and instructor SKAs.
- A procedure must describe training requirements for each employee. It should be possible to construct a job-to-training matrix for all company jobs.
- There must be training records for employees evidencing that each employee has completed required training.
- Records should show the company conducts timely reviews of employee training needs.
- Procedures should include a way to evaluate learner outcomes and describe strategies to ensure all job-related training needs are met.

Q-Project Action Items

To meet the ISO standard and guideline and to devise an effective and efficient training program for employees and trainers, a company needs to develop a two-part training structure. The first part is the training program, and the second is the record-keeping system.

GROUP TRAINING CATEGORIES

A convenient way to structure training programs is to group activities into key categories. The categories might include generic training for everyone, specific task training for some individuals, and special requirements or certifications for selected individuals. In most companies, everyone will need some element of common training, some will need specific job-related training, and some will need special certifications.

- Generic training consists of training everyone should receive, such as company orientation, safety overview, regulatory or environmental training, and introduction to ISO and quality assurance.

- Job-specific categories include topics such as computer data base training or telephone service skills. Formal education, work experience, apprenticeships, military experience, and other skill-specific activities satisfy much of this.

- Special training for specific jobs may be certifications in regulated environments or for individuals who have completed a skill-based apprenticeship, such as welders. Others in this category are management training, certified quality auditor or engineering programs, advanced skills courses, re-qualification, formal courses, seminars and professional meetings, and special certificates.

MATRIX JOBS TO REQUIREMENTS

Once a category system is established and types of training are assigned to each, develop a simple matrix of jobs-to-training. This matrix provides management with a structured, fact-based foundation to develop an action plan to budget and schedule training. This matrix can be an attachment to the company's training procedure.

SELECT ACTIVITIES

Most companies must use resources carefully and maximize value for resources spent. Return on investment means employees learn needed skills to improve productivity, perform jobs safely, and reduce errors and waste. Here are two strategies to select training:

■ List deliverables or outcomes expected based on a clear description of what employees will learn. Specify how objectives will be applied at work. If trainers cannot specify a practical application before training begins, there is a good chance the activity will not deliver needed value. Deliverables should be part of the contract review process and reflect agreement from employees' management and supervisors.

■ Ensure each attendee has the required experience to benefit from the activity. Too frequently, training goes over some individuals' heads because they do not have either necessary pre-training or experience to understand the material. Even worse, sometimes employees already have the SKAs and find training a boring waste of time. Two simple ways to ensure training is neither above nor below employees' heads is to review the material with their supervisors and observe employees working.

TAKE CREDIT FOR NON-TRADITIONAL TRAINING

Non-traditional activities typically are not done in a classroom. Many companies have a difficult time structuring and capturing records for informal activities such as on-the-job training, safety meetings, shift turnover meetings, tailgate meetings, team meetings, required reading, and company meetings. These activities are legitimately counted as training because they provide learning for participants. Here are practical strategies to help structure these events and capture these records.

■ Work instructions and inspection records can be used as a pretest to see what employees already know, as a training tool and a training record. Have the supervisor observe an employee complete the work or inspection and sign a copy of the work instruction or inspection record. Include it in the employee's training record. Include a statement they observed the activity/inspection, and the employee satisfactorily completed the activity/inspection. A rubber stamp with blanks for date and signature is an efficient way to set up this tactic.

- Use on-the-job training and work instructions as a performance test. There are several advantages to this strategy. First, work is accomplished as trainees are being trained. Second, employees get practical experience and confidence at work. Third, employees can immediately see the relevance of training when they can apply learning to tasks on the job. Again, a sign-off by the instructor on a work instruction serves as a training record.

- If an equipment vendor provides training as part of a purchase, the contract should require them to provide a training guide so trained employees can conduct future equipment training for employees. Also, the vendor should provide a record the employee completed necessary tasks and is qualified to operate the new equipment.

- When employees attend training seminars, professional meetings, or industry group meetings, they should prepare a simple memo report to include in their records. A fill-in-the-blank form can include date, general topic, and short description of learned objectives. They should submit the memo/report as part of their expense report. Employees will take an interest in completing this form if their expense paycheck is contingent on submitting it.

- If the company conducts routine safety meetings, end-of-shift, turnover, or tailgate meetings, a simple set of minutes, along with attendance sheets,

190

can quickly capture this training. Also, make provisions in the procedure to catch those individuals who are absent on meeting days.

KEEP RECORDS SIMPLE

Record keeping ought to be the simplest element in the training program. Unfortunately, records typically are a weak area for many companies. Although records are a critical element of an effective quality program, companies should definitely avoid the temptation to make the system elaborate by attempting to create hooks to track and retrieve everything. The net result of this approach is a monumental and unusable mess. A straightforward, well-considered, simple system works best.

DECIDE WHO SHOULD MAINTAIN RECORDS

- Training Department

Trainers are interested in ensuring that records are well maintained, but in small companies they may be too rushed to tackle this task adequately.

- Human Resources Department

An advantage is that they are accustomed to dealing with records and can include training records in their daily routine. The downside, however, is they tend to be small departments and usually busy with what they perceive as more pressing concerns. If training records become a secondary, "we will get to it when we can" chore, such a situation would result in a negative audit finding. Also, it is important to ensure that personnel and training records are separate.

- Employees' Departments

The advantage of having employees' departments maintain training records is that they are readily available to each supervisor. There are several downsides, however. Inconsistencies invariably will occur across departments. If a particular supervisor perceives training records as unimportant, records will receive minimal attention. If record keeping is to serve its purposes when departments maintain records, the company must establish a procedure and conduct in-house audits to make sure record keeping is accurate, current, and a corporate priority.

■ Employees

When employees maintain an individual copy of their own training records, it improves the likelihood they will take personal interest in them. This motivation is usually based on the record's perceived importance when performance is reviewed or when promotions are considered.

DETERMINE RETENTION TIMES

Generally, records must be maintained for the entire time the individual is employed. If there is a potential for legal action resulting from a product failure or a health-related disability, it is a good idea to maintain training records in perpetuity.

Reality Check

Training's most strategic payoff is a more productive work force. Other payoffs include higher accuracy, fewer rejects or downtime, a stronger safety record, and reduced legal liability. Organizations frequently undervalue and fail to support training activities because management does not understand and cannot readily observe or measure value for training resources invested. Because value is often equated with return on investment, the benefit must be evident and demonstrable to management.

The ISO 9000 training and record-keeping requirements provide trainers an excellent opportunity to structure a well-conceived and a well-executed training program and show value of training to management.

CHAPTER 24

Element 4.19

Servicing

Service, according to ISO, is a product. Practitioners in service industries using the ISO standards are advised to think of their product as the interface point between supplier and customer where they perform an activity, generate results, and satisfy a need. ISO started in the manufacturing sector, and application to service industries is relatively new. Therefore, much conceptual underpinning and language of ISO appear to fit manufacturing environments. Readers will gain some help and direction on how to apply ISO to service industries in the Chapter 35 discussion of ISO Guideline 9004-2 for Services.

Servicing is not the same thing as service. This element in the standard refers to servicing as a contractual agreement between customer and supplier in which the supplier provides support for a product. Servicing is similar to product warranties, which are covered in other elements of the standard. Servicing may be a post-warranty agreement or be part of an equipment rental agreement. Companies renting large copy machines or fleet vehicles are familiar with servicing contracts. For example, a company rents a copier and the servicing contract provides routine maintenance plus repairs at an agreed cost. Usually, a significant part of a servicing agreement covers guaranteed availability of parts and time-sensitive response to eliminate lengthy equipment downtimes. Servicing agreements may include a guaranteed four-hour response time, for example.

This narrow definition of servicing is applicable to only a few companies, and it has a very narrow application to training organizations. However, it does have a significant hook into the instructional design process and can be directly related to the evaluation of training.

What the ISO 9001 Standard Says

This is a very short element. Companies providing servicing contracts must have procedures explaining how they perform these functions. This requirement is consistent with Element 4.9, Process Control. They must also verify and report that servicing meets specified requirements. Again, this is covered in Element 4.3, Contract Review, and Elements 4.4.7 and 4.4.8, Design Verification and Design Validation. Finally, it is consistent with Element 4.10.4, Final Inspection and Testing.

What ISO Auditors Look For

If a company does not manufacture a product and only provides servicing, auditors would use all other elements of the standard to assess how well the company meets servicing requirements. In fact, there is little guidance and nothing unique in Element 4.19 that auditors cannot adequately assess using the remaining elements.

What the Education and Training Guideline Says

Because the guideline equates ongoing post-training support as servicing, it has more value for trainers than the standard has for most companies. Again, it begins with the caveat that limits application to contract agreements. However, the guideline authors have given trainers an excellent tool to help them avoid some typical post-training evaluation barriers.

Too frequently trainees return to their jobs and do not apply learning to their daily activities. The guideline encourages trainers to consider long-term application of skills, knowledges, and attitudes to jobs. It provides a mechanism for ongoing support by indicating trainers should specify how the training organization will provide this kind of ongoing support and how they will monitor this support. It suggests post-training impact evaluations are one way to monitor success.

What Training Assessors Look For

As part of the assessment of the instructional evaluation step, assessors will want to see how trainers accomplish post-training evaluations. Assessors want to know how trainers assess trainees' abilities to apply learning on the job. If the program routinely includes ongoing training, they will assess post-training support from initial analysis and design steps through the final evaluation processes.

Q-Project Action Items

Develop Application Plans

Consider including a trainee plan or application contract as part of every training activity. The application plan is simply a list of tasks or activities trainees undertake upon returning to their jobs. Application plans should include spe-

195

cific tasks and dates and goals for individuals to accomplish during three- or six-month periods that help them apply learning on the job.

BUILD IN REFRESHER TRAINING

As part of ongoing support, some training programs should include refresher training. Skills-based or procedure training is often a good candidate for refresher training. Safety and environmental topics are candidates for routine upgrading or ongoing support.

DEVELOP READING PROGRAMS

Consider a reading program as an ongoing project to support former trainees. Send former trainees articles of interest or self-study assignments for such things as procedure revisions, changes to regulations or requirements, or industry topic information. If this tactic is adopted, assign one individual to coordinate it and include it as part of routine scheduling of training resources. Otherwise, it will become a catch-as-catch-can activity and receive low priority.

TIE NEEDS ASSESSMENT TO EVALUATION

Tie needs assessment, part of the analysis phase, into the evaluation step. As part of the post-evaluation process, be sure to survey trainees and their supervisors about needed ongoing training plus additional topics requiring training. There is nothing wrong with using this tactic to build demand for additional training.

Reality Check

In many companies, post-training evaluation receives little emphasis. Trainers who are pressed to produce training may have difficulty finding enough time to do adequate needs assessment, and post-training evaluations are probably last on most priority lists. This element of the guideline gives trainers an opportunity to develop post-training evaluation as a valuable addition to their arsenal to obtain resources and make a contribution to the strategic mission. Evaluation of application of training to jobs and a good ongoing support program will add to trainers' credibility by showing impact and added value to the strategic mission.

There is a double downside, however. There is always the possibility evaluations will reveal that training had no impact or value. Additionally, such evaluations may be perceived as interfering with line management's responsibility to assess employee job performance for such things as pay increases and promotions. Tread carefully in these politically sensitive areas by having the Training Quality Team actively support and participate in this portion of the training evaluation.

CHAPTER 25

Element 4.20

Statistical Techniques

Statistics is a shorthand communication language. A few numbers, carefully organized and presented, can express a wealth of information. When companies establish goals and objectives, they are usually expressed, at least in part, in numerical terms. The raw data, arranged in a logical display, can communicate trends and progress toward achieving goals. Useful statistics help control processes and help companies figure out how to improve processes. Not everything can be reduced to numbers, of course, and arranging numerical data to present a positive reflection of reality where none exists is certainly possible. However, most managers understand numbers and rely on statistical information to help them control business.

The Education and Training Guideline authors have defined a much more detailed and useful element in their discussion of statistics than have the ISO 9001 authors. The ISO 9001 Standard is so generic that it is difficult to apply. It is primarily oriented toward manufacturing processes and statistical process control. ISO also publishes a statistics handbook useful to practitioners with experience in mathematics or statistics.

What the ISO 9001 Standard Says

This element makes two simple statements. It says, first, organizations should figure out if they need to use statistics. Second, if organizations decide they need to use statistics, they should document how they gather them and what they do with them.

Despite the simplicity of this focus, a couple of points are worth noting. First, the element refers to statistics. It does not refer to statistical process control or SPC. Second, there is no requirement for an organization to explain how it determined whether it needs to use statistics. Neither is there any requirement to explain how the company selected the statistics it uses. Finally, convincing auditors a company does not need or should not use statistics to control its quality assurance process is almost impossible. There are several places in the standard where statistics and trend analyses are needed, including, among others:

- Element 4.1, where companies define their goals and objectives, establish responsibilities for eliminating problems, commit resources, and establish management reviews of the effectiveness of the system.
- Element 4.2, where companies develop plans based on their customers' needs and their capability to deliver.
- Elements 4.3 and 4.6, where companies determine their own and their subcontractors' capabilities.
- Elements 4.4, 4.9, and 4.10, where companies conduct design control, process control, inspection and testing.

■ Elements 4.17 and 4.14, where companies do internal quality audits and take corrective and preventive action.

What ISO Auditors Look For

Most elements in the standard suggest some kind of statistical component. Generally, ISO auditors will not specifically look at statistics. As they do with documentation and record keeping, they will view statistics as part of every other element within the standard. The preceding list suggests statistical areas of concern for auditors. Most assuredly, auditors will be interested in trend analysis for Element 4.1.1, Quality Policy, particularly as applied to goals, objectives, and resources. They will also, most assuredly, look at trends for Internal Quality Audits, Element 4.17, and Corrective and Preventive Action, Element 4.14.

What the Education and Training Guideline Says

This element of the guideline is much more detailed than the standard and as a result more directive and useful for trainers. The guideline, unlike the standard, directly connects statistics to customer satisfaction to ensure that the quality system and processes are in control. Further, the guideline encourages the use of trend analysis and variability as a means to evaluate both trainees and training process. The guideline categorizes statistics as either quantitative or qualitative, listing about a dozen characteristics in each category. Capturing numbers, such as time spent on instruction, examination validity, and training resources, should be easy. A computerized data base can be used to track these numbers. The qualitative characteristics data are not particularly more difficult to gather. For example, responses about trainers or training characteristics, such as credibility, responsiveness, courtesy, and usefulness, can be gathered through trainee evaluation forms and interviews conducted with former trainees and their supervisors some time after training is completed. It states statistical techniques should apply to each part of the quality system and therefore to every aspect of the instructional system and also to trainees. If, as the guideline suggests, trainers have structured their processes according to an Instructional Systems Design (ISD) model, then trainers should apply statistics as part of the process to analyze, design, develop, deliver, and evaluate training. They should also apply statistics to evaluate trainee performance in training activities.

The guideline suggests statistics should be ongoing throughout the ISD process. It correctly notes that outcomes, such as trainees' ability to apply learning on the job, can only be assessed after training is completed and they have returned to work. However, trainees need to be confident that training activities will meet their needs. The 25 measures identified in the guideline will help trainers assure trainees their needs will be met. Finally, this element of the guideline, as do several elements of the standard and guideline, requires the organization to maintain records showing how statistics are used to reduce errors and improve the quality assurance process.

What Training Assessors Look For

Training assessors will probably have more interest in how statistics are used and will address this element more directly than will ISO auditors. Their primary concern is that trainers clearly tie their statistics to quality assurance both in terms of training processes and in terms of trainee performance. Besides a procedure, assessors will expect to see:

- Statistical analysis of performance indicator variability reflected in reports to management and as part of Element 4.1.3, Management Review.

201

- A method to gather both quantitative and qualitative data. Two paragraphs in the element suggest a list of 25 data categories of interest to trainers that reflect effectiveness of the quality assurance process.
- Data gathered before, during, and after training activities.
- An obvious data trail showing how statistical results are incorporated into changes in training activities.

Q-Project Action Items

ASSESS AVAILABLE DATA

Determine what data are currently being gathered or are already available. Much may already be available from various sources both inside and external to the training function. Assess the lists of kinds of data provided in the guideline and determine which of them would be useful for the particular needs of the organization. The needs of the organization include both training and total organization. Develop simple, efficient ways to gather and maintain needed data without creating a cumbersome monster.

SEPARATE TRAINEE FROM TRAINER DATA

Develop a structure to identify and separate data reflecting both participant performance from training organization performance. There is a direct correlation between the two. Trainee success is a reflection of trainers' efforts. However, many factors affect trainee performances beyond the scope and/or control of trainers. Training is not a panacea for organizational or process problems. Conversely, some trainees succeed in spite of the training provided.

INVESTIGATE INTERVIEWING AND SURVEYING

Quantitative data appear easier to gather than qualitative data. More importantly, quantitative data appear easier to report and understand. Fortunately, growing interest in total quality management (TQM) has spurred interest in customer interviewing and surveying techniques. There is an increasing body of accessible information in the quality literature about how to conduct interviews and surveys. The automotive and service industries are heavily involved in these efforts, and trainers can benchmark these experiences-to-training processes.

USE NUMBERS CAREFULLY

Avoid numbers for the sake of numbers. They can backfire. Such things as total number of hours spent by trainees in training or percentage of payroll spent on training may only give management a budget cutting tool. These summary numbers have no meaning. Consider every piece of statistical data as an opportunity to show improved trainee job performance or increased productivity and/or profitability.

CONNECT TO ISD

Make sure each step in the Instructional Systems Design model has specific statistical data associated with it to show how that step adds to effective and efficient training and trainee job performance. There is a quality assurance process associated with each of the five steps in the standard ISD model: analysis, design, development, delivery, and evaluation. Evaluation, in particular, gets short shrift from many trainers. Post-training interviews (at perhaps three months) with trainees' supervisors will directly connect training activities with trainees' abilities to apply SKAs on their jobs.

CAREFULLY SELECT STATISTICS

Carefully consider what statistics to report to management. Most data are useful only to the training function itself. There is no requirement to tell everyone everything. Carefully consider how to present statistics to management.

203

A few charts and graphs showing trends and improvements are far more informative than many numbers and/or laboriously written and detailed reports. Statistical reports should have two purposes: to keep management informed and, as importantly, to build support and credibility for training.

Reality Check

What gets measured gets attention. Information is power. Like evaluation, statistics frequently get passed over in the rush to do training. That is a mistake. Politically savvy trainers know this element gives them a powerful tool to build credibility and gain needed resources to contribute to their corporate strategic goals and objectives.

Part Three

The Malcolm Baldrige National Quality Award Criteria

These chapters describe the Malcolm Baldrige and Education Pilot Criteria, explain how they are organized, describe what an examiner might look for, and provide practical ideas to help implement these quality ideas.

CHAPTER 26

Introduction to the Malcolm Baldrige National Quality Award and Education Pilot Criteria

For trainers and educators, an important and timely element in the Malcolm Baldrige National Quality Award (MBNGA) and Education Pilot Criteria (EPC) material is their discussion of award eligibility. Organization training departments cannot apply independently for the Baldrige Award since the eligibility criteria specifically disallow "company units performing any of the business support functions" from applying. However, in 1995, the National Institute of Standards and Technology (NIST) and Department of Commerce issued the Education Pilot Criteria against which applications by educational institutions could be evaluated. Public and private, for-profit, and not-for-profit schools and universities at all levels are eligible to respond. Congress must change the enabling law to create an award for educational institutions. It is not clear yet which organizations will be eligible for this award and whether profit-making education institutions or independent training functions within large corporations, such as in-house universities and colleges operating within large corporations, will be eligible.

Despite these limits, there are important reasons why both training organizations and academic institutions should structure and operate their training functions to meet the MBNQA and EPC principles. The criteria recognize that one of their values is for "self-assessment, planning, training, and other purposes." Many organizations use the criteria as a foundation for their internal quality processes without intending to apply for the award. They view the criteria as an excellent philosophical foundation and view the exercise of applying the criteria as useful for their own organizational development. The process of considering how the organization fulfills the criteria and expressing this understanding in the written MBNQA application or EPC response reveals a good deal about the organization values and philosophy, its processes, and its strengths and weaknesses. It also provides a template for improvement and growth.

The Malcolm Baldrige National Quality Award (MBNQA) and Education Pilot Criteria (EPC) introductory materials reflect their shared philosophies. The introductory documentation establishes areas that organizations should address within each of the seven criteria and adds explanatory information in note sections. It explains how the Department of Commerce and NIST administer the award, how companies can apply, and how eligibility is determined. It includes a definition of the public law and some administrative information.

Companies apply for the MBNQA or respond to the EPC by preparing a document of no more than 70 pages. In it they describe their *approach* to the item requirements in the criteria, that is, the methods they use to meet the requirements. They also describe their *deployment*, which is the extent to which the approach is applied to all requirements across the organization. Finally, they describe the results of their deployment.

Examiners score MBNQA applications and EPC responses based on a numerical value assigned to each subparagraph. This value serves as a weighting device for the criteria. Some categories are considered more important and therefore have a higher point value within the 1,000 total possible points. Scoring reflects how well the quality management system meets the criteria. Organizations that score more than 601 points may receive a site visit. All applicants receive a written appraisal of their submittal. This written appraisal is useful as an external evaluation of their quality system. Receiving such an evaluation is a useful learning exercise even for companies that do not wish to apply for the award.

The Baldrige documentation is organized into four topic areas which establish how examiners view the criteria and how they score applications. These four are as follows:

- The 11 core values and concepts.
- Key characteristics of the award criteria.
- Linkage of the criteria to key business issues.
- The scoring system.

The remaining sections of this chapter discuss these four topics and explain how to relate them to education or training organizations.

The 11 Core Values and Concepts

Some of the most useful information in the document describe the 11 core values and concepts. A significant body of literature is available about these concepts; however, in three pages, this section summarizes these ideas well and provides a philosophical grounding on quality management. Educators and trainers can translate these core values and concepts in developing a quality system to support their organization business plans. The core values represent a way for education and training organizations to declare or articulate their strategy and guiding principles and to show the value training resources add to an organization's strategic mission.

Trainers and educators who plan to model their process to meet the Baldrige criteria should carefully study and discuss these core values and concepts. In particular, they should agree on how to interpret and apply them in their own organization. The Q-Project team should revisit these core values and concepts regularly through the course of the project to sustain a focus around the fundamentals. By describing their approach, deployment, and results in terms of the specified criteria, the organization reflects these core values and concepts. This summary of the MBNQA values and corresponding concepts from the Education Pilot Criteria is followed by suggestions on how to apply them to education and training organizations.

MB CUSTOMER-DRIVEN QUALITY
EP LEARNING-CENTERED EDUCATION

Customers judge the value of products or services on how well they fill a need. Customers then express their satisfaction, trust, confidence, and loyalty to the provider by becoming repeat customers. The highest compliment for an organization—and the most important indicator of customer satisfaction—is repeat business. Customer retention and market-share gain are evidence of success in this strategic area.

Trainers' customers include employees, their supervisors, and corporate management. All training customers need training to enhance their job performance. Employees and their supervisors must be satisfied with the investments of time and energy they make to attend training activities. Corporate management will be satisfied if there are tangible benefits from economic and human resources devoted to training. If training, or any part of training, does not contribute to enhanced job performance, it is, in the language of the criteria, an error. Beginning with its vision statement, therefore, a training organization should address the question of customer-driven quality and state what trainers do to meet this core value. A sentence or two in the vision statement such as "we design quality training programs to enhance employees' job performance" is a good start toward expressing this core value.

Educators' customers are their students, students' families, potential employers, feeder schools, and their communities. The EPC tie learning effectiveness to teaching effectiveness and argue education should "translate marketplace and citizenship requirements into appropriate curricula." That is, educators should determine what students need to be productive employees and good citizens and provide education focused around those ends. The EPC recognize students will become knowledge workers who need to be problem solvers in a rapidly changing marketplace. Schools and universities can provide learning-centered education by:

- Setting high standards and expectations.
- Valuing and accommodating different learning styles and rates.
- Providing active learning approaches involving students.
- Using formative and summative assessments.
- Encouraging students and families to use self-assessments.
- Focusing on transitions between schools or from school to work.

MB LEADERSHIP
EP LEADERSHIP

This core value refers to visible activities by organization leaders supporting their organization quality initiatives. Just as corporate management must provide visible leadership to support their quality initiative to the entire organization, education and training management must provide clear and obvious leadership throughout the organization to support its commitment to quality.

Visible leadership requires managers to commit substantial time and energy. Leadership activities cannot be left to chance. Trainers must plan them as part of their daily, routine activities. Reviewing lesson materials under development, observing training presentations, being a presenter for some part of the training program, reviewing instructor and course evaluations, and conducting interviews with trainees and their supervisors all are visible training leadership activities. In addition, finding ways to publicize department and individual achievements to training staff and the entire company are visible activities that display and support the training department's quality program.

Academic leaders can establish directions and set high expectations by participating actively in the education process, as through teaching a course, and by observing and recognizing teachers' efforts and student success. They can work to encourage excellence through continuous improvement of teaching approaches, tools, and programs. These active contributions establish and reinforce a learning climate. Also, academic leaders link their schools and universities to their communities through outreach and community service.

MB CONTINUOUS IMPROVEMENT AND LEARNING
EP CONTINUOUS IMPROVEMENT AND ORGANIZATIONAL LEARNING

The core value of continuous improvement must be an element of every activity. The MBNQA and EPC define continuous improvement as an element of daily work. Besides reflecting a search for opportunities to improve performance and solve problems at their source, a continuous improvement mentality reflects efforts to diagnose the potential for problems and prevent them. Continuous improvement is aimed at improving outcomes by better use of time and human resources. Faculty, staff, trainers, and customers—the students and trainees—are rich sources for fact-based and quantifiably measurable improvement ideas. So is learning from others with similar goals through benchmarking other education and training organizations. Other sources of continuous improvement ideas are a needs analysis before training, evaluations of employees' abilities to apply new SKAs on the job after training, and formative and summative evaluations of student performances.

Trainers and educators can benchmark and gain information about learning processes and improved performance by establishing liaisons with outside academic organizations and corporate training groups to share information and ideas. A good way to establish these liaisons is to attend meetings and conferences of local and national professional organizations.

MB Employee Participation and Development
EP Faculty and Staff Participation and Development

This core value addresses improving skills and motivation of organization members. Just as all employees and students need to improve their SKAs, faculty and staff as well as corporate trainers and staff need ongoing training both in instructional skills and content or SME topics. They must work to remain current on topics they are teaching. Moreover, MBNQA and EPC link these training work processes (training and education) and tie it to organization performance indicators. Thus, the criteria call for trainers and educators to have established plans to increase their own competencies. Development plans for faculty, trainers, and students should be based on objective evidence gathered from results. For example, if school or training department results reveal difficulties in meeting fast turnaround requirements or implementing new curricula, or a high student turnover in a program, evidence may provide a link between these problems and such things as lack of skills by instructors or inefficient work practices.

MB FAST RESPONSE
EP FAST RESPONSE

Fast response means rapid, flexible action to meet customer needs and short cycle time. The hallmark of a well-structured, efficient training organization is its ability to provide fast response to corporate training needs or student and community needs. Although changes to curricula or programs typically take several semesters in schools and universities, responsiveness to changes in society and the needs of both students and hiring organizations remains critical in the view of the EPC. Improvements or simplification of work processes, including planning and decision making, are ways to shorten response time. An ultimate goal of the entire effort to align education and training process to the Baldrige criteria is prompt response to customer needs. A commitment to prompt response should be part of the school or training department mission statement.

Meeting the core value of prompt response requires adequate resources. A structured training department or educational organization with its processes clearly in control can more easily justify the need for additional resources than one which does not demonstrate control. Out-of-control processes are quickly evident in the form of missed deadlines or missed instructional targets. These result in loss of credibility and increasing resistance at the management or oversight level, whether these are executives, boards of directors, or state governments, to support education and training activities.

MB DESIGN QUALITY AND PREVENTION
EP DESIGN QUALITY AND PREVENTION

This core value reflects the need for quality to be built in beginning with initial design. The criterion refers to *robust* or *error-resistant* processes and products. *Concurrent engineer-*

213

ing, which means that engineering, production, marketing, and other support personnel are involved in the design process, and emphasis on upstream interventions to correct problems early are tools to apply this core value. *Upstream* interventions are those that occur early in the process. The Education Pilot Criteria reinforce this emphasis on effective design of both curricula materials and learning environments and tie design process to evaluation process.

By conducting needs analysis and job-task analysis with production personnel and their supervisors before designing training activities, trainers demonstrate concurrent engineering and upstream intervention. Also, piloting programs or parts of programs before conducting training are good ways to ensure that programs are robust.

MB LONG-RANGE VIEW OF THE FUTURE
EP LONG-RANGE VIEW OF THE FUTURE

This core value requires organizations to make a long-range commitment to all stakeholders. Stakeholders include students, trainees, their families, customers and employees of the organization, suppliers, stockholders, as well as the public and community. Training organizations help companies achieve this goal by supporting corporate investment in employee development. Schools and universities support society's investment in future generations by preserving knowledge, generating new knowledge, and teaching new generations of students. Adopting these criteria to enhance educational and training effectiveness and efficiency demonstrates commitment to this long-range outlook.

MB MANAGEMENT BY FACT
EP MANAGEMENT BY FACT

This core value has three aspects: measurement, data, and analysis. *Measurements* must be pertinent to and derived

214

from key organization goals, strategies, and processes. *Data* are facts or numbers gathered from internal sources about such things as use of resources and from external sources on such things as customers' response and their intention to repeat business. *Analysis* and interpretation of data provide information to help organizations understand current performance, and the results support decision making. Measurement in education and training organizations should include quantitative and qualitative data about both processes and outcomes. Data analysis leading to thorough evaluation of the effectiveness and efficiency of education and training processes is the equivalent of MBNQA's management by fact. Relying on end-of-course evaluations that ask how participants liked the course is an insufficient basis for decision making. Rather, evaluating changes in trainees' job performance is necessary. Schools and universities need to evaluate such things as how well their students do in successive courses or grades and how well they are placed at graduation. Management by fact is a key opportunity for trainers and educators to show the value of training and education and to align their activities to overall corporate strategies or needs of communities and society.

MB PARTNERSHIP DEVELOPMENT
EP PARTNERSHIP DEVELOPMENT

This core value seeks to encourage schools, universities, and companies to establish internal and external partnerships with other organizations to advance their strategic mission. Partnerships with customers and suppliers provide opportunities for collaboration to improve products and services, including improved flexibility and customer-oriented responsiveness. Trainers' customers are the corporation's employees. Students, their families, potential employers, local communities, and the larger society are customers of educational institutions. Partnering and sharing information during needs analysis and job-task analysis activities are ways to show this core value. Also, using a Quality Team to review training results and evaluations will help apply this core value to training activities. Working with other institutions or companies to learn how they manage their training and education processes also reflects this core value. Efforts by schools and universities to work together with communities and other area institutions to determine how they may respond to community needs similarly reflect the partnership development core value.

MB CORPORATE RESPONSIBILITY AND CITIZENSHIP
EP PUBLIC RESPONSIBILITY AND CITIZENSHIP

This core value reflects concerns for public health, safety, and environment, and in addition reflects the expectation the corporation will behave ethically in meeting customer product and service expectations. This core value goes beyond mere compliance and requires a commitment to citizenship. Schools and universities serve as important role models for this value in all their activities. They must prepare their customers to be citizens and to live and work effectively in society. Similarly, training organizations have an excellent opportunity to support this core value in all their programs. Just as attitudes toward such things as safety should be an integral part of all training programs, attitudes toward quality and corporate citizenship should be incorporated into all training programs.

MB RESULTS ORIENTATION
EP RESULTS ORIENTATION

This core value reflects the award criteria focus on results and improvement. Both sets of criteria call for a balanced set of measurements and performance targets in which needs of both students and other stakeholders are integrated. A quality program oriented around performance results should be structured to communicate requirements and

216

expectations, to monitor performance, and to marshal broad-based support for improving results.

Key Characteristics of the Award Criteria

The six key characteristics of the MBNQA and EPC are almost identical in the framework they provide to think about the meaning of the criteria. The characteristics reflect the intent of the criteria to help quality practitioners focus on quality issues. These six ideas should be center points for the Q-Project team as they develop ways to describe and manage their training processes.

RESULTS ORIENTATION

The criteria are directed toward results. The MBNQA identifies seven key results which help organizations determine whether they are meeting their strategic goals: customer satisfaction and retention; market share; product and service quality; financial indicators; human resource performance and development; supplier performance and development; and public responsibility or corporate citizenship. Of these, customer satisfaction and productivity, operational effectiveness, and responsiveness are particularly important to training and educational organizations. The EPC identify five areas of school performance: student performance, student success, and satisfaction; stakeholder satisfaction; school performance relative to comparable schools; and effective and efficient use of resources. A fundamental idea is that results are important. Trainers and educators should be interested in outcomes of their activities: Did the activity meet established needs and achieve desired goals?

NON-PRESCRIPTIVE

The criteria are non-prescriptive, that is, they do not tell companies how to address quality needs or how to satisfy the criteria. The criteria identify issues that organizations must address if they expect to have a well-functioning quality program. It is up to each organization to decide how to structure its activities to serve the needs of its customers. Training organizations have freedom to select a variety of methods to address and meet needs in terms of their corporation characteristics, style, and goals. The EPC also focus on results, not procedures, tools, or organizations, since these elements may vary based on the school's size and type, its focus, and capabilities.

COMPREHENSIVE REQUIREMENTS

The criteria are comprehensive, that is, they address all internal and external requirements of the organization. This means activities and efforts of all members involve and affect quality. Quality is everyone's job.

INTERRELATED LEARNING CYCLES

The criteria address interrelated (process-results) learning cycles. In the MBNQA criteria, all processes are interrelated and mutually supporting. Processes and results feed back into one another and enhance continuous improvement and learning cycles. Therefore, all processes need to be mutually supporting. Four learning steps support this characteristic: planning, execution, assessment, and revision. Total Quality Management practitioners recognize this four-step cycle as a form of the Shewart Improvement Cycle: Plan, Do, Check, Act.

Q-SYSTEM ALIGNMENT

The fifth characteristic is an emphasis on quality system alignment. It reaffirms the idea quality is an integral part of daily routine. Core values and concepts should be evident in every task and activity. Alignment means all elements are interconnected and consistent. Thus, all organizational activities should interconnect and support strategic goals. This characteristic makes training organizations responsible for supporting their organization strategic goals and all school divisions or departments responsible for supporting their organization objectives.

DIAGNOSTIC VALUE

Finally, the sixth characteristic is the diagnostic value of the criteria. That is, the criteria can be used to diagnose and identify quality needs and opportunities for continuous improvement. Moreover, the criteria provide a conceptual framework to build a quality management or quality assurance system. Both the Baldrige and EPC and the ISO standards provide guidance to construct such a structure. The purpose of this book is to help trainers and educators use either or both to develop an effective, efficient, customer-oriented organization.

Linkage of the Criteria to Key Business Issues— MBNQA

This section of the criteria discusses the connection between the criteria and corporate performance centered on business strategy and financial performance. It also ties together innovation and creativity and breakthrough improvements. Linking the award criteria to corporate performance is a way to show how the criteria enhance rather than hinder progress toward organization goals. Some companies perceive quality as external to their work of producing a product or providing a service. A production supervisor once said he was totally conscientious about quality 27 days each month. The last three days of the month, he was heard to say, we "ship the trash." That statement unfortunately reflects a common way of thinking, that quality is fine if it does not hinder production.

Integration of Key Education Themes—EPC

The themes in the EPC similarly focus on school performance results. The areas respondents to the criteria should address in their document fit into a framework with these themes:

- Excellence is demonstrated by value added performance. That is, improvements are measured against prior performance or benchmarked against comparable organizations.
- The specific mission objectives provide a framework for interpretation of strategic and operational planning and results.
- Customers include students and their families as well as faculty, staff, employers, and community.
- Primary emphasis is placed on teaching and learning rather than research or service, although these are included as well.
- An on-going, well-conceived, and well-executed assessment strategy, especially how assessments will and will not be used, is fundamental to success.
- Assessments are tied to the organization mission as well as to student and faculty performance and are criterion-referenced and curriculum-based.
- Assigned criteria point values provide an initial way to score participants; however, an overall pattern of strengths and demonstrated performance improvement progress are valued.
- The criteria are integrated and mutually supporting and require a systems-thinking approach that stresses cause and effect and performance improvements.

The Scoring System: Approach, Deployment, Results

The MBNQA and EPC scoring systems help Q-Project teams evaluate how well their organizations meet the goals

220

they establish. Baldrige uses four categories to judge the value of a process or the success of a function: approach, deployment, results, and relevance.

- *Approach* refers to how the criteria are addressed. It asks: are the methods used appropriate and useful to the needs of the organization?
- *Deployment* refers to how well the techniques are used across all relevant work units. It asks: are all units using the same techniques and are all units working together?
- *Results* refer to the outcomes of processes to achieve the purpose. It asks: is the organization succeeding?
- *Relevance* or importance is an attempt to tie approach, deployment, and results directly to the business needs of the company. This final factor asks: does the activity move the process forward toward corporate goal achievement?

The application documentation provides a list of examples to help define these four factors. The factors ask the questions: what are we striving to do, how are we going to do it, what is the result of the effort, and is what we are doing helping us or is it important to our mission?

Award Criteria Documentation

The MBNQA Criteria documentation provides Q-Project training team members with a philosophical and operational basis on which to design and structure their processes by focusing on issues that help improve training quality. Although the document is short, it is dense, with much information and some complex philosophical issues to understand, digest, and discuss. Team members should not expect to be able to understand the contents totally on the first reading.

CHAPTER 27

1.0
Leadership

The Malcolm Baldrige National Quality Award Criteria ask applicants to address three elements in describing leadership in their organization, including how leaders establish values and expectations, and how the organization addresses public responsibilities and corporate citizenship.

MB 1.0 LEADERSHIP (90 POINTS)
EP 1.0 LEADERSHIP (90 POINTS)

This criterion focuses on senior leadership and the management system. Senior leadership includes the Senior Administrative Leadership in a school or the Chief Executive Officer and all senior managers in a corporation. The senior trainer for a corporation would be included in this group. These senior executives establish the organization vision, and all senior managers must be actively involved on a daily, personal level to encourage employee performance that reflects the organization values.

MB 1.1 Sᴇɴɪᴏʀ Exᴇᴄᴜᴛɪᴠᴇ Lᴇᴀᴅᴇʀsʜɪᴘ (45 ᴘᴏɪɴᴛs)
EP 1.1 Sᴇɴɪᴏʀ Aᴅᴍɪɴɪsᴛʀᴀᴛɪᴏɴ Lᴇᴀᴅᴇʀsʜɪᴘ (40 ᴘᴏɪɴᴛs)

Senior managers demonstrate leadership through three activities: establishing the organization values and expectations, devising strategic plans to reach these goals, and reviewing performance results. Baldrige examiners expect to see active and ongoing involvement by senior executives in these three areas. *Active* means executives find opportunities to communicate directly with employees and customers. Executives should be actively involved in learning customer needs and promoting the company quality policy to customers and reinforcing values and expectations within the organization. Promoting quality both in-house and to customers thus is not the sole responsibility of the Vice President for Quality. Every senior manager must be involved in this effort. Examiners are interested in learning about the kinds of quality-related activities all senior managers undertake and how much time is spent on these activities.

The EPC expand the focus from senior managers to the entire administration and add a fourth task for academic leaders. In addition to creating values and expectations, devising the strategic plan to reach goals, and reviewing performance, Senior Administration Leadership must maintain a climate conducive to teaching and learning, including safety and equity. Like the first three items in the MBNQA, this fourth item added to the EPC is the responsibility of all senior executives who set the tone and environment within which all organizational members participate.

Examiners want to learn how senior executives regularly review both goals and achievement of goals. This is a double requirement. Senior executives should routinely look at trend analysis and performance statistics that show goal achievement. They should also routinely review the quality system in terms of its underlying vision and goals, since vision and strategies should change in response to changing competitive conditions and quality processes must be structured to meet these changing requirements. Academic leaders should evaluate several important and interrelated systems: student performance, faculty performance, business or administrative practices, and learning environment. Examiners would expect to see descriptions of practices in these areas and efforts to improve these processes.

What MBNQA and EPC Examiners Look For

- There is a vision statement with clear and concise values that all employees throughout the organization know, understand, and act on; that senior administrators are actively involved in setting the vision and creating the environment to support participants' achievement of the organization goals.
- Process and system evaluations directly link the vision and goals to students, faculty, and staff achievements; that job performance expectations based on these values are communicated to all faculty, trainers, and staff.
- Senior leadership is actively involved with both employees and customers to provide quality products or services.
- Activities and processes are in place to create a safe and supportive environment to encourage learning.
- Senior leaders routinely and frequently review performance indicators and evaluate the effectiveness of their quality system. Routine assessments of outcomes lead to process changes which affect results and meet changing requirements.
- Employees believe leaders clearly communicate important issues to them and model and support expected quality outcomes.

These items are pervasive in an organization and

224

examiners will get to this information by looking at a variety of management activities, including planning and decision making, customer contact and outreach, collection and analysis of data, as well as organizational structure and workflow designs. This subclause is the first of many throughout the criteria that asks for specific measures that reveal how the organization gathers and uses data to change its quality processes in response to changing conditions. Examiners would expect to see that the organization gathers this data proactively rather than reactively, through collecting such data as customer complaints. In response to this item, applicants and respondents need to describe specific, measurable indicators that demonstrate effective leadership. Data for these indicators must be both routinely gathered and systematically used to effect changes. Importantly, examiners are interested in seeing that senior leadership looks at the entire organization rather than just selected areas or departments.

MB 1.2 LEADERSHIP SYSTEM AND ORGANIZATION (25 POINTS)
EP 1.2 LEADERSHIP SYSTEM AND ORGANIZATION (30 POINTS)

This clause asks the organization to explain how it integrates its values and expectations in three ways: to the leadership system, to the organization, and to its policies. The key word in the clause is integrates. *Integrated* means as part of, not as an add-on. Too frequently, quality and performance initiatives are add-on programs rather than shifts in organizational culture that integrate quality and performance values and practices into daily routines. Contests, slogans, and flavor-of-the-month programs have no lasting effect. These values are integrated into an organization when leaders set the vision and take an active role in implementing it and reviewing performance toward it. These values are integrated within the organization when its structure and processes support quality outcomes. Too frequently, structures work against individual efforts to achieve quality out-comes, as when non-value steps delay a process and prevent timely delivery to customers. Finally, policies are integrated in the quality system when they reward rather than punish desired performance.

The second part of this clause asks organizations how they communicate and reinforce their values and expectations so everyone knows and understands them. Ways to communicate values vary from posting them or having them printed on a wallet card or back of an employee identification badge to specific intensive training programs. Whatever method or media are used, the key requirement is that expected performance is positively reinforced. *Reinforced* means more than reminded; it means rewarded, or at a minimum, not punished. Rewards need to be consistent with organization values and valued by the recipient.

The final subclause in both criteria asks the organization to conduct effectiveness and efficiency reviews of their entire quality process. Such routine (monthly or at least quarterly) meetings are an opportunity to step back and ask if the quality and performance excellence system is helping the organization achieve its goals. This review should be more than a summary of the quarterly performance and assessment of trends. Although these are important issues, this subclause asks the organization to close the circle, tying results to performance to policies and structures to see the quality assurance/performance excellence system in total as a contributor to the organization goals.

What MBNQA and EPC Examiners Look For

■ The organization is structured logically to support its quality and performance policy. Logical processes and procedures help employees meet performance expectations.

- Specific measures for performance have been identified and expectations of job performance have been communicated to all participants, that good performance is rewarded and reinforced.
- All members understand the quality policy and know how their individual performance contributes to the organization success.
- There is a structured way to review effectiveness of processes routinely to ensure they support quality/performance and help the organization achieve its desired goals.

MB 1.3 PUBLIC RESPONSIBILITY AND CORPORATE CITIZENSHIP (20 POINTS)
EP 1.3 PUBLIC RESPONSIBILITY AND CITIZENSHIP (20 POINTS)

This clause recognizes that organizations are neighbors in their communities. Good neighbors contribute to the well-being of the community and cause no harm to it. This criterion asks organizations to explain how they predict trends and plan for contingencies in areas of safety and well-being of their neighbors and customers. In this section, there are three primary areas of concern: how operations impact the environment, how product and services impact customers, and how contributions to community quality of life organizations and charities are encouraged. Employee health and safety are covered under Item 4.4. Statutory requirements and ethical standards are useful in establishing environmental effects and effects of products/services on customers. The third area to address, quality of life, directly affects employees and others who live and work in their communities. The EPC are concerned that educational organizations act both as learning-oriented and role models. Trainers and educators, by the nature of their jobs, have an excellent opportunity to be learning-oriented role models. Good citizenship contributes to employee well-being as well as to the well-being of all members of the community.

What MBNQA and EPC Examiners Look For

- Systematic planning process within strategic planning considers how operations affect the environment and how products and services affect customers.
- Corporate and school community citizenship is a priority, a part of the overall organization goal, and is encouraged.

Q-Project Action Items

PRACTICE FOLLOWERSHIP

Trainers and educators need to support leader involvement in the day-to-day processes. Such support often is welcomed by senior executives because good leaders appreciate good followers and good ideas. Participation by senior leadership in training and classroom teaching should be encouraged and enabled. For example, corporations that move beyond the five-minute videotape of the CEO as part of employee orientation and have senior managers participate in orientation or quality system classes provide a powerful message that training and quality/performance goals are important. To facilitate this, the training staff might conduct the lecture and case study part of management classes, and senior managers could join as discussion leaders. At a minimum, a senior executive should make a brief appearance at any program that lasts more than one day. Senior administration leadership in schools should be visible participants in classes, either teaching whole sections or contributing to a variety of classes on a regular basis.

PROMOTE TRAINING SUCCESSES

Savvy trainers use the MBNQA emphasis on senior management evaluation of organizational processes as a way to promote training effectiveness. Brief, well-designed

228

assessment reports from the TQT not only help management honor the criterion requirement, but also provide a medium for trainers to tout their successes and campaign for needed resources. Similarly, educators can make sure senior administration as well as external bodies such as legislatures are aware of their successes and requirements.

PROMOTE EMPLOYEE INVOLVEMENT

Financial help provided by organizations to the arts or charities is important to these recipients. However, the real resources needed by most community and charitable organizations are time and effort. Organizations that encourage and help their members find time to participate in community and charitable activities are truly good neighbors.

Reality Check

The concerns identified in this section of the criteria seem obvious and straightforward. They are more profound than that, however. When considered in the context of the 11 core values and concepts, leadership issues reflect a rich philosophical and practical approach in achieving organizational goals. The remaining six sections of the criteria build on this first section, since good leadership and clear values and quality performance concepts are at the heart of a quality assurance process. A failure in leadership or lack of clear values and goals sentences an organization to mediocrity.

CHAPTER 28

2.0
Information and Analysis

Applicants must describe in their MBNQA application or EPC response how their organization addresses three areas: management of information and data, competitive comparisons and benchmarking, and analysis and use of company-level or school-level data.

MB 2.0 INFORMATION AND ANALYSIS (75 POINTS)
EP 2.0 INFORMATION AND ANALYSIS (75 POINTS)

Educators and trainers familiar with Instructional Systems Design needs analysis, job and task analysis, and evaluation will recognize the structure and purpose of this criterion. In its simplest terms, this category asks companies to describe how they gather and use data, including quality and comparative data, to make decisions. Although this category is worth only 75 points, it establishes a foundation for all remaining categories. Data and information underpin strategic planning, human resource allocation, process management, results, and customer service orientation. Three subclauses in this category ask companies to describe how they:

- Select and manage data and information for planning, management, and evaluation.
- Use comparative data and information for improvement.
- Analyze and use data and information for review.

In all three subclauses, the MBNQA and EPC criteria wording is almost verbatim, with a few appropriate word changes, slight differences in emphasis in a few places, and small differences in point value. However, the two reflect the same essential focus.

MB 2.1 MANAGEMENT OF INFORMATION AND DATA (20 POINTS)

EP 2.1 MANAGEMENT OF INFORMATION AND DATA (25 POINTS)

This section of the criteria sets the stage for remaining sections, especially for Process Management and Business Results. Good decisions about what kinds of metrics to gather and how to relate them to key business drivers will help companies improve their whole range of planning and operations processes. *Metrics* here means measures. For the Baldrige criteria, metrics include all data gathered and used, not just data about quality functions. For the most part, metrics refer to quantitative data. Qualitative data, including comments from customers, also are valuable, but they do not serve as well as numerical data to make trends and changes visible. Examiners want to see that the organization gathers information that is relevant and important, not just what is easy to measure or what has traditionally been gathered. In addition to having a systematic way to gather and analyze data, companies need to ensure that users get information in a timely fashion and information then is available for analysis and use in planning and decision making.

Educators and trainers need to determine what metrics will help them evaluate how well they are doing and how or where they can improve their processes. Validity of the data is key in this. *Validity* means the data measure what it says it measures and reveal information that helps organizations understand what is happening. To enhance validity, educators and trainers should objectively gather a variety of metrics from a variety of sources. A balanced set of metrics, including long- and short-term measures, can demonstrate current status and highlight change. This information can serve as the basis for performance improvement initiatives. Finally, educators and trainers need to find efficient ways to summarize and report data so that it is timely, available, and easy to use.

The second subclause in this element focuses on how the company evaluates and improves its data-gathering processes. In order to have appropriate data and information to support decision making in Section 5.0, Process Management, and Section 6.0, Business Results, companies need to evaluate how well they gather and compile data, how they present and compare them, how they relate them back to customer needs and forward to key business drivers, and how they disseminate them to users. Feedback from users is a critical element in determining whether data and information are appropriate and revealing. The criteria apply the term *user friendly* in referring to well-selected and used data and suggest it may be necessary to train individuals how to use the information.

What MBNQA and EPC Examiners Look For

- There is a systematic way to gather and analyze relevant customer-driven data pertinent to the key business drivers or objectives. There are ways to disseminate information to users in a timely and user-friendly fashion.
- Data gathered support the organization plans and strategies and help the organization improve its process management and performance results.

- Data are valid, that is, that they are drawn from a variety of sources, are objectively gathered, and are of sufficient depth/amount.

- Metrics represent data in all areas of the organization, in addition to financial and performance, including data related to customer satisfaction, safety, employee satisfaction, and other work climate issues.

- Methods used and data and information gathered are assessed for their usefulness to the organization.

MB 2.2 COMPETITIVE COMPARISONS AND BENCHMARKING (15 POINTS)
EP 2.2 COMPARISONS AND BENCHMARKING (15 POINTS)

This challenging subclause is particularly useful to educators and trainers. Two different activities are called for—comparisons and benchmarking. They have separate outcomes. *Benchmarking* means examining and understanding a function or series of functions that represent best practice and adapting and adopting them for use. *Competitive comparisons* mean measuring performance against competitors or other similar schools or programs. Educators and trainers may compare themselves to other academics and trainers; however, they need to benchmark their individual functions against any of a wide variety of companies and industries outside of the academic or training community. Business comparisons should be against organizations of the same size, providing the same products or services, or in the same markets. Benchmarking, in contrast, is done against any function in any company that can be judged as world-class. Comparisons tell what must be done to meet the competition; benchmarking reveals what is possible to do and how to achieve it. A key challenge for educators and trainers is to expand comparisons and benchmarking beyond the academic or training industries and draw improvement ideas from a wide variety of sources and different industries.

Examiners want to know how the company selects companies to compare and benchmark and how the company uses this information to improve its own processes. The clause mentions *stretch targets*, which mean improvements beyond incremental change. Stretch targets should not be arbitrarily chosen. Instead, through benchmarking, trainers and educators can determine what targets are possible and develop strategies and tactics to achieve them.

The final subclause requires companies to develop specific plans to evaluate and improve their comparisons and benchmarking processes and enhance application of the information they gather through these activities.

What MBNQA and EPC Examiners Look For

- The company has a systematic way to research and select companies and functions to benchmark and compare.
- The company either has individuals who know how to gather and use data to support analysis and improvement or provides training toward this goal.
- A plan is in place to use benchmarking and comparison data, and the plan includes an evaluation of their process.
- Benchmarking and comparison data are valid, appropriate, and useful for the organization.

MB 2.3 ANALYSIS AND USE OF COMPANY-LEVEL DATA (40 POINTS)
EP 2.3 ANALYSIS AND USE OF SCHOOL-LEVEL DATA (35 POINTS)

This subclause is easy to understand and difficult to apply. Essentially, the clause asks organizations to gather data from all of its operating areas, particularly areas identified in the seven sections of the Baldrige criteria, assimilate all divergent data, and interpret how they fit together. The outcome of this interpretive approach is to discover root causes and influences, that is, what is really going on. Aggre-

234

gate performance measures go beyond simple information gathering and trend analyses to help companies understand how their processes are interwoven and how the organization as a whole is performing. Both the MBNQA and EPC list a variety of measures to consider.

Trainers and educators should be interested in several specific suggested metrics relating to cost of quality and cost of training in terms of outcomes. The MBNQA criteria suggest three areas: how benefits and costs are associated with education and training, how net earnings are derived from quality initiatives, and how resource performance improvements related to quality affect financial performance.

Beyond gathering and interpreting data, examiners would expect to see ways information is communicated to individuals within the organization to help them understand how their jobs and their performance affect the overall success of the company. Also, companies need to show how they use these interpretations to set their strategic plan and develop their tactical initiatives.

What MBNQA and EPC Examiners Look For

- There is a systematic way to compile aggregate measures and metrics to understand root causes and to use this information for fundamental business decisions.
- Employees understand how to gather and use these kinds of data and how their performance influences data and performance outcomes.

Q-Project Action Items

MATRIX METRICS TO GOALS

A well-balanced set of metrics will help trainers and educators evaluate their performance in key performance drivers. A matrix of key drivers to metrics will reveal if adequate measures are being collected to evaluate all activities.

RESEARCH SOURCES

Finding organizations to benchmark or conduct competitive comparisons against is difficult. National and state quality award winners and winners of various professional organization competitions are places to start. The business press carries success stories and provides leads to find such companies. Participation in professional organizations also can help identify organizations. Most important for trainers and educators is to find ways to benchmark and compare outside of the academic and training community.

GIVE DATA MEANING

But it is easy to fall into a trap of simply gathering data, doing a quick trend analysis, and assuming the meaning of data is clear. In their regular assessments of performance and quality, educators and trainers should routinely seek new ways to interpret available data, looking beneath the surface of any single measure to see more subtle or interrelated relationships. They should seek new ways to apply their interpretations to strategies and tactics for challenges and opportunities.

SEEK TO BECOME WORLD-CLASS

Trainers and educators should settle for nothing less than world-class performance in their own organizations. But it is incumbent on trainers who are called upon to support quality and performance initiatives in commercial organizations to walk their talk. But it is equally critical that educators model the behaviors and attitudes they teach. A focused plan to learn from comparison and benchmarking and improve instructional processes will give trainers and educators great credibility with their customers.

Reality Check

Little is more useless than unapplied data. It is easy but a waste of effort to collect irrelevant, readily available data. Organizations should either make use of data or eliminate the effort to collect it. Further, even good data can support poor decision making or be misused. It is tempting to rush to a conclusion based on inadequate data, but it also is tempting to draw a hasty conclusion based on only cursory study of good data. Failure to consider alternative interpretations or to question the validity and pertinence of data supports quick patches for symptoms rather than considered solutions for causes. Thoughtful data analysis is critical; common sense, careful use of information, and knowledge of the organization are valuable spices to the decision-making stew.

CHAPTER 29

3.0
Strategic Planning

There are two sections in this category: development of strategy and deployment of strategy. Applicants or respondents should address how their organizations set strategic directions and determine key requirements and how requirements are translated into a performance management system.

MB 3.0 STRATEGIC PLANNING (55 POINTS)
EP 3.0 STRATEGIC AND OPERATIONAL PLANNING (55 POINTS)

A classic definition of the difference between strategy and tactics is that *strategy* asks the question, "Where are we going?" and *tactics* asks the question, "How do we get there?" Trainers and educators are familiar with questioning what their learning objectives and curriculum and training activities are supposed to achieve (where are we going?) and then deciding on instructional methods (how are we going to get there?). These Baldrige criteria ask educators and trainers to take a broader view and question what the education organization is supposed to achieve to support its community or the training organization to support its corporation, and what methods it will use to achieve those goals. In addition to planning for the future, this criterion asks organizations to develop key business drivers that translate strategy into operations. The first part of the criteria asks an organization to describe its strategy planning processes. The second part asks it to describe how strategy is deployed, how it is translated into performance. The deployment concept is consistent with the military definition of *deployed* as placing troops in battle positions. Only a few appropriate word changes and differences in point values distinguish the MBNQA from the EPC.

MB 3.1 Strategy Development (35 points)
EP 3.1 Strategy Development (45 points)

There is no one right way to do strategic planning. The complexity of planning processes depends upon a number of factors, such as the organization size; the complexity of its products, services, and processes; and the maturity of the organization and industry. How formal the planning process is depends upon the individual organization approach. This criterion asks the organization to describe the system it uses to plan strategically, rather than a formal process. The organization should be able to flowchart its planning process and identify who does what. The criterion asks organizations to explain how they gather data and integrate data into the planning process. They should address how they use information about changing competitive conditions, customer expectations, risks, and organizational capabilities as part of their strategic planning.

Organizations also need to describe how the plan is translated into business drivers. *Business drivers* are those primary, major routine, or special operational activities and requirements performed by business units and individuals within the organization that are critical to meeting its goals.

239

Key business drivers might be to expand into new geographical markets, increase market share, reduce waste, introduce new products, or drive down costs. It is usually possible to summarize the business drivers on one page. Business drivers represent the deployment of the strategic plan, how the organization will allocate troops and make tactical assignments. The plan should be carefully reviewed routinely (at least quarterly) and updated as necessary in response to changing conditions. Mechanisms for reviews should be indicated on a planning process flowchart.

A basic theme throughout this criterion is the organization's orientation toward the future, toward determining what it needs to do to meet needs of current customers now and in the future as well as the needs of future customers. Through the strategic planning function the organization can assess its capabilities, allocate resources, and develop ways to respond to anticipated or unexpected competition or customer requirements.

This criterion, like many other criteria, asks the organization to assess how well it accomplishes its planning process. This is not an evaluation of the plans themselves, but rather an evaluation of the planning process. The idea is to review who does what and to flowchart planning to make sure they use plans in ways to help the organization. Evaluation helps ensure that strategy development is working for the organization.

What MBNQA and EPC Examiners Look For

- There is a systematic way to develop strategic plans. A flowchart describes the processes, and authorities and responsibilities are established. The process is efficient.
- Planning includes consideration of data and factors which affect the organization success.

- Planning includes a way to translate key business drivers into individual and department action plans, assign resources, and establish priorities.
- There is an established and routine evaluation and update of the plan to meet changing conditions and competitive challenges, and to reflect on past successes and anticipated needs.
- There is an evaluation of the planning process itself to ensure the organization strategy development process is effective and efficient.

MB 3.2 STRATEGY DEPLOYMENT (20 POINTS)
EP 3.2 STRATEGY DEPLOYMENT (30 POINTS)

This part of the Baldrige criteria asks organizations to describe how they deploy or integrate their strategic plan throughout the organization. They also are asked to project where they expect their organization to be in the future, particularly in terms of key measures or indicators. The obvious link between these two ideas is that what happens today affects future success. In order to predict future success, the organization needs to predict future markets, future customer needs, and future industry directions. The organization can then understand how these changes will affect it and select and focus on key business drivers to help it move forward and meet these challenges. Once these priorities are established, it is possible to assign appropriate resources. In fact, it should be possible to link connections visually between the budget and planning processes and see how resources are assigned to priorities. The idea is to translate the organization vision into manageable, assignable, and achievable activities. One way to show how key business drivers are deployed throughout the organization is to construct a chart relating key business drivers, organization objectives, performance measures, department responsibilities and authorities, and activities and tactics used by individuals and internal units to achieve the goals.

What MBNQA and EPC Examiners Look For

- There is a realistic and specific business plan for the next two to five years based on anticipated future customer needs and industry competitive factors.
- An easily understood deployment plan links key business drivers, company objectives, performance measures, and activities assigned to units and individuals within the organization.

Q-Project Action Items

MAKE THE PLANNING PROCESS VISUAL

Develop a flowchart of how plans are made, resources are assigned, and activities are defined and deployed. Connect this flowchart to the budget preparation flowchart. Good integrated plans are the foundation of good processes and good execution. Helping organization members see the connections makes the process immediate and accessible to them.

FOCUS ON EFFICIENT PLANNING

Good plans are the foundation of good processes and good execution. Good processes provide educators and trainers with time and resources to accomplish goals and support trainee and student success. Have routine, at least quarterly, update reviews of plans. Evaluate past performance and adjust plans in response to changing conditions and anticipated requirements.

FOCUS PROCESS IMPROVEMENTS

Select high priority processes based on key business drivers and find ways to improve them. Either completely and radically re-engineer the organization or focus resources and energy on a few improvement projects at a time. This may avoid confusion and permit steady and incremental change. Process improvements should help training or education organizations improve their service and prepare for future customer needs.

Reality Check

Strategic plans sometimes are considered akin to budgets, a nasty hoop to jump through and then forget. Some organizations spend much time and effort through several formal iterations to develop and approve strategic plans and then do not use the plan. It is like the German term, *Sturm und Drang*, loosely translated as lots of noise and commotion. Budgets and strategic plans may lie gathering dust until the next year when they are pulled out and used as a basis to repeat the frustrating and essentially futile exercise. In contrast, good budgets and good plans are used; they are enacted and implemented. They also serve as a basis for response to the final Baldrige criterion, Customer Focus and Satisfaction.

CHAPTER 30

4.0
Human Resource Development and Management

This category asks applicants and respondents to describe the integration of their human resources processes to the organization's strategies. There are four items directed toward creation of a high performance workplace to address. The term *high performance* is eliminated from the title of the EPC criterion but is incorporated in the body of the clause.

MB 4.0 HUMAN RESOURCE DEVELOPMENT AND MANAGEMENT
   (140 POINTS)
EP 4.0 HUMAN RESOURCE DEVELOPMENT AND MANAGEMENT
   (150 POINTS)

Different companies express different attitudes about their employees. Some state that employees are their most important resource. Some include as part of their vision statement that they want employees to believe the company is a good place in which to work. Still others acknowledge that employees are the company. Some of the ideas associated with building an environment in which employees value

244

their association with their company include empowerment, opportunities for career growth, pay for achievement, self-directed work teams, and company payment of academic and training tuition. The Baldrige criteria are founded on the concept that employees are the means to achieve all organization goals.

For this MBNQA criteria, trainers need to distinguish between human resources activities they provide (i.e., training activities for the company and its employees) and the human resources activities related to themselves. Like the cobbler's child who has no shoes, sometimes trainers focus exclusively on company training demands and ignore their own development and processes. When training organizations apply MBNQA to their processes, they need to ensure their focus is on human resources in terms of how this function supports trainers and the training function.

MB 4.1 HUMAN RESOURCE PLANNING AND EVALUATION (20 POINTS)
EP 4.1 HUMAN RESOURCE PLANNING AND EVALUATION (30 POINTS)

This criterion challenges the organization to describe how its work force is encouraged to develop its full potential and how programs to accomplish this are integrated within the organization vision. There must be a direct link between human resource programs and the organization mission. There are some differences between the MBNQA and EPC: the MBNQA criteria is worth 20 points and the EPC 30 points. Additionally, there are a few shifts in focus in the first section. The two primary issues in this item are:

- How the company ties human resource planning and evaluation to strategic goals.
- How the company ensures the well-being of its work force.

The first area addresses how the organization translates performance needs into its human resources plans. The relationship between performance needs and human

ISO 9000 AND MBNQA

resource plans is reciprocal. Organizations need to help personnel develop the capability to meet corporate goals, and the goals and strategies organizations undertake affect employees. For example, a corporate decision to right-size or refocus into a market niche will change work loads and job performance expectations. This reciprocal relationship requires organizations, therefore, to update human resource plans routinely to reflect changing business environments and corporate strategies in response to those changes. Training plays a major role in implementing change. For example, if a decision is made to expand into a new market, human resources will need to help the company acquire or develop individuals with expertise in that market, and trainers will be called upon to update current employees' SKAs to enter that market. Similarly, educational organizations must integrate human resource concerns into their strategic plans, including faculty and staff development, promotion, compensation and benefits, and expectations of faculty and academic units.

Once the primary link is made between human resources plans and strategic business plans, detailed activities can be tied to human resources. These plans should look at both long- and short-term outcomes. The criteria include four outcome areas to address:

- Changes to work design to improve flexibility, innovation, and rapid response.
- Employee development, education, and training.
- Changes in compensation, recognition, and benefits.
- Recruitment.

The second area to address—how the organization assures the well-being of its employees—focuses on collection and use of employee-related data in order to improve job performance and tie job performance to organizational goals. This section is tied to Section 2.0, Information and Analysis. There needs to be a consistent and systematic way to gather

246

and use data to improve training processes. Educators and trainers are familiar with gathering results data as part of both the analysis and evaluation ISD steps. In addition to feedback given to individual trainers concerning their performance, these data should be used to improve workflows and help educators and trainers support the organization strategies. MBNQA and EPC examiners want to see how that data is used to:

- Assess development and well-being of employees.
- Link human resources to key business results.
- Ensure reliable and complete human resources data are available to support organizational strategic planning.

Although there are a few minor word changes in the EPC, the basic focus remains the same. Where the MBNQA specifies that human resources plans need to be tied to strategic and business plans, the EPC tie human resources plans to overall performance improvement plans. In any case, education and training organizations need to connect their overall performance plans with their human resources plans and address the quality of their relationships with faculty, trainers, and staff. In the first area to address, the EPC acknowledge an additional need to consider and plan for expected demographic changes in faculty and staff.

What MBNQA and EPC Examiners Look For

- Long-term and short-term goals are established for the training organization and these goals are directly linked to the overall strategic business plan. These plans are developed concurrently with rather than as a separate activity from organization strategic planning.
- Specific goals are established to train and empower faculty and trainers so they can support their

strategic mission. Goals include SKAs for both specific subject matter content and instructor capabilities and are based on identified corporate needs linked to individual job needs.

■ Specific and measurable goals are established to improve work design, improve flexibility, and encourage and reward/recognize rapid response.

■ Opportunities and assignments allow trainers to go beyond their current SME and trainer SKAs, and these improvements are tied to reward, recognition, compensation, and benefits.

■ Data are collected and used. Data collection activities are systematic and simple to use, and data analyses are a routine, ongoing part of ISD processes used to improve training activities and trainer performance.

MB 4.2 High Performance Work Systems (45 points)
EP 4.2 Faculty and Staff Work Systems (30 points)

This section is new to the 1995 criteria. It combines two notions previously treated separately, employee involvement and employee performance and recognition. However, it adds new ideas related to how jobs are designed and how work is accomplished. Educators and trainers familiar with ISD needs analysis and job-task analysis processes have a philosophical foundation to address this part of the criterion. Examiners want to see how workflows are designed and structured and how these structures make it easier for educators and trainers to do their work. There are two areas to address:

■ How job design promotes high performance.

■ How compensation and recognition reinforce job design.

The changes in this section have eliminated the previously used terms *empowerment, employee involvement,* and *teamwork*. The focus on these elements remains, however. Organizational members need opportunities to take initiatives and responsibility. Faculty and trainers need to be encouraged to contribute ideas on how to make their own jobs more effective and efficient, how to help their organizations support corporate strategies, and how to promote flexibility and short cycle-times. In addition, organizational structures need to promote cross-functional communication.

One way to encourage and foster high performance is through compensation and recognition efforts, and the second area in this item addresses this. Whereas most compensation packages are based on employee tenure or short-term financial results, particularly for upper management where quarterly results frequently drive compensation calculations, there have been significant efforts to connect compensation clearly to performance. Pay-for-performance approaches remain in the category of innovative, leading edge programs. They are in contrast to traditional compensation packages based on financial measures such as net profits or sales rather than on quality improvements. In this category, examiners are looking for a description of how compensation packages are applied across the entire organization and how the compensation package is linked to the key business drivers. They are seeking to learn how performance measures and rewards are tied to strategic goals.

Employee recognition has as much effect as compensation. Employee-of-the-month programs, gift certificates or T-shirt awards, while well intended, often are perceived as popularity contests or quota events. Many are mundane and formulaic. Recognition is not a program; effective recognition is management's response to specific achievements at appropriate times and in appropriate formats and environments. For example, recognition for team efforts should be directed to the team, not to selected individuals within the team. There can be no one-size-fits-all approach to recognition

249

because individuals find different rewards motivating, and different kinds of recognition are appropriate for different kinds of achievements.

The EPC adds two additional ideas in this criterion: student focus and cross-functional cooperation. The first area shifts focus from improving educator and trainer performance to focusing on improving trainee or student performance. The EPC defines student success as a reflection of good work by faculty and trainers. This subclause focuses on how institutions approach faculty evaluation, compensation, promotion, and recognition as a way to help faculty and trainers improve student performance. The second idea, cooperation across functions, refers to internal cooperation or partnerships with employee organizations such as unions or teams, as well as partnerships with external companies to develop faculty and staff. This item is essentially the same as the MBNQA, with a few appropriate changes in terms to refer to faculty and students.

What MBNQA and EPC Examiners Look For

- There is evidence faculty and trainers are satisfying both their internal and external customers. Job designs and workflows support efforts to communicate both within the organization and to external customers.
- Work is designed to support teamwork, open communication between trainers or faculty and their customers, as well as flexibility, rapid response, empowerment and involvement, and customer satisfaction.
- Work designs are evaluated and changed or improved to encourage trainers and faculty to contribute to the design of their own work. Work design changes are evaluated to ensure activities

250

are effective and efficient.

- There is a connection between trainers' morale and motivation and continuous improvement of their work structures that reward them, award them credibility, and help them achieve personal and organization goals.

- Both compensation and recognition processes are used and open to all, and trainers and faculty help design these programs.

- Compensation and recognition programs are consistent with jobs and performance, and faculty consider these programs a fair measure of their contribution to their organization success.

MB 4.3 EMPLOYEE EDUCATION, TRAINING, AND DEVELOPMENT (50 POINTS)

EP 4.3 FACULTY AND STAFF DEVELOPMENT (50 POINTS)

This criterion asks organizations to describe how they link their education and training efforts to their business plans. Education and training should contribute to employee motivation, progression, and development. There are two areas to address:

- How training and education builds company and employee capabilities.

- How training and education are designed, delivered, reinforced, and evaluated.

Even though trainers and educators can probably easily describe how their activities support employees' achievement, they may have difficulty showing how they apply these same activities to their own development. Faculty needs education and training in both what topics or content they teach and on how to be good teachers and trainers—their own skills, knowledges, and attitudes. One way to connect key business results and trainer SKA development is to develop a strategic training plan for all individuals involved

251

in training processes. This includes individuals in the training organization and line individuals who support training activities either as participants in job-task analyses and/or as on-the-job trainers. This strategic plan might include a matrix of SKAs and learning opportunities to individual participants. Just as trainers do needs analysis for employees before they design training, educators and trainers should start with key organizational goals and work back to identify SKAs educators or trainers need to help them meet those goals.

Finally, in addition to tying employee education, training, and development to key business goals, examiners want to see how education and training will help individual careers and development. The 1995 MBNQA has expanded this criterion to emphasize employee development. Future job needs, improved training processes, and succession planning are all factors to consider within this criteria.

Although the MBNQA does not require an ISD process, this element in particular would be well supported by such a process. Examiners would expect to see the following four areas addressed:

- How employees and line managers help determine training needs and design training activities.
- How training activities are delivered/conducted; specifically, how the delivery methods are appropriate to ensure transfer of acquired SKAs back to daily job practices.
- How SKA learning is reinforced and maintained on the job.
- How training and education activities are evaluated and improved.

Because trainers tend to be a small group within their organizations, it may be difficult for them to provide their own instructor SKAs. They may need to hire vendors or attend external workshops for these focused activities. However, trainers can and should participate in content SME training with employees. Regardless of the venue, training and education opportunities for trainers must be selected based on identified SKAs determined through a systematic job-task analysis. Groups and individuals should be interviewed to identify specific tasks trainers must do to perform their jobs. These tasks must be directly tied to organization key performance goals.

The EPC and MBNQA criteria are almost verbatim throughout this criterion. The EPC do not use the word *motivation* but add a requirement for orientation of new faculty. There are a few other wording changes.

What MBNQA and EPC Examiners Look For

- There is a strategic training plan or some systematic method to assess education and training needs for all individuals involved in training processes. That plan includes opportunities to develop both subject matter and teacher or trainer SKAs.
- Trainer education and development plans are tied to key performance goals, predicted, prepared for, and updated regularly as these key targets are changed.
- Needs analysis and job-task analyses are used to develop individual training and education plans for faculty and staff. Plans are job-specific and linked to individual career development plans.
- Faculty development efforts are evaluated and improved to meet their own and organizational needs.

MB 4.4 EMPLOYEE WELL-BEING AND SATISFACTION (25 POINTS)
EP 4.4 FACULTY AND STAFF WELL-BEING AND SATISFACTION (40 POINTS)
These clauses in the MBNQA and EPC are almost verbatim. However, the EPC value it at 40 points, whereas the MBNQA values it at 25 points. Essentially, the clause con-

cerns how organizations, whether schools or corporations, maintain a work environment conducive to employee well-being. There are three areas to address:

- How the company ensures a safe and healthy work climate.
- What services are available to enhance employee well-being.
- How the organization assesses employee satisfaction, well-being, and motivation.

In addition to adhering to OSHA requirements, organizations should have proactive accident prevention programs. *Proactive* means programs which detect potential accidents and health-related conditions. Lost-time accidents and safety posters are appropriate but insufficient. Trainers and educators have an excellent opportunity to affect employee attitudes which in turn affect employee behaviors through training activities that routinely and systematically include attitude objectives such as safe work practices and health issues.

Health issues include human factors engineering programs, gym or health clubs (either on-site or memberships at reduced rates), assistance to locate child care or provide it on-site, family issues, and Employee Assistance Programs for drug, alcohol, legal, marital, or other problems. These routine programs support the second topic to address, services to enhance employees' well-being. The third and final element focuses on frequent, systematic data gathering to determine current employee attitudes, satisfaction, and well-being. Such surveys will help the organization judge how effective its programs are and how well it is maintaining these programs.

What MBNQA and EPC Examiners Look For

- There is a proactive health and safety program to

detect potential accidents and help employees deal with family and personal matters.

- There is easy access to services, such as child care, and health improvement and maintenance activities, such as gyms or smoking cessation programs, are available.
- Data concerning employee satisfaction and well-being are routinely and frequently gathered. Satisfaction surveys, along with data, such as turnover, absenteeism, illnesses, and the like, should be used to evaluate program effectiveness.

Q-Project Action Items

TIE HUMAN RESOURCES PLANS TO STRATEGIC PLANS

Trainers and educators need to be prepared to respond to their organization needs, with both subject matter or content and instructor SKAs to plan and present training and teaching. This capability requires some lead time to ensure it is available when needed. A way to ensure lead time is to make sure human resources planning is routinely included early in the planning process, what the Baldrige criteria refer to as *upstream*. The senior training manager in a corporation should be involved in or have a direct and early connection into the corporate strategic planning process. Education and training leaders need to seek the help of their senior administrators to advise them how the training organization can best support evolving and changing needs. A TQT of senior managers should routinely incorporate this issue into their discussions.

MAKE HUMAN RESOURCES GOALS SPECIFIC

Goals need to reflect specific needs identified by consistent data gathering. Instead of the arbitrary goal—"Trainers will receive 10 hours of training per year"—specific goals for individual faculty or trainers allow the organization to apply its resources toward goals tied to its performance objectives.

IDENTIFY INTRINSIC AND EXTRINSIC REWARDS

Educators and trainers, just like other organization members, are motivated to succeed by appropriate intrinsic and extrinsic rewards. In addition to tying together performance indicators and compensation, organizations should identify non-financial forms of recognition and reward. Credibility within the organization and an opportunity to see students and trainees succeed in their application of learning also are rewards. Successful managers know management by walking around, taking an active interest, and catching people doing things right also are significant motivators.

DESIGN TRAINER WORK SYSTEMS

The Baldrige criteria do not require an Instructional Systems Design (ISD) model be employed to design work systems for trainers and educators. However, without good process management which results from application of ISD or similar systems, it is exceedingly difficult to develop motivating awards or rewards for trainers and educators.

INCLUDE ATTITUDE OBJECTIVES IN EDUCATION AND TRAINING

The *A* in SKA is attitudes. Attitudes are the beliefs and values learners gain while attending education or training activities. In corporations, practicing good housekeeping, following safety precautions, using the right tools, following work instructions, communicating effectively with and respecting fellow workers, and desiring to do a good job and be a capable employee are all examples of possible attitude objectives which can be incorporated into training programs. Trainers should routinely seek to identify and include such attitude objectives in every training activity. In the same way, educators can identify attitudes to nurture through classroom work, including following instructions, working to communicate effectively in writing and speech, practicing good citizenship behaviors, and fostering the desire to integrate the material from this class with other classes and apply it.

Reality Check

Many organizations state in their vision or mission statement that employees are important to the organization, and most organizations want to be good places to work. Implementation of these notions is not always so easy. Pressures to achieve short-term financial results, preoccupations with production at the expense of human concerns, and more dramatic changes like downsizing make employee support and development an afterthought in some organizations. Educators and trainers in all organizations must make a concerted effort to sustain human resources and development initiatives. Such efforts, along with good leadership and planning, help trainers and educators sustain a supportive work climate.

CHAPTER 31

5.0
Process Management

These criteria are focal points for key work processes. MBNQA items to address here include design, prevention orientation, evaluation and continuous improvement, linkages to suppliers, and overall high performance. EPC items are, similarly, education design and delivery, school services, and business operations.

MB 5.0 PROCESS MANAGEMENT (140 POINTS)
EP 5.0 EDUCATION AND BUSINESS PROCESS MANAGEMENT (150 POINTS)

This criterion is the capstone of the first four MBNQA criteria. Leadership sets the vision, information and analysis gather necessary data to support strategic planning, and human resources puts people in place to do the work. This section concerns process management, which refers to how work gets accomplished and how goals are met. Process management includes design of a product or service and its production and delivery. It also includes subcontractor management and research and development. Finally, and most importantly, it covers integration of all work units. It ought to be possible to flowchart key processes and identify major steps and responsibilities for each. Business results, the section after this, evaluates outcomes of these first five steps.

Educational and Business Process Management focuses on the same concerns as the MBNQA Process Management. However, ten extra points are assigned to this criterion, and there are two extra subparagraphs. One of the differences is that the Education Pilot Criteria equate design and production to instructional activities rather than business administrative processes, as the MBNQA does. The pilot criteria focus on the process of providing education, and each of first four subclauses use this frame of reference to match MBNQA clauses. The EPC have two additional subclauses focused on the business of administering an education institution: enrollment management and business operations.

MB 5.1 DESIGN AND INTRODUCTION OF PRODUCTS AND SERVICES
   (40 POINTS)
EP 5.1 EDUCATION DESIGN (40 POINTS)

In the MBNQA, this subclause focuses on how new products are designed and how existing products are modified. In both settings, examiners expect to see key product or service characteristics identified and coordination among and contributions from affected work units. There are three areas to address:

- How products/services and production/delivery are designed.
- How process designs are reviewed and tested.
- How designs are evaluated and improved.

The first area is the linchpin between this criterion and criteria on information and analysis and strategic planning. How products/services are designed begins with gathering information from customers concerning key characteristics, that is, what customers want from the product or service. It also requires the company to draw affected work units that will contribute to the production and delivery of the product or service into the design process. They must be included early enough to affect the design phase.

In addition to a systematic product or service design and development process, the criterion calls for a second area, reviews and tests, that focuses on prevention rather than correction in the design stage. A fundamental preventive technique is to include all relevant work groups early in the design phase so their input contributes to the design and avoids changes later. These work groups can determine how to meet key product characteristics identified by customers and help the design group determine ways to fabricate the product or produce the service to include those key customer characteristics. A second way to establish preventive rather than corrective action is to conduct pilots or produce mock-ups to test products or services under development. A number of tests need to be conducted during both design and production phases to ensure design meets customer needs and can be fabricated or provided. Testing is done during both phases, and outcomes of these tests are used to refine and improve design and fabrication processes.

The third MBNQA area to address focuses on methods used to evaluate design processes and ways the company improves its design process by reducing the time it takes to design, test, produce, and introduce new products and services. Examiners expect to see a systematic process to ensure effectiveness and efficiency in the design process. This education criterion focuses on educational programs rather than on business processes, looking at how training programs and curricular materials are designed and introduced. There are three areas to address:

- How educational programs are designed.
- How the design supports delivery of instruction.
- How the design process itself is evaluated and improved.

How educational programs are designed reflects several concerns. First, just as characteristics of other products or services must meet customer needs, education programs must meet student or trainee needs. Similarly, the presence of product or service characteristics implies a standard must be met, and the EPC specify that education programs must establish high standards. Second, no education program or training activity exists in a vacuum. Although curricular materials may support only one activity or program, each activity and program are part of an educational whole. That means activities and materials must be sequenced and linked to support desired outcomes. Third, educational organizations must establish an evaluation process to determine if desired goals are met; and fourth, faculty and trainers must be prepared to and capable of conducting instruction and helping participants succeed.

The second area respondents to the EPC must address is how design supports delivery of instruction. Various delivery strategies—lecture, demonstration, self-study, discussion—demand different instructional designs, and different instructional strategies support different individual learning styles among participants. Most participants learn most readily when they are actively involved in a learning process. Instructional designs that support active participation address and support a variety of individual learning rates and styles. This criterion also requires description and evaluation of the organization's use of formative and summative evaluations and adequate faculty contact with trainees/students. Finally, in addition to systematic ways to gather formative and summative information, there needs to be an established way to ensure this information is fed back to faculty and instructional designers to improve both design and delivery of curricular materials and training activities.

The third area ties information gathered during the evaluation process to design improvement. Factors to address include what information is gathered and how frequently, what sources are solicited for feedback, and how this information is tracked and fed back into the process to improve both specific activities and materials. Another key in this area is how information is applied to improve design and delivery processes.

What MBNQA and EPC Examiners Look For

- Appropriate sources and sound statistical methods are used to identify customer requirements; information can be translated into product and service characteristics which in turn can be translated into instructional activities and curricular materials.
- Data are objective, and valid reflections of customer requirements and inputs come from all relevant stakeholders.
- There are direct links between gathered customer information and design of instructional materials and activities. Design process translates needs into instructional characteristics and strategies to meet participants' needs.
- Relevant affected work groups and stakeholders have been identified and their input has been solicited and used early in the design process; there is evidence groups who will work with instructional materials are involved early in the design process.
- Both design and curricular material development process are evaluated; they are effective, efficient, and thorough and meet needs of instructional designers, faculty, and trainers.
- Instructional programs are structured, sequenced, and integrated using appropriate instructional strategies to meet learner needs.

- A systematic plan is in place to use formative and summative assessments during both design and development phases as well as during instructional delivery phases; outcomes of these assessments are communicated to appropriate parties and are used to improve processes.

MB 5.2 PROCESS MANAGEMENT: PRODUCT AND SERVICE PRODUCTION AND DELIVERY (40 POINTS)

EP 5.2 EDUCATION DELIVERY (25 POINTS)

This MBNQA subclause focuses on operational processes companies use to fabricate products or provide services. Control of processes is an outcome of design steps and needs to be linked back to design processes. There are two areas to address:

- How the company controls its key performance processes.
- How the company evaluates and improves its production processes.

In addition to developing flowcharts and procedures to describe major processes, companies need to explain how they control their processes and measure their effectiveness. Controls require more than procedures; there should be self-assessment by workers of their own work as well as a quality control, inspection, or statistical process control evaluation to help keep production in control. Measures should include standards or targets tied back to customer requirements.

In addition to measuring and controlling processes, examiners are interested in knowing how companies deal with process control failures as well as continuous improvement opportunities. There needs to be a systematic way to analyze causes of process breakdowns, and, although the criteria do not specifically ask for root-cause analysis or statistical process control, many of these standard problem-solving quality tools can be applied to this criterion. A basic tenet of quality theory is fact-based decision making. Therefore, objectivity and thoroughness in data gathering and decision making are important concerns for examiners.

Finally, in addition to using a variety of problem-solving approaches and detailed and thorough analysis of failures, companies should also conduct both short-term and long-term follow-up of corrective actions taken. All these initiatives will help the company reach and maintain desired performance goals. Trainers should remember that, just as procedures are insufficient to control production, training is insufficient to measure and control individual behaviors. Individual performance measures should include established standards against which to provide feedback to employees and motivation (either positive feedback or negative consequences) that encourage employees to meet these standards.

The second part of this clause goes beyond maintaining processes and looks at how companies improve processes. Usually, a good way to start improving processes is to flowchart them. Once stakeholders are able to see what is actually occurring, they are usually able to find ways quickly to eliminate non-value-adding steps. Other ways to improve processes are to research design and development, find new or improved technologies to automate or speed work, and benchmark improved processes used by other companies. A less esoteric but equally useful approach is to solicit input actively from both internal and external customers of the process. A subset of using systematic ways to improve processes, and one that usually get short shrift, is how the company considers and discards alternatives before selecting a best approach or single solution. Rushing to solution without adequate consideration of alternatives is contrary to good quality assurance practice.

This EPC clause addresses the same two concerns as the MBNQA clause:

- How the school ensures that programs and offerings meet design requirements.
- How programs and offerings are evaluated and improved.

This clause directly ties back to the previous one and looks at how instruction is delivered, linking design of instruction to delivery of instruction. Observation and objective measures or indicators help educators and trainers make sure delivered programs and offerings fulfill customer-defined requirements. Many assessment techniques are available, including observing trainers in instructional settings and conducting formative and summative evaluations of trainees as instruction progresses. To meet Baldrige criteria, organizations need an established way to feed the outcomes of these observations and evaluations back to instructors/trainers and students/trainees. Feedback must be timely and generate improvements in instruction. For example, instructors should grade papers or assess trainee projects and return results to them quickly. Similarly, instructor evaluations should provide a basis of facts on which faculty can improve their teaching effectiveness.

In addition to controlling their instructional processes, education and training organizations need to find ways to improve their instructional processes. Feedback from trainees, benchmarking best practices from other education or training institutions, as well as benchmarking practices from non-education companies are ways to improve these processes. Additionally, peer faculty evaluations, additional instruction training, research and application of new training techniques, and introduction of new technologies are all ways to improve instruction delivery.

What MBNQA and EPC Examiners Look For

- All primary processes are identified, described

(flowcharts or procedures), and controlled; specific measures are in place to make sure production or operations meet design.

- Process management controls, based on measurable outcomes, are in place and effective. Controls rely on more than procedures and training, including preventive as well as corrective action. Positive and negative consequences are built into the control process.

- Stakeholders are identified and responsible for production and operations outcomes. They are included in problem-solving processes, and they receive timely feedback from evaluation processes.

- Quality problem-solving tools are used to support fact-based evaluations and decision making, sufficient data acquired from a variety of resources and alternative solutions are thoroughly considered, and root causes of problems are identified and corrected.

- Systematic and ongoing effort to improve processes is based on evaluation outcomes, research, improved technology, benchmarking, input from internal and external customers, and other techniques.

MB 5.3 Process Management: Support Services (30 points)
EP 5.3 Education Support Service Design and Delivery
(25 points)

Whereas clause 5.2 looks at how line operations control and improve their processes, this MBNQA clause focuses on how support functions and administrative departments, such as purchasing, human resources, and legal departments, work to support operations groups. In addition to linking their goals to the line operation, support functions must be controlled and improved. This subclause looks at three areas:

- How support departments provide their functions and link their service to their internal customers.
- How support functions control their processes.
- How support functions evaluate and improve their performance.

The first area to address is similar to requirements for line operations groups described in clause 5.2. Support groups must design and provide their services based on needs of their internal customers. In addition to being defined and described through flowcharts and procedures, these processes need to be evaluated regularly and have measurable outcomes. There needs to be a direct link between line operations and support functions. Support groups need to understand line or operational group's needs and provide services that help operations groups achieve corporate goals. Support groups must understand key requirements of operations groups and must identify their own key requirements to support those needs. Support functions must have process management controls in place to translate their key requirements into products or services for their operations or line customers. Support functions should have quality project plans for their work and should evaluate both their plans and their work. Finally, support functions should be early participants in product and operation design and goal setting so they can be prepared to support line groups.

The second and third areas to address look internally at support functions themselves. Support functions should identify and control their own key processes. Just as the operations groups must measure and plan their processes, support groups should have measurement plans in place to ensure their process performance meets expected levels. This third area concerns ways to improve support processes. The same techniques used by operations groups are appropriate here. The support groups should use quality problem-solving tools and fact-based decision making. Thorough data gathering and consideration of alternative solutions, benchmarking, alternative technologies, and information from internal and external customers should be factored into the evaluation processes. Timely feedback of results of evaluations to participants should be a routine feature of the evaluation process.

The EPC are similar to the MBNQA criterion, although there are two rather than three subclauses. Support services in the educational setting include libraries, counseling, placement, and tutorial services, among others. It is important to note that administrative or business support services are not included in this subclause but are addressed separately in Clauses 5.5 and 5.6 of the EPC. Support services in this clause are confined to education and training-related activities. The subclause looks at two areas:

- How support services are designed.
- How support services are evaluated and improved.

Support services should be designed to complement instructional activities and support established goals of the education or training organization. Their processes should translate organization goals and be directly linked to the goals of the organization. In addition to flowcharts and procedures, these support groups need to control their own internal processes to ensure they are performing effectively and efficiently. Similarly, there should be systematic evaluation of support services processes, and feedback should be gathered from a variety of sources, including trainees, families, operations groups, and faculty. Benchmarking, observations, and peer evaluations are all ways to gather data. Quality problem-solving tools should be used to assess and improve processes.

What MBNQA and EPC Examiners Look For

- Support processes are identified, described (through

flowcharts or procedures), and controlled; specific measures are in place to ensure they meet design and support operations requirements.

- Support service personnel are identified and responsible for process outcomes; problem-solving and feedback processes are in place.

- Quality problem solving tools and fact-based evaluations and decision making are used; sufficient data are acquired from a variety of resources, and alternative solutions are thoroughly considered.

- Systematic and ongoing efforts to improve processes are based on evaluation outcomes, research, improved technology, benchmarking, input from internal and external customers, and other techniques.

MB 5.4 MANAGEMENT OF SUPPLIER PERFORMANCE (30 POINTS)

This MBNQA subclause does not have a corollary in the EPC. This subclause is a logical progression from the preceding two subclauses. Where sections 5.2 and 5.3 look at operations and support processes, this subclause focuses on suppliers or vendors from outside the company who provide products or services. The same kinds of concerns are evident in relationships with these external suppliers. There are two areas to address:

- How communication and relationships with suppliers work.

- How improvements in relationships are achieved and supplier performance is improved.

The company should first determine what it needs from external suppliers and then have a process in place to select suppliers and communicate requirements to them. These requirements should include not only descriptions of the products or services, but also what critical measures will be used to judge the quality of products or services supplied.

Establishing critical measures necessitates establishing a way to monitor and evaluate supplier performance and provide feedback to suppliers. Evaluations and feedback should come from internal users of the product, which means the procurement function must solicit feedback from within the company and be a conduit for this information to external suppliers.

The second area concerns how the company improves its relationship with its suppliers. Many companies take a partnership approach with their suppliers and develop effective communication links with them. The MBNQA specifically asks companies to improve their own procurement processes and internal feedback to strengthen and improve relationships with external suppliers.

The Education Pilot Criteria omission of this particular subclause probably reflects the EPC focus on schools and universities. Corporate training organizations need to address this issue since many corporate training groups have significant expenditures for external vendors including purchasing training programs. Both groups do have procurement processes and use external vendors for supplies and services and should have a quality assurance process to control these activities.

What MBNQA Examiners Look For

- Controlled processes are in place to identify, evaluate, and contract with external suppliers of products and services.
- Suppliers are identified, critical measures are communicated, evaluations of external suppliers are based on internal customer satisfaction, and results are communicated to suppliers.
- The company has an active, continuous improvement process in place to help both external suppliers and its own procurement process.

EP 5.4 Research, Scholarship, and Service (20 points)

Whereas the MBNQA subclause 5.4 looks at the procurement relationship between companies and vendors, the EPC 5.4 focuses on research, scholarship, and service. Most of the areas in this clause concern colleges and universities; however, secondary schools involved in community outreach programs, GED high school equivalency programs, and other services to their communities would describe those services in this section of the criteria. Other outreach activities related to community citizenship should be addressed in Section 1.3, Public Responsibility and Citizenship. Similarly, commercial organizations can find ways to meet this criterion. There are three areas to address:

- How research, scholarship, and service contribute to knowledge creation and transfer to external communities.
- How research, scholarship, and service contribute to internal customers, such as faculty and trainees, and to the organization mission.
- How research, scholarship, and service activities are evaluated and improved.

On the college and university levels, research is accomplished by individuals working alone or in small groups. Scholarship usually is measured in terms of publications in refereed scholarly journals published by professional organizations. These publications are the medium of communication to transfer knowledge to external communities. This EPC criterion encourages colleges and universities to create environments and structures to help individuals or small groups conduct and publish research. Commercial organizations also contribute to knowledge creation and transfer by participating in benchmarking activities with other companies, supporting professional groups, and allowing employees to present at professional meetings and conventions.

The second area, how research, scholarship, and service contribute to individuals within the organization (that is, faculty, students, and staff), should also be addressed by colleges and universities, as well as secondary schools and commercial organizations. Members from all three groups should have access to relevant journals and professional publications. Programs should be in place in all three environments to help members go to professional seminars and conventions to gather new information. Also, members should participate in additional learning opportunities to gain SKAs that will help them improve their job performance. Commercial organizations with focused learning organization processes can use research, scholarship, and service to aid them in achieving their mission objectives.

The third and final area concerns how research, scholarship, and service activities are evaluated and improved. Again, peer evaluations and feedback from participants as well as benchmarking evaluations are appropriate ways for all three kinds of institutions to improve their research, scholarship, and service processes.

What EPC Examiners Look For

- Specific programs are in place to encourage research, scholarship, and service both to the community and organization.
- Funds and time are available to allow trainers to conduct research and publish findings as well as to attend professional organization meetings; there is a way to capture learning from these meetings and transmit it back into the organization.
- Organization practices encourage organizational learning to improve its operations continuously and meet its vision and goals.

EP 5.5 ENROLLMENT MANAGEMENT (20 POINTS)

This clause is primarily focused on colleges and universities; however, secondary schools and commercial organizations also need to have processes in place to attract capable participants and manage enrollments. Managing enrollment includes the actual administration of admission or entry processes and ways the organization helps potential and new trainees prepare for transition into the organization. There are two areas to address:

- How the organization communicates admission requirements.
- How the organization manages its interactions with external organizations, potential trainees, and their families.

Usually secondary school admission is based on a geographical service area, but such things as required inoculations, records, and transportation must be managed. Commercial organizations conduct orientation programs for new employees, and commercial training organizations communicate prerequisites and learning objectives to prospective attenders. Colleges and universities provide activities such as tours of libraries, how-to-study workshops, meetings, and orientation to college life that fall into this category. Universities and colleges also need to ensure equity in their admissions processes, conduct orientation and placement for new students, provide additional services such as housing or health services, and provide feedback to *feeder schools,* which are other institutions that supply students or trainees, such as high schools or junior colleges. In commercial organizations, feeders may be supervisors who send their employees to training programs.

The second part of this clause concerns the organization's relationship with its feeder schools. In the past, colleges and universities have expected to find students waiting to enroll when they open their doors. However, changing

273

populations and increasing competition have resulted in more outreach programs to attract students. Training groups within commercial organizations have also suffered when they expected employees to line up to participate in training activities. Therefore, both universities and training groups have discovered they must improve their recruitment methods. In addition to evaluating customer needs and providing high quality training, they must have outreach programs to attract capable trainees and participants, and they must provide good support to new participants to help them succeed in the learning environment. Finally, they must provide feedback to feeder schools and other sources and organizations that supply trainees/students to their programs.

What EPC Examiners Look For

- Comprehensive administrative admission process is in place; admission requirements are communicated to potential attenders; feedback is provided to feeder schools and other feeder sources.
- Programs are in place to help attenders prepare for transition into the organization and help them succeed in the learning environment.
- The organization uses a self-evaluation process to ensure that its programs meet new attender needs, and communication and admissions processes are effective and efficient; results of these self-evaluations are used to improve recruitment, admissions, and initial support processes continuously.

EP 5.6 BUSINESS OPERATIONS MANAGEMENT (20 POINTS)

This final clause focuses on the business or administration of running an education organization. Although there is no comparable clause in the MBNQA, concerns here are similar to those of any business or administrative operation. Essentially, this clause asks the organization to explain how it conducts business. There are two areas to address:

- How the organization manages its key business or administrative processes.
- How the organization evaluates its business operations to improve its performance, reduce costs, increase productivity, and reduce cycle time.

This clause is similar to clause 5.2, which looks at the process of managing instructional processes. Clause 5.6 addresses the process of managing the organization's business processes. There must be defined goals set, measures and standards established, and processes monitored. Second, operations must be evaluated and improved using customer feedback, benchmarking, and good process analysis tools. Purchasing activities must be included in these business processes.

What EPC Examiners Look For

- Procedures and flowcharts describe business processes; business processes are defined, measured, evaluated, and improved.

Q-Project Action Items

LINK ISD STEPS

The Education Pilot Criteria do not require an Instructional Systems Design (ISD) model. However, process management includes each of the five steps in an ISD model: analysis, design, development, delivery, and evaluation. The key is to link these five elements together so each step in the process mutually supports each other step. That is, analysis supports design, design supports development, etc. All steps are supported by the evaluation step, and each step should be evaluated in turn. And, most importantly, the evaluation step itself should be evaluated. A master flowchart of the instructional processes will show interrelationships among the five steps.

MAKE PROCESSES SYSTEMATIC

There must be a systematic quality plan to support process management. In addition to flowcharting primary processes, development of curricular materials should be based on project plans identifying individual sub-steps, individuals who will contribute to each process, and how feedback will be used to improve both product or service.

IMPROVE PRODUCTS AND PROCESSES

Effective and efficient processes will help produce high quality products and services with characteristics customers want. However, process management must go beyond simply evaluating the product or service. The process itself must be evaluated and improved. Improved processes are evidenced in fewer errors, less downtime, quicker cycle time, and education and training targeted to participant needs.

EVALUATE INSTRUCTIONAL STRATEGIES

Many kinds of instructional strategies are available to trainers. These range from simple lectures to sophisticated simulators such as those used to train airline pilots; each has its specific uses. Trainers should select a specific instructional strategy based on curriculum content and trainee needs. No one strategy can be applied in all cases; however, most often, strategies that actively involve trainees and demonstrate an immediate and obvious usefulness will appeal to trainees. As part of design process evaluation, trainers may consider conducting pilot programs to test the effectiveness and efficiency of a few different instructional strategies. For example, some trainees could receive one-on-one instruction from a SME supervisor, and other trainees could participate in demonstrations and role plays. Trainee success in mastering the activity could then be evaluated, and one strategy selected for the entire population.

276

EVALUATE FACULTY, TRAINEES, AND TRAINING

The final step in the five-step ISD model calls for evaluation. Evaluation includes faculty, trainees, and training programs. All three must be incorporated into an effective process control and continuous improvement program. Resources spent on evaluation activities can be considerable; however, the payoff in improved employee SKAs and job performance should more than offset these costs. Just as there is a need to establish learning objectives for training programs, an evaluation process needs to be in place to ensure that goals have been reached and continuously find ways to make training more effective and efficient.

INCLUDE SUPPORT SERVICES AND SUPPLIER SERVICES

Support and supplier services should be an integrated part of every quality assurance system. Flowcharts and procedures related to both support and supplier services should directly tie into line and operational functions. High quality organizations have figured out how to integrate all functions within their quality assurance processes.

CONSIDER RECRUITMENT AND PREPARATION CRITICAL

Just like other first impressions, recruitment and admissions processes set the tone for participant response to an education organization. Admission processes may mean helping college students register for a new semester of classes or helping employees sign up for a training program. In addition to establishing recruitment and admissions processes, organizations need to communicate prerequisites and help participants be prepared to gain the most from their learning experiences.

SEPARATE BUSINESS FROM INSTRUCTION

Training organizations, colleges, and universities face two separate quality assurance issues. One is to provide effective and efficient education and training to trainees/students and employees. The second is to administer a business, including such things as paying bills, ordering office supplies, and preparing payrolls. Education and training organizations must focus on both of these disparate functions in order to be successful. The best efforts of trainers will not succeed in a poorly administered setting, and conversely, great administrative processes will not redeem poorly designed and delivered training activities. They must function to support each other.

Reality Check

Of the seven criteria, process management is probably the most difficult both to understand and apply. Quick fix or add-on approaches will not work. Process management that meets MBNQA or EPC criteria requires a fundamental change in thinking and approach in doing the day-to-day tasks involved in creating and delivering high quality instruction. Success in this area leads directly to success in the education and training settings and demonstrates cost-effective solutions to customer needs. Process management techniques help control processes and link desired outcomes identified in the analysis and design stages. Evaluation of process management steps can be both scary and confusing. If management uses process management evaluations to assign blame or punish participants, then the quality process itself will break down.

CHAPTER 32

6.0
Business Results

MB 6.0 BUSINESS RESULTS (250 POINTS)

EP 6.0 SCHOOL PERFORMANCE RESULTS (230 POINTS)

This criterion may be the most unfamiliar and difficult for educators and trainers to address. Trainers and educators have focused on teaching processes rather than business outcomes of their activities. Typically, only student classroom performance is measured and reported. In contrast, business traditionally evaluates processes and measures results at three points: at the start with input, in mid-process, and at the end with output. These evaluations demonstrate whether processes are in control. They are inward-looking, focused on internal activities required to produce the product or service. The outward-looking activities are addressed in the next criterion, Section 7.0, Customer Satisfaction.

The structures of the MBNQA and the EPC criteria are rather different in this section. They ask for similar kinds of information, but focus and organization of the subclauses are expressed differently in each. The MBNQA 6.2 covers the same ideas as the EPC 6.4, for example. Therefore, presentation of criterion elements in this chapter is not in numerical order.

The MBNQA criteria ask organizations to address three areas or subclauses, evaluating inputs, in-process results, and outputs:

- Product and Service Quality Results (outputs).
- Company Operational and Financial Results (in-process).
- Supplier Performance Results (inputs).

Inputs represent more than just external supplier or vendor materials. Inputs also include contributions of labor, products and services, and ideas and concerns from internal suppliers and customers. All three subclauses ask the company to provide data on current key measures and assess trends, using graph and table formats and including appropriate comparative data. The criteria reflect an assumption that trends and comparisons with other organizations will show improvement arising from efforts to enhance quality and performance. However, it is a fact of life that not all organizational results always reflect positive trends or change. Presenting nothing but positive results would call into question an organization's credibility. Explanations of anomalies and/or negative trends should be provided.

MB 6.1 PRODUCT AND SERVICE QUALITY RESULTS (75 POINTS)

This section asks for data and trends on outcomes, results of organization processes, to provide customers with goods or services. Results should show a clear connection between customer indicators described in Section 7.0 and the organization's quality and performance. Both current results and trends in product and service quality and comparative information are specified for this section. Examiners will expect data reported in response to this section to be:

- Comprehensive, covering a broad range of processes and indices.

- Long-term, including as many years or reporting periods as possible.
- Objective, drawn from a variety of sources and including a variety of types of data.
- Used to analyze company performance, including benchmarking comparisons of competitor performance and comparing company performance against its own goals and standards.

Charts and graphs are efficient ways to translate data into information. *Data* are numbers, whereas *information* represents interpretation of data so they can be used to assess results and formulate plans. Note the old saying: "Figures don't lie, but liars figure." Charts and grafts can be constructed to present a positive picture of even negative data through selection of overall size, scale, and type of chart (pie, histogram, graph) by making it fancy or colorful or selecting the number of data points and the number of indices per chart. Baldrige examiners are alert to such spin-doctoring.

EP 6.1 STUDENT PERFORMANCE RESULTS (100 POINTS)

The EPC criteria consider student performance to be the product or outcome of education and training activities. Like the MBNQA, the EPC expect presentation of longitudinal measures over several years (at least three). Additionally, examiners expect to see data compared to national or related populations and/or benchmarked against best practice organizations. Educational institutions are fortunate in this area because national school and university numbers ordinarily are available for these comparisons. Trainers in commercial organizations will have greater difficulty comparing their trainee results to groups external to their organization.

In addition to showing improved results on such traditional measures as national standardized tests or average GPA, the EPC expect educators and trainers to conduct holistic appraisals of students. *Holistic appraisals* go beyond simple

281

trends and measures of typical scores on curricular studies, such as reading and mathematics, to include a wide variety of factors including creativity, self-expression, health, growth, maturity, social skills, and other human development factors affected by the school but generally not specifically identified in the curriculum or considered typical measurement criteria. For example, attitudes toward learning and ability to participate as a team member are learned in school settings but are not measured by routine test scores. The emphasis in this criterion on holistic measures continues as an emphasis in the next section on education climate.

What MBNQA and EPC Examiners Look For

- Data and information are comprehensive (many indices), relevant (important), and long-term (several years).
- Charts and graphs are clearly presented and easy to understand. They present information fairly and accurately.
- Information is usable. Trends demonstrate improvement and goal achievement or opportunities for improvement.

MB 6.2 COMPANY OPERATIONAL AND FINANCIAL RESULTS (130 POINTS)

Whereas clause MB 6.1 is focused on products and services, clause 6.2 focuses on the in-process company activities. Areas of process management covered in clauses 5.1, 5.2, and 5.3 would be reported as results in clause 6.2 in two broad categories, operational results and financial results. The MBNQA suggests at least a dozen typical operational measures including cycle time, innovation rates, machine capability and availability, safety records, reduced waste, and improved efficiency in overhead usage. Operational results should address key operating issues. Financial results include operating expenses, net profits, return on investment, revenue per employee, revenue per product, and the like.

One item that is not specifically identified in this MBNQA criteria should be addressed. This is the cost of quality. Companies routinely devote significant resources to efforts to improve products and services, but they frequently have a difficult time identifying financial returns for these investments. Performance excellence is expensive. A study of operational and financial results should address return on investment in quality.

EP 6.4 SCHOOL BUSINESS PERFORMANCE RESULTS (40 POINTS)

The MBNQA and EPC address the same issue in different subclauses within this criterion; the MBNQA 6.2 is the equivalent of EPC 6.4. It is interesting to note MBNQA awards 130 points for this criterion and EPC only 40 points. The difference in point value reflects the EPC's primary focus on student and trainee outcomes rather than business and financial outcomes for education organizations. Key indices in EPC 6.4 are the same as in MBNQA 6.2 and include cycle time, waste reduction, and environmental improvements. Financial results might include cost per credit hour, revenue per credit hour, overhead expenses, and cost of instruction, focusing on key cost elements—personnel, materials, energy, and capital.

What EPC Examiners Look For

Examiners have the same kinds of concerns in this subclause as in 6.1. Typical operational and financial results are important, as are results related to cost of quality.

MB 6.3 SUPPLIER PERFORMANCE RESULTS (45 POINTS)

Supplier or vendor performance results are not included as a separate item in the EPC. They should be reported as part of EPC 6.4, School Business Performance

Results. However, commercial organizations that purchase curricular materials or consultant instruction or services should consider this MBNQA criterion important to their quality process. This criterion asks companies to focus on how vendors are evaluated and selected, how relationships and communication between the vendor and company are conducted, and what steps are taken by the company to help vendors meet expectations and improve their relationship with the company.

Organizations that purchase training need to evaluate carefully their needs and select suppliers, vendors, and consultants who can meet those needs. Companies often spend considerable resources providing outside training for employees. The cost includes employee time away from work in addition to the actual price of seminars or training programs. It is incumbent upon the company to communicate clearly their needs and expectations to suppliers and work to contribute to their success. This section should describe how the organization manages and improves these relationships.

EP 6.2 SCHOOL EDUCATION CLIMATE IMPROVEMENT RESULTS
(50 POINTS)

This criterion does not have an equivalent section in the MBNQA. Even though it focuses on areas relevant primarily to schools and educational organizations, these issues are also relevant to commercial trainers and their organizations, although not as directly. Items under this category extend the concerns covered in EPC 6.1, Student Performance Results. Educational climate is difficult to measure, but a number of quantifiable indicators can reflect how school leadership, policies and practices, and commitment contribute to educational progress. Teacher and student absenteeism as well as student drop-out and faculty turnover rates reflect school climate. Student, parent, and faculty participation in extracurricular activities, student discipline problems, use of health facilities and counseling services, results of satisfaction surveys and surveys that measure optimism for the future are additional reflections of how the organization climate contributes to or impedes learning.

What EPC Examiners Look For

Examiners expect to see the same kinds of data-gathering efforts and evaluation of results, using graphs and charts, as are used for student performance results and school business performance results. Educational climate evaluations should go beyond quantitative and include qualitative data. In all areas examiners will expect to see clear and positive efforts to use results to improve processes.

EP 6.3 RESEARCH, SCHOLARSHIP, AND SERVICE RESULTS (40 POINTS)

This criterion is more applicable to colleges and universities than primary and secondary schools. Essentially, research and scholarship refer to knowledge creation and dissemination. However, these activities are relevant in lower grades, as well as among commercial training organizations. Often primary and secondary school teachers can develop case studies and report results of innovative or pilot curricula programs to include in this criteria. Commercial trainers who present at professional organization meetings or participate in professional benchmarking of their training activities across companies would include those efforts as part of creation and transfer of knowledge.

Both education and training organizations should assess and improve their commitment to service under this criterion. Trainers who support professional development activities, act as judges for teams or other application awards and prizes, serve on committees related to training, and provide assessments of training outcomes to other companies qualify under this service criteria. Similarly, primary, sec-

285

ondary, and college and university faculty may take credit for service to their schools, students, and community by participating in committee work, organizational projects, and student activities outside the school setting. This item, like the others, calls for comparative and benchmark data. This information should be framed in terms of number of faculty to make the comparison one of apples to apples.

What EPC Examiners Look For

This data may be difficult to capture because participants often are volunteers in these kinds of activities. Companies and schools may help connect individuals to projects by serving as a communication link to worthwhile projects and allowing their trainers and faculty time to work on these projects. For example, a company may allow a trainer time to serve as an award judge or present at a local professional chapter meeting. Encouraging use of physical facilities for health fairs, community meetings, and use by service groups or charities is an example of service. Schools often encourage service by their own students by organizing training or charitable fund-raising activities. Outreach and scholarship programs also reflect service results.

Q-Project Action Items

STUDY CHART/GRAPH CONSTRUCTION

Graphs and charts present a great deal of data in little space and help users assimilate it quickly. In planning graphic data presentation, consider what story needs to be communicated. Carefully use titles, headings on each axis of a graph, and the like to clarify and cue the user. Whereas collecting and calculating are the science side of chart and graph making, there is an art side, also. The art of chart or graph design is the process of finding interesting, accurate, and informative ways to translate the data into understandable and useful information.

ESTABLISH ROUTINE DATA GATHERING

Efforts to gather data after-the-fact are doomed to create frustration and lead to failure. Data gathering and reporting should be an integral part of daily activities. If data gathering becomes burdensome, people may find ways to short-circuit the process or "magic" the data. *Magic* here means becoming creative and extrapolating or producing lovely numbers from thin air. A major Q-Project Team challenge is to develop effective and efficient means to gather useful data that will help continuous improvement processes.

COLLECT USEFUL DATA

It is exceedingly easy to fall into the trap of collecting only the obvious or readily available data, regardless of its usefulness. Measurement indices, like goals, need to help organizations improve their product or service. In the same way establishing easily achieved or non-challenging goals is not in the spirit of improving quality and performance, simplistic data does not spur an organization to achieve world-class status. Just good enough isn't good enough.

DETERMINE ROI FOR QUALITY

There is a payoff for resources devoted to quality programs, but it often is difficult to demonstrate that payoff, especially in readily understandable financial terms. Cost-of-quality and return on quality programs are difficult to assess because improvements come from a wide variety of causes, and it is difficult to credit outcomes to particular activities. However, the difficulty of assigning credit to particular activities should not deter trainers and educators from seeking ways to determine both quantitative and qualitative (using anecdotal information) value of their efforts in the quality arena.

STRUCTURE VENDOR SELECTION

Commercial organizations purchase instructional

287

materials, training supplies, and consultant training services. These purchases should be based on a structured way to select vendors and suppliers. Companies need first to identify the need for vendor-provided training activities and the outcomes they expect from these services and then communicate these expectations clearly. As the customer in this case, organizations have the right and responsibility to state what products or services they expect and establish ways to assure that they get them.

Reality Check

Just as there is a temptation to set easily realized goals, there is always a temptation to report just the most obvious data, the data that are readily available. Neither is appropriate for organizations that take seriously the objective to be customer-driven, improve continuously, and be world-class. Although gathering data to discover how the organization is really performing may be difficult or frustrating, it is a critical underpinning to an organization's ability to achieve its goals. This section on performance results should reflect a direct connection to earlier sections in which vision, goals, and strategic plans are identified as part of a fully deployed and integrated approach to continuous improvement of quality and performance.

CHAPTER 33

7.0

Customer Focus
and Satisfaction

MB 7.0 Customer Focus and Satisfaction (250 points)
EP 7.0 Student Focus and Student and Stakeholder
   Satisfaction (230 points)

Customer satisfaction is the philosophical basis and driving motivator behind the Baldrige criteria, linking together all of the other sections. This section of the Baldrige criteria closes the circle created by the previous six sections. The importance of this section is obvious from its length—it contains more subclauses than any other section—and number of points assigned to this area, about 25% of the total. A training or education Q-Project team would find it useful to start with this section, using it as a guide to structure their training organization and address the remaining six sections of the criteria.

Essentially, Customer Focus and Satisfaction asks organizations to explain how they determine what their customers want, then how they use that information to organize their processes to provide a service or produce a product. Organizational leaders and members gather and analyze information about markets (Section 2.0), set the vision (Section 1.0), develop the plans (Section 3.0), guide people who do the work (Section 4.0), manage processes to produce or provide the product or service (Section 5.0), and track results of their efforts (Section 6.0). All these sections and subclauses are focused on satisfying customers (Section 7.0). References in many of the notes in each subclause of Section 7.0 ask the organization to tie customer focus to information contained in previous sections.

MB 7.1 Customer and Market Knowledge (30 points)
EP 7.1 Current Student Needs and Expectations (40 points)
EP 7.2 Future Student Needs and Expectations (30 points)

This section of the EPC is organized slightly differently from the MBNQA, modifying the numbering system and subclauses. The MBNQA refers to near-term and longer-term customer needs, whereas the EPC contain one extra subclause which emphasizes the difference between current student needs and future needs. Other than this distinction, similar ideas are contained in similar subclauses throughout this section.

The first subclauses ask organizations how they go about listening to and learning from customers. Trainers and educators should have a systematic way to learn about their current and future customer needs. In addition to describing methods used to gather information from a variety of sources, it is important to explain how customer groups are categorized according to their needs. For example, members of different age groups, students with different learning styles, or attenders with special challenges represent groups that have varied needs and expect different outcomes from their learning experiences. Some groups need particular features in products and services. Some instructional features are more valued or important to some groups than to others. The MBNQA provides a list of nine listening and learning strategies educators and trainers can adapt to gather information about their student populations. This information then should be used to determine what employees or students need from their learning activities and how to structure activities to meet these requirements.

The MBNQA then asks organizations to explain how they prepare for the future, what trends they predict, and how the organization learns about and prepares to meet these changes. The EPC address future student needs in a separate section. Future needs should be based on anticipated changes in student populations, from demographic and societal changes. Changes in work environments would require new SKAs to help graduates succeed in their work lives, for example. This subclause also emphasizes the possibility of meeting education and training challenges through alternative education or training resources. This reflects a major shift in thinking about competition among schools and corporate training groups.

Traditionally both schools and corporate training organizations consider they have captive audiences, and their approach to customer satisfaction, therefore, has been less than aggressive. Competition is increasing, however, and organizations are experimenting with new ways to attract and retain students and be innovative in meeting their needs. Some corporations are experimenting with allowing their training groups to offer services to outside groups while allowing internal groups to seek training help from outside the corporation. Universities and colleges are approaching recruiting and retention in new ways, and legislative changes are allowing some secondary schools to compete openly for students. The goal of all these changes reflecting heightened competition among education and training groups is to provide students and trainees with alternatives to meet their individual needs and at the same time spur quality improvements among providers.

Both the MBNQA and EPC ask organizations to explain how they translate information they have gathered about needs into action items that will help them improve their processes. Both ask how organizations evaluate and improve processes they use to gather and apply data. One way to show how information is used is to construct a three-way matrix of customer groups to expectations or needs and then to action items or services provided. Such a matrix will distinguish common and special needs and provide trainers with a framework for structuring their offerings and prioritizing their improvement processes.

What MBNQA and EPC Examiners Look For

- Systematic ways exist for the organization to gather data and translate information into action items to help them produce products or provide services to meet individual customer group needs and expectations.
- A variety of data, including customer complaints and less obvious or more difficult-to-gather data, such as lost customers, are used to determine needs.
- Systematic and routine ways to evaluate and improve processes are used to listen, learn, gather, and use customer satisfaction information.

MB 7.2 Customer Relationship Management (30 points)
EP 7.3 Stakeholder Relationship Management (40 points)

This subclause asks organizations to explain how they provide information to customers and how they allow customers easy access to comment or complain to the company. Whether the customer contact is a complaint or a question, contacts offer organizations opportunities to learn about their customers' needs and expectations. There must be a way to resolve complaints quickly and additionally to feed information about customer complaints back into the process to improve the product or service and to avoid future problems. Obviously, in order to judge how well they are doing, the company needs to have established standards against which to assess their performance.

Customer contact or service representatives frequently are referred to by the military term *front line*, which suggests they are the ones catching the bullets. The MBNQA notes section of this clause says these customer contact employees should be well trained to handle customer inquiries and complaints and lists specific SKAs these individuals should possess. If training organizations are going to provide such training to their corporate customer service representatives, they certainly should have the same SKAs within their training organization.

Customer management is more than responding to initiatives made by the customer. Many customers do not bother to complain; they simply take their business elsewhere. The organization should have a systematic process to solicit feedback from customers concerning their satisfaction. This feedback should be evaluated both to improve current products and services and predict future needs for products and services. The EPC add an important additional point to the MBNQA requirement, suggesting educational organizations need to have ways to communicate their needs to their customers. Schools, like churches and charities, are in business to serve their customers; however, these organizations also need support from their clients and communities. This support helps the school do their work. Such two-way support is inappropriate in commercial organizations because customers do not expect to be concerned about company needs; they want and expect a quality product or service with features that satisfy their needs at a competitive price.

Finally, as in most of the other sections and subclauses of the MBNQA and EPC, there is a requirement to assess routinely the effectiveness of the process itself. Here again, organizations need to evaluate their customer relationship management process to determine if these processes are providing information they need about customers; if the organization is effectively and quickly resolving customer complaints; and if the organization is feeding this information back into its own improvement processes to avoid problems and improve products and services.

What MBNQA and EPC Examiners Look For

- Quick response mechanisms are in place and knowledgeable customer service personnel are available to answer customer questions and resolve customer complaints.
- Information gathered from customer contacts is systematically captured, evaluated, and fed back into process improvement initiatives.
- Customer service representatives are well trained, knowledgeable, and empowered to resolve customer difficulties, and they have ways to influence outcomes to help avoid future problems.
- Routine and systematic evaluation of customer relationship management results are gathered during these evaluations and are used to improve processes.

MB 7.3 CUSTOMER SATISFACTION DETERMINATION (30 POINTS)
EP 7.4 STUDENT AND STAKEHOLDER SATISFACTION DETERMINATION (30 POINTS)

Whereas the previous subclause asks organizations to describe how they respond to customer complaints and inquiries, this subclause asks organizations what proactive steps they take to solicit data from customers concerning their satisfaction with the product or service and determine their customers' future purchasing intentions. The MBNQA equates customer satisfaction to repurchase decisions relative to competitors; that is, customers are satisfied when they plan to purchase more goods or products from the organization rather than buying from the competition. Organizations are not required to ask that question directly of customers; but, the MBNQA lists 14 customer dissatisfaction indicators that will help the organization predict a customer's likely future market behavior. The organization also may increase objectivity of comparisons between themselves and their competition by employing an outside market research service to gather such data. The EPC have a shorter, but equally revealing, list of indicators of customer satisfaction, including dropout rates, complaints, claims, refunds, repeat services, and litigation.

Both the MBNQA and EPC ask for descriptions of methods and scales used to measure satisfaction, the frequency of these efforts, how objectivity and validity are assured, how differences among customer groups are handled, and how this key information is captured and fed back into improvement processes. The EPC separate and apply these same questions to both current and past students in addition to other key stakeholders. The EPC do not emphasize competition but ask organizations to assess themselves against comparable schools. After data are gathered and assessed, the organization should have ways to use information, that is, turn information into action items to enhance processes to improve products or service and maintain customer loyalty. And, as in many other subclauses, the organization should have a way to assess the effectiveness of its customer satisfaction determination process to ensure it is obtaining information it needs.

What MBNQA and EPC Examiners Look For

■ Proactive processes are in place, and varied methods are used to solicit customer satisfaction feedback relative to competitors, helping determine customer repurchase intentions.

- Established data indicators are collected and translated into action items to improve specific product and service features as a way to improve ratings and influence customers' likely future market behavior.

- Training and education organizations gather information from current and past trainees/students as well as from other stakeholders and assess their performance against comparable organizations.

- The organization routinely assesses the effectiveness and efficiency of its customer satisfaction determination processes.

MB 7.4 CUSTOMER SATISFACTION RESULTS (100 POINTS)

EP 7.5 STUDENT AND STAKEHOLDER SATISFACTION RESULTS (50 POINTS)

There is a significant difference between the MBNQA and EPC in point values assigned to this clause. Part of the reason for this difference is that the subclause added elsewhere takes some points. More significantly, the concept of student and stakeholder satisfaction results is relatively new in many education and training organizations. Until they have an opportunity to evaluate the response to these issues, the EPC writers were probably wise to limit the number of points for this subclause.

Quite simply, this section asks organizations to report satisfaction results and trends against key measures. Essentially, the criteria ask for the same kinds of reports as in Section 6.0, where the organization reported its internal results for operations, financial outcomes, and improvements. In Section 7.0 it reports external results, that is, customer satisfaction results. Results should be segmented by appropriate customer groups. The criteria assume results will show high current customer satisfaction and trends will show improvement. It is appropriate to report adverse indicators along with analysis of their cause and plans to correct or overcome dissatisfaction.

What MBNQA and EPC Examiners Look For

- A variety of customer satisfaction indices are reported from different customer groups.
- Reported results indicate high current customer satisfaction and several years of improving satisfaction trends.

MB 7.5 CUSTOMER SATISFACTION COMPARISON (60 POINTS)
EP 7.6 STUDENT AND STAKEHOLDER SATISFACTION COMPARISON
(40 POINTS)

This MBNQA clause asks companies to compare themselves with their competitors, and the EPC clause asks organizations to assess themselves relative to comparable schools. As in the previous clause, levels and trends are important. Indices in this section include gains or losses in market share, competitive awards, and other external ratings and recognitions. A quality award or a high rating from a consumer information group is evidence of such success. The EPC note that some education organizations face competition through alternative learning methods, such as home schooling or corporate educational programs.

What MBNQA and EPC Examiners Look For

- Several indices are reported to show gains in market share and compare the organization against several organizations, including world-class competitors.
- Current levels are high and trends are positive; anomalies are explained.

Q-Project Action Items

FLOWCHART THE BIG PICTURE

The Baldrige criteria do not require an Instructional Systems Design (ISD) model; however, a flowchart of the seven steps in the Baldrige easily equates to the five steps in Instructional Systems Design: analysis, design, development, implementation, and evaluation. A flowchart of the big picture, showing how the organization does its major functions related to the seven criteria, will help trainers and educators understand their own processes and communicate how they do business with both internal and external customers. Such a model will also help trainers and educators evaluate and improve how they go about doing their business.

PREPARE FOR THE FUTURE

Sometimes it is difficult enough just trying to keep up with current needs. Too frequently, trainers and educators find themselves behind the power curve because they are not included in strategy planning sessions and have insufficient forewarning or time to develop training activities and help their organizations prepare for the future. Instead, they find themselves playing catch-up and rushing to meet current needs. The Q-Project Team needs to have at least one member with access to the corporate strategy level so this kind of information can be available routinely. Some training organizations attempt to offer JIT, just-in-time training. *JIT* means delivered when needed, not prepared when needed. Good JIT requires good prior preparation, design, and development to have training activities ready to go when needed.

FOLLOW-UP

End-of-course evaluations are inadequate tools to gather the range of comments, complaints, and other customer satisfaction information that are required to evaluate and improve training and education. Because the hallmark of quality training is the trainees' ability to use newly acquired SKAs, corporate trainers should definitely include a loop-back at approximately three to six months to find out if training met trainee needs and if trainees are using newly acquired skills on the job. Quick personal interviews, a phone call, or short visit with both trainees and their supervisors are ways to gather this information. Educators should similarly follow up on student performance. Although some of this is reflected in overall enrollment and enrollments in higher level classes, follow-up with students will reveal much important information.

TRAIN REPRESENTATIVES TO VALUE CONTACTS

Train customer service representatives to use every customer contact as an opportunity to increase knowledge about customers and improve customer relationships. The subclause notes of MBNQA offer a list of six specific SKAs representatives ought to possess. In addition, establish a systematic and routine way to gather this data and feed it back into a continuous improvement project process.

USE CHARTS, GRAPHS, AND TABLES

Responses to each clause in this section should include charts, graphs, and tables to summarize information, make it accessible, and capture trends. Used along with written descriptions, visual representations can show how processes work, how data is transformed into information, and how results are employed to improve processes, in addition to results and trends. Additionally, trainers and educators can and should use these same charts, graphs, and tables to report positive results to their organization management to show the value of the quality assurance process applied to training and education activities and also the value of training and education to customers.

Reality Check

Employee empowerment and good customer service are not satisfied by the presence of young customer service representatives with smiles in their voices who are told to do whatever it takes to resolve a complaint, or more bluntly, to do something to get the customer to shut up and go away. Good customer service means every representative of the organization has the appropriate SKAs to use any customer contact as an opportunity to build customer satisfaction, customer loyalty, and repeat business. Empowerment further means the representative has the wherewithal to influence operations to improve processes and avoid future errors.

Training and education organizations typically have little time to consider customer satisfaction. They frequently are burdened by the traditional view that they have a captive clientele and by limited resources to focus primarily on their daily activities. In the past, relatively few resources have been devoted to evaluating training or education organizations. However, schools and universities are discovering that dissatisfied customers, particularly dissatisfied communities and potential employers, are becoming more vocal and demanding that graduates have the academic SKAs to succeed in the work environment. Additionally, corporations are placing increasing demands on their trainers to demonstrate the value of resources spent on training. Typical end-of-course trainee questionnaires that ask if trainees liked the training are insufficient demonstrations of customer satisfaction.

It is easy to agree that good customer service is the hallmark of a quality organization and that organizations practicing good quality processes should be able to deliver high quality products and services. Customer satisfaction is the underlying theme and support for all other sections of the criteria. Customers are the final judge of performance and repeat customers are the highest compliment. However, it is significantly more difficult to structure processes according to quality criteria and operate within a quality environment than it is to talk about quality. Creating an organization that actually operates on quality principles is neither easy nor inexpensive. Frequently processes grow up helter-skelter based on needs of the moment and quick fixes to end symptoms rather than finding solutions to problems. Effort, time, and resources must be spent to make processes simple and focused on defined outcomes. The seven sections of the MBNQA and EPC give trainers and educators tangible tools and practical ways to implement quality initiatives.

Part Four
The ISO Guidelines

This section discusses ISO guidelines of interest to trainers and educators and discusses how to maintain the energy and enthusiasm for a quality program after ISO registration or receipt of a Baldrige Award.

CHAPTER 34

ISO Guidelines and
Other Standards

A wealth of information is available for trainers from the International Organization for Standardization. In addition to the 9000 series, ISO publishes thousands of standards and guidelines related to many specific products and services and lists and updates these annually in the ISO Bulletin. More than 180 technical committees are charged with writing and updating individual standards and guidelines usually once every five years. Trainers will find standards relating to their own industry and company's products an important resource, and this information can help them structure activities to support corporate goals. Ideas contained in product standards and guidelines also help trainers structure training processes to meet the Z-1.11, Education and Training Guideline.

This chapter focuses on the three ISO 9000 Standards and several guidelines of interest to trainers. The standards are compliance contracts, that is, a company must address each element in the standard, whereas the guidelines provide additional information to help companies and auditors interpret the standards. There is no need to address items in the guidelines, and auditors will not attempt to audit a quality assurance process against a guideline.

Companies may elect to be registered against any of the three standards. ISO 9001 and ISO 9002 are exactly the same except that ISO 9002 does not address Element 4.4, Design Control. Companies that do not have an engineering or product design function usually elect to register to ISO 9002. ISO 9003 contains significantly fewer elements, and some elements that it shares with 9001 are less stringently defined or applied. Generally, companies adopt the 9003 standard for either final inspection and testing or as a way to structure receiving inspections. As of January 1995, fewer than 400 U.S. companies were registered to ISO 9003. Most U.S. registrations are either to 9001 or 9002.

ISO also publishes the 9000-x series and the 9004-x series of guidelines. There are several guidelines in both categories and, in recent years, ISO has been restructuring and renumbering them. Here is a brief summary of each as of August 1995.

The 9000-x Series

ISO 9000-1 SELECTION AND USE

This guideline helps managers understand basic ideas about quality assurance and how to select a standard to apply to their company. It describes the goals of a quality assurance process and how management should go about reviewing the effectiveness of its quality assurance process. It also gives some basic information about the value and role of procedures, work instructions, and quality plans required for ISO. The guideline writers make clear that they intend these documents to be dynamic, i.e., changing frequently according to need and "high value-adding." *High value-adding* means that these documents are supposed to help give the organization confidence that its processes are in control and help it reliably measure its current performance and desired improvements. The high value-adding language should help companies decide what is important and needs documentation while limiting the excessive paperwork that sometimes plagues companies who attempt to adopt ISO.

ISO 9000-2 GENERIC GUIDELINE FOR APPLICATION

This guideline should definitely be in every trainer's library and available to every member of the Q-Project team as they set up a quality assurance process. This guideline elaborates ideas behind each of the 20 elements in the ISO standards and interprets and explains each element. The guideline writers maintain a neutral and generic approach so their explanations can apply to a broad spectrum of companies. Unfortunately, many of the examples continue to focus on manufacturing and products rather than on service-related industries. For example, the explanation of Element 4.20, Statistical Techniques, is oriented primarily toward manufacturing and is frustrating to apply to a service industry. On the positive side, however, as more service industries apply ISO, more experience and information are becoming available to service organizations. This guideline gives examples of concerns that need to be addressed in each element of the standard and thus provides significant insight into the fundamental ISO concepts.

ISO 9000-3 SOFTWARE

This guideline applies to development and maintenance of software. Companies that develop software, whether for computers or as a control device in machinery and equipment, will find it helpful. Trainers who work in such companies also will find it helpful as they provide training to their employees.

ISO 9000-4 DEPENDABILITY PROGRAMS

This guideline relates to dependability program management, focusing on product life-cycle characteristics that ensure equipment dependability. Interestingly, ISO 9001, Element 4.9g, briefly mentions suitable maintenance of equipment. Many quality practitioners recognize the value of an effective preventive maintenance program in concert with an equipment design process that emphasizes product dependability and reduces equipment and product failures. This guideline will be of interest to trainers who work in companies interested in equipment design and, more broadly, in companies interested in effective preventive maintenance programs.

The 9004-x Series

ISO 9004-1 ISO GUIDELINES

This guideline is useful for companies wanting to begin a quality assurance system within their organizations but who do not have customers who require ISO registration. Like ISO 9000-2, it provides insight into the intention behind each element in the standard and helps explain how to think about many issues in a quality assurance process. Besides information about the elements in the standards, it also talks about such topics as documentation, financial considerations, quality planning, configuration management, and marketing, among others.

ISO 9004-2 SERVICES

This guideline discusses each element in the standard as it applies to service-related industries. There is a full discussion of this guideline in Chapter 35.

ISO 9004-3 PROCESSED MATERIALS

This guideline discusses processed materials, usually fungible products, such as coal, or any product delivered by pipeline, drums, tanks, or cans. There is heavy emphasis on statistical sampling and product evaluation, process control and product specifications, and control and maintenance of equipment used to store and ship these items. Trainers working in these industries will find the information contained in this guideline helpful as they analyze their employees' training needs.

ISO 9004-4 QUALITY IMPROVEMENT

This guideline is the ISO answer to the concern for continuous improvement seen in the Malcolm Baldrige National Quality Award and Total Quality Management movements. Companies with strong continuous improvement processes in place will find that information in this guideline is basic.

ISO 9004-5 QUALITY PLANS

This guideline focuses on quality plans. Although the 1987 version of the ISO standard did not require companies to produce quality plans, they have become a requirement in the 1994 version of the standard. The requirement for quality planning is not a radical departure from the 1987 guideline and is not particularly demanding in its basic requirements. Many companies, except those flying strictly by the seat of their pants, will discover they probably already meet many of the requirements for quality plans. They may need to formalize, structure, and document the processes already in place; however, the guideline and standard should not place an undue burden on current process in many companies.

ISO 9004-7 CONFIGURATION MANAGEMENT

Configuration management is defined as "functional and physical characteristics of a product as set forth in technical documentation and achieved in the product." This guideline is useful for companies with strong research and development and/or design engineering functions. Trainers in these companies are usually familiar with more technical topics and will find this guideline of special interest.

Other Guidelines

ISO 10011-1,2,3 QUALITY AUDITING

This three-part guideline on quality auditing is covered at length in Chapter 36. They are must-have documents for every trainer's library. Every trainer will find these documents important to help structure internal quality audit processes for both their training function and their corporate-wide quality auditing program.

ISO 10012 MEASURING EQUIPMENT

This guideline covers instrumentation. Most companies have some type of measurement equipment or instrumentation that they must calibrate according to the ISO standard Element 4.11, Control of Inspection, Measuring and Test Equipment. Trainers will find the guideline informative as they help their companies address this significant area of concern. Also, trainers who are using the Z.1-11, Education and Training Guideline, will find ISO 10012 useful in their validation of trainee performance measures and examinations.

ISO-10013 QUALITY MANUALS

Many books, seminars, and computer software programs are on the market to help companies develop their quality manual and procedures. This guideline, available from ANSI, is the ISO approach to writing these documents. Knowledgeable trainers and individuals with experience writing these documents will find that the information covered in the guideline is basic and geared to individuals with limited experience.

Other Standards

SHINGO PRIZE FOR EXCELLENCE IN MANUFACTURING

Dr. Shingo was the President of Japan's Institute of Management Improvement, author of the Toyota Production

Study, and father of SMED (Single Minute Exchange of Dies) system. The five major parts and several subparagraphs in the criteria reflect the concept of *lean manufacturing* processes. Large or small manufacturing companies, whole companies or divisions or business units, or single plants within a large company may apply for this prize. The prize and criteria are limited to manufacturing companies. There is a 1,000-point scoring system, and applications receive a detailed feedback report. Information is available from the College of Business, Utah State University, Logan, Utah 84322-3520.

NATIONAL ACADEMY FOR NUCLEAR TRAINING

NANT publishes the Objectives and Criteria for Accreditation of Training in the Nuclear Power Industry. The document includes eight objectives and 58 criteria. The ISO Z-1.11, Education and Training Guideline, refers to this document, and there are obvious similarities between the two. The Institute for Nuclear Power Operations was created after the Three Mile Island incident; it established NANT to help nuclear utilities develop personnel training programs. This standard is probably more useful for trainers in technical rather than service industries. Further information is available from NANT, 1100 Circle 75 Parkway, Suite 1500, Atlanta, Georgia 30339-3064.

NUREG-1220

The U.S. Nuclear Regulatory Commission published a document titled Training Review Criteria and Procedures. Despite its ponderous title, it is an excellent document for trainers in all industries. It follows a modified Instructional Systems Design (ISD) model and includes interview protocols and checklists for each step in the model. The checklists alone are worth the $7.00 cost of this document. Information is available from the Superintendent of Documents, U.S. Government Printing Office, P.O. Box 37082, Washington, D.C. 20013-7082.

CHAPTER 35

ISO 9004-2
Guidelines for Services 1991

Guideline 9004-2 is a guideline to help service organizations find ways to apply the 9001 standard. ISO based the initial development of its standards primarily on manufacturing processes and products, and many registrars and quality assurance auditors have come from manufacturing backgrounds. Fortunately, service industries are now learning about ISO and beginning to apply the standards to achieve excellent customer service. Additionally, registrars and auditors are gaining experience dealing with service organizations.

Readers who compare the Education and Training Guideline to the Guideline for Service Organizations will be grateful for the detail provided by the former. Because the service guideline is so generic, it is difficult to interpret and contains little specific helpful guidance. A review of the service guideline may give trainers some ideas and help them interpret the Training and Education Guideline. The following discussion is not thorough, and Q-Project team members should devote time to reviewing and discussing it for additional insight and ideas.

Defining a service organization is problematic. It may be large or small and deal with a range of services, such as house cleaning, a service provided with the purchase of a product (such as warranty work on an automobile), or provision of annual information by a mutual fund company. Within organizations, the scope of service processes includes all activities from initial marketing to final delivery. As in manufacturing settings, internal and external customers are the ultimate recipients. In many training situations, the customer is internal to the corporation.

The authors of the guideline recognize the diversity of types of organizations and types of service within organizations. Therefore, much of the guideline language refers to characteristics of service. The guideline says, in paragraph 4.1, that service has these (and more) characteristics:

- "The requirements of a service need to be clearly defined in terms of characteristics that are observable and subject to customer evaluations."
- "The processes that deliver a service also need to be defined in terms of characteristics that may not always be observable by the customer, but directly affect service performance."

Trainers can satisfy these two characteristics in several ways within their ISD process. For example, trainers define training requirements by conducting needs analyses and job-task analyses. Coordination with supervision and the Training Quality Teams (TQTs) serves as a contract review. Both of these ISD activities help satisfy the first characteristic. The second characteristic is familiar to trainers, who know that much of the process of delivering the training happens before the instructor enters a classroom. The service guideline supports the Education and Training Guideline by saying that customers can evaluate many qualitative characteristics when the organization finds ways to measure these characteristics quantitatively. This idea expands on Element 4.20, Statistical Techniques, and provides further incentive for seeking statistical data to measure processes and quantifying quality in products and services.

The guideline describes three quality system principles for service; these are repetitions of the ideas contained in the ISO 9001 Standard. These discussions elaborate on the requirements in the standard and give the Q-Project team insight into the authors' thinking about these issues. There are several "should" statements in this part of the guideline. However, the entire discussion centers on the basic needs for a good quality process. The three principles are as follows:

- Management responsibility, including establishing quality policy and objectives, responsibility and authority, and management reviews.
- Personnel and material resources, including encouraging personnel motivation, training and development, communications, and providing adequate material resources.
- Quality system structures, including establishing needed procedures, documentation, internal quality audits, and interface with customers.

The final portion of the guideline discusses operating elements from marketing to final delivery. This discussion is a restructuring of the ISO elements on process control and its related elements of design control, inspections and testing, and delivery. Again, this section of the guideline emphasizes the need for a structured approach and quantitative data to verify that the process is in control and the customer is receiving quality service.

Trainers will find value in this guideline because it correctly recognizes that service organizations frequently have difficulty carefully structuring processes they use to deliver their service. As organizations grow and the demand for service increases, company personnel cobble together their service processes while interacting with individual customers. Frequently, service occurring at the interaction point between the customer and company's service representative is one person in response to the moment, the problem, or the customer. Organizations have difficulty gathering this experiential learning of its members, organizing it, making sure it is repeatable, improving it, and passing it on to other individuals who provide service. At the same time, the structure of the organization is constantly changing and growing; it is reinventing itself as the demand for service increases or changes. Too often an organization's approach may be haphazard. They know that they want to provide good service, but there is little time to make sure a workable process is in place to provide it. Also, there tends to be little time to implement quantitative measures to help management understand how well they are serving the customer and help discover ways to improve the service.

Good service is sometimes defined as fixing a customer complaint. Good service is not responding to complaints; good service means there are no complaints. In fact, good service should be seamless; good service is just there. Unfortunately, it is often the youngest, least experienced members of the organization who provide service. Companies may successfully grant these individuals authority to fix a complaint and satisfy a customer's needs. However, companies frequently do not grant these younger service providers authority to fix the system that delivers the service.

Like customer service providers, trainers are frequently younger and have a more narrow focus on the company's operations. A training organization that structures its process to meet the ISO 9001 Standard and Education and Training Guideline will help trainers overcome some of these inherent difficulties by attacking the root cause of problems and fixing processes rather than reacting with a Band-aid solution by narrowly focusing on the customer's complaint.

CHAPTER 36

ISO 10011
Guidelines for Auditing

The ISO 10011 series consists of three guidelines. Like all guidelines, they suggest issues and ways to think about standards. Since they are not standards, they do not contain requirements that must be met. However, these guidelines will help practitioners understand and apply Element 4.17, Internal Quality Audits, and Element 4.14, Corrective and Preventive Action. The guidelines provide help on three topics:

- How to organize a quality assurance audit process. (Guideline 10011-1)
- Qualifications for quality auditors. (Guideline 10011-2)
- How to manage quality audit programs. (Guideline 10011-3)

Trainers should be familiar with these three guidelines to:

- Participate as an auditor in organization-wide internal quality auditing processes.

315

- Develop an internal quality audit process for the training function.
- Organize and write a procedure to meet ISO 9001, Paragraph 4.17, Internal Quality Audits, for the training function.
- Prepare for and undergo audits of the training function by external agencies.
- Conduct training for internal auditors to support corporate quality assurance programs.

This chapter does not contain a comprehensive discussion of all issues in these guidelines. Rather, it briefly describes major points of interest to trainers and offers some ideas about how they can meet these issues in training procedures and practice.

ISO 10011-1 PART 1: AUDITING

This guideline is the most comprehensive of the three. It "establishes basic audit principles, criteria and practices . . . for establishing, planning, carrying out and documenting audits." One advantage of internal quality audits is that, since internal audit teams consist of personnel who are intimately familiar with the processes and opportunities for improvement, they can make changes and help their continuous improvement process. The guideline identifies responsibilities of participants in the audit process and gives a procedure writer an easily adaptable set of tasks that can be tailored to the training organization's internal audit procedure. It also includes definitions that can be incorporated into the procedure.

ISO 10011-2 PART 2: QUALIFICATION CRITERIA FOR QUALITY SYSTEMS AUDITORS

This guideline lists qualifications for auditors. Because the guidelines are written for international application, the first requirement is that the auditor must be able clearly and fluently to express ideas orally and in writing in the officially recognized language of the audit. Besides a secondary education, auditors must:

- Know the standard(s) against which they conduct the audit.
- Have skills and knowledge about how to conduct an audit.
- Have appropriate workplace experience (line experience) and auditing experience.
- Possess a list of personal, common sense attributes, including the ability to get along with people.

There are two particularly interesting points here. First, the guideline authors point out that experience must be practical, and they include the statement: "not including training." They correctly establish the need for practical experience, both line experience and experience in quality assurance. In the same spirit, ISO 9001, Element 4.18, Training, requires that all personnel performing activities affecting quality are trained to do their jobs. The guideline authors rightly recognize, just as all trainers do, that training is necessary but not sufficient to ensure individuals can do their assigned tasks.

The second interesting assumption is clear in the list of auditor attributes. That assumption is that auditing is usually not much fun. Experienced auditors know that conducting an objective and effective audit is a major mental and physical challenge. The list of auditor grievances is long, including:

- Usually there is not enough time to do a thorough job.
- Frequently, auditees are defensive and would prefer the auditor would go away and allow them to do their work.
- Auditors are always involved with auditees. There is never a quiet moment where auditors can collect their thoughts and catch their breath.

■ The audit is highly interactive, so auditors must constantly be thinking and interacting with auditees. More important, auditors must be constantly on guard not to offend auditees.

ISO 10011-3: PART 3: MANAGEMENT OF AUDIT PROGRAMS

This guideline covers all types of audits: internal, external, and extrinsic. It is particularly helpful when establishing an internal audit process and will help trainers and their management focus on some fundamental organizational and management issues. Issues presented in this guideline also serve as points to consider when writing the company's quality manual. Here are some suggestions and ideas for implementing such a procedure.

Q-Project Action Items

MAKE AUDITS SYSTEMATIC

There are two parts to this requirement. At the global level, audits should include all elements of the system. This does not mean that everything should be audited every time, but it does suggest that the entire system should be audited over a specific period, usually one year. An annual audit schedule can be developed to identify which elements are audited at which points in the year. A good plan is to schedule short audits once per month so that at the end of the year, all areas and elements of the standard have been audited. The advantage of this plan is that quality is seen as an ongoing, daily activity rather than a once-per-year, special occurrence separate from ongoing work.

The second part of the requirement to be systematic concerns the level of individual audits. The scope (that is, what is looked at, what is to be included, and what is to be excluded) of an audit should be carefully established. A schedule of events and assignments for individual auditors should be laid out. Finally, a checklist of items and questions to be assessed should be established.

USE INDEPENDENT ASSESSORS

The quality audit should be an independent examination of the quality system. A specific note in this paragraph says that individuals who work in an area should not be involved in an audit of that area. This note refers only to second- and third-party audits and formal compliance or regulatory audits. It does not mean a training organization cannot set up its own internal system to audit its own processes.

There are several ways such an auditing process can remain independent. First, if the training organization is large enough, individuals representing various functions within the department can audit areas over which they have no responsibility. Second, persons from other departments can be drawn in to serve on an internal audit team. Finally, drawing help from training departments in external organizations may be possible.

IDENTIFY AUDIT OBJECTIVES

The general objective of a quality audit is to decide whether the planned processes are both suitable and effective in meeting established goals. The guideline lists possible specific objectives of audits. They are used to:

- Determine accomplishment and conformity with a requirement.
- Determine effectiveness of a quality assurance system.
- Initiate opportunities to improve processes.
- Meet regulatory requirements and achieve registration.

The first part of this definition focuses on compliance, whether established procedures are being followed. This second part takes auditors beyond objective examination of evi-

319

dence and places a burden on them to evaluate the quality assurance system itself. Specifically, they must decide how well the process meets the needs of the organization. That requirement seems reasonable in theory. In practice, however, it places individuals outside a process in a position of trying to decide its adequacy. To complicate the matter further, once auditors decide a process is not satisfactory, they might be drawn into deliberations about what an adequate process would be.

It is at this point that auditors could possibly be placed in a position where they are no longer objective, external observers. The second and third objectives, to determine effectiveness and improve processes, take the guideline beyond the typical audit requirements to decide compliance. It links the auditing process with a continuous improvement process. The guideline authors recognized the inherent conflict when taking auditing beyond its traditional role when they included an interesting footnote at this point in the guidelines. It says, "Quality audits should not result in a transfer of the responsibility to achieve quality from operating staff to the auditing organization."

ASSIGN ADEQUATE RESOURCES

Top management must ensure there are sufficient resources, particularly time and experienced personnel, available to conduct internal audits. They must also send a clear message to everyone in the organization that they support the quality auditing process. They should require supervisors and managers to coordinate time for their personnel to work with the auditors and cooperate with the audit process.

ELIMINATE THE BLAME GAME

Top management must make it clear that they expect nonconformances will be found and NCRs will be written because these are a part of the auditing process. These reports are not cause for blame. Rather, they are opportunities for the organization to improve its production and service processes. Management also must emphasize corrective action and follow-up as part of the audit process. Corrective actions also provide opportunities to improve processes.

TRAIN AND EVALUATE AUDITORS

Management must evaluate auditor experience and training requirements. The goal is to have consistency across all auditors and all auditing activities. Given the same operation or process to audit, well-trained, experienced auditors can probably arrive at similar conclusions. From a practical standpoint, auditors have different experience backgrounds and different perceptions that affect their judgment; nevertheless, they should generally arrive at similar conclusions and outcomes when auditing a process.

EMPHASIZE CONTINUOUS IMPROVEMENT

There is no such thing as a process that cannot be improved. That includes auditing processes. Management and auditors should be alert to possible improvements in the auditing process. The goal of these three guidelines is to have an effective auditing process. Just as other processes are reviewed to assess how well they are meeting standards and achieving desired results, quality auditing activities should be reviewed routinely to ensure they are achieving their objectives.

PUBLISH AN ETHICS POLICY

In several places throughout these three guidelines, the authors refer to potential, actual, or perceived conflicts of interest that might hamper or influence an effective auditing process. The last statement in this guideline suggests that management include a code of ethics for all personnel involved (both auditors and auditees) in an auditing program. The code of ethics might be included in the quality manual or as an initial statement in the auditing procedure. A code of ethics can help management establish the auditing process as a way to help the organization improve its processes and achieve its goals. Given this orientation, it is in the best interest of all employees to work to make the auditing process as effective and as efficient as possible.

Reality Check

ISO auditors know an effective internal quality audit process is one hallmark of management's commitment to producing high quality products and services. In addition to the corrective action process and management review, ISO auditors will always and routinely review a company's internal audit process (see Chapter 22).

CHAPTER 37

ISO 8402
Vocabulary Guideline

There is a story among training auditors concerning a company undergoing its first quality audit. The outcome should make trainers believers in paying attention to terms and vocabulary. The training organization had created what they believed were several excellent procedures, each of which had a section containing definitions. Unfortunately, the auditors were quick to point out that the training organization had defined the same terms differently in several procedures. That is, they had failed to maintain consistent definitions across all procedures. The simple, but time-consuming, solution was to delete all definitions from individual procedures and place them in one document which became the training department glossary of training terms.

The International Standards committee has wisely chosen the same approach. It provides users of the ISO 9000 series with Guideline 8402, Vocabulary. This short, but useful, guideline is designed to:

■ Define basic terms related to quality ideas.

- Help writers of the standards prepare international standards.
- Promote understanding in international communication.

The guideline consists of nine pages separated into three columns. Each column defines the same terms in three languages: English, French and Russian. If the document were only in English, it would be less than four pages.

The guideline defines 22 terms. Interestingly, it does not include in its list of defined terms either *product* or *service*. However, definitions of these two terms appear in the early discussion in the guideline. The guideline proves useful in establishing groundwork and emphasizing the overall value of definitions.

Q-Project Action Items

Here are some ideas of how trainers might use the guideline:

- Read the guideline carefully. It is short and worth the half-hour or less necessary to study in detail.
- Decide if a glossary is appropriate for the training organization.
- If terms and definitions are included in individual procedures, decide if consolidating them into one glossary of terms is appropriate. If so, begin the process of revising these procedures.
- Begin identifying terms unique to the organization and writing definitions.
- Reread Chapter 3 of this book to understand some training terms. These definitions were developed specifically for this book, and they can provide a start for a glossary.

- Establish a process to help the organization achieve consensus in identifying and defining terms.
- Establish a limit for the number of terms to be included in the glossary. Start with 25.

Reality Check

Few people are really interested in designing or developing a glossary as they see this exercise as a waste of time. However, when talking about or applying terms, individuals will usually put their own unique twist on their understanding and explanation of terms. They often pay little attention to the glossary or its development until they encounter a disagreement on terms. Achieving consensus on definitions may be difficult at best since people naturally think they understand terms they use frequently, and they assume others understand those terms similarly.

Limit the number of terms in the glossary. This will reduce the chance that the glossary will balloon into a monstrous and unmanageable document. A strict limit will reduce the tendency of some individuals to try to define every term in the universe.

CHAPTER 38

Retrospective and Prospective Issues

This book has argued that trainers and educators will reap several benefits from applying the quality and performance ideas contained in the ISO 9000 Standards and the Malcolm Baldrige Criteria to their organizations. First, their work will work better. That is, their courses and programs will be more focused on the needs of both trainees and students and the larger body of the organization or the community. With effective and efficient processes, training and educational organizations can spend more time on their primary task of designing and delivering programs that get the right job done. Second, implementing ISO or Baldrige principles is a powerful opportunity to demonstrate the value of training to the wider group of stakeholders—senior managers, supervisors, prospective trainees, parents, prospective employers, and the community. Particularly in response to pressures to demonstrate results and accountability, implementing a quality and performance system validates the efforts of schools and training organizations. This validation, this heightening of credibility often support trainers' and educators' requests for cooperation, input, and additional resources. Finally, it should be emphasized that implementing a quality and performance program is fun. It's exciting to see ISO or Baldrige teams take fire and relish the opportunity to make such a clear difference in their organizations. There is a deep satisfaction in being part of such an organizational transformation.

This book also has argued that trainers and educators should seriously consider implementing ISO before attempting the Baldrige. The Baldrige criteria assume an organization has completed a great deal of interconnected work in all of its operating areas, focusing both on processes and results. Although not all areas necessarily are at the same stage of quality implementation, the relationships among items in the Baldrige criteria make it difficult to present a very strong application without extensive and fairly consistent deployment throughout the organization. In contrast, ISO focuses on getting control of basic activities. Therefore, although an organization-wide effort is an ideal goal, ISO can be implemented area by area. In particular, the training function can serve as a model for the rest of the organization by implementing ISO for its own activities and demonstrating the value of the approach. Hence, this book has argued that trainers and educators should begin by implementing ISO and then move on to the Baldrige.

Quality and performance systems serve all the organization's stakeholders. Beginning with its customers, who are necessary for the continuation of the organization, and its employees, who are supported through such systems in doing what the organization needs, through to external stakeholders, such as suppliers and communities, everyone benefits from more efficient and effective organizations. Similarly, trainers and educators can serve their organization and customers by aligning their process to the ISO standard and/or to the Baldrige criteria.

Finally, as if it isn't enough to weather the challenges of a Q-Project, there is the aftermath of a major quality project to consider. Whether the project has resulted in organizational self-assessment, ISO registration, a written evaluation by Baldrige examiners, or the Baldrige Award itself, each organization must grapple with sustaining and enhancing its quality and performance program.

For some organizations, the effort to keep the quality effort a high priority is particularly difficult because organizational members approached the Q-Project as a single-shot effort. They may have considered it something to be completed and put behind them so they could move on to tasks that were more familiar, less challenging, or those they (erroneously) felt were more directly connected to the organization's needs—or their own. The Q-Team must help all members of their organization understand that efforts to improve quality and performance are on-going. Just like flavor-of-the-month quality programs which fail because they have no staying power, viewing ISO or Baldrige projects as one-time efforts will frustrate organizational members and impede the organization from reaching its growth objectives.

In order to combat the too-human tendency to revert to familiar ways of thinking as soon as the stimulus for change recedes, Q-Team members also must persuade the organization that quality and performance programs produce ongoing rewards. These rewards are improved organizational performance, good training, and education programs that satisfy trainees and students, and perhaps most importantly, heightened trainers' and educators' personal satisfaction with their own work. Here are some additional ideas to help trainers and educators maintain and improve their quality assurance processes after completing the initial registration or award project.

PLAN FOR CHANGE

Change is one of the things we can count on in the world. Virtually all change offers opportunities for growth. Trainers and educators can support their organizations by reminding them of this—from the beginning and throughout the process—and helping them build solid and workable opportunities for review and adjustment into their new systems.

MODEL CONTINUOUS IMPROVEMENT

A training or education organization has a singularly good opportunity to learn, experiment, and incorporate the ideas of continuous improvement expressed in ISO 9004-4, Guidelines for Quality Improvement, and section "c" in each of the Baldrige clauses. By demonstrating the power of these ideas in their own efforts, trainers and educators can help their organizations integrate continuous improvement efforts. Trainers should establish their own strategic plan and tie it clearly to the organization's strategic plans, quality goals, and objectives. As a starting point, at least one training management review meeting per year should focus on these overall goals.

DEVELOP STATISTICAL EVIDENCE

Careful data gathering and statistics will demonstrate payoffs for resources spent on training and help build continuing support for these expenditures. A helpful ongoing activity is to continue development of statistical outputs that prove immediate, intermediate, and long-term benefits. Benefits include both financial and psychological gains to the organization. For example, it may be possible to show reduced errors in work processes, faster learning cycles for employees, and increased customer satisfaction as results of learning achieved through training activities. Trainers should continue to seek better ways to measure the effectiveness of their quality system and present their results. Each monthly or quarterly Training Quality Team review meeting should include brainstorming to identify new ways to gather data that help show value from training.

EMPOWER TRAINERS

Employee empowerment is a cornerstone for many quality initiatives. However, empowerment is sometimes wrongly defined as giving employees authority to initiate action to satisfy a customer complaint, providing a special service to a customer, or short-circuiting quality requirements to complete a rush order or to satisfy a special need. This approach is based on an inaccurate definition of customer service, that it is a quick response to complaints. Good customer service is actually delivering a product or service that meets or exceeds customers needs or desires and thus avoids a complaint. A good employee empowerment program is one that encourages employees to:

- Identify problems or potential problems and initiate a fix to the system to avoid them.
- Improve the system so that products and services are readily available when needed and cycle and wait-times are reduced.
- Improve relationships with vendors and customers.

A strong contract review and purchasing review process, along with good training analysis, design, and evaluation processes will identify needs and improve understanding between the training function, its vendors, and its customers.

CLEAN HOUSE

An ISO or Baldrige quality initiative is an excellent housecleaning activity. The implementation project should include ruthless elimination of unused or outdated documentation and processes. Processes should be scrutinized and flowcharted and wasteful or non-value-adding steps eliminated. A simple but relentless strategy of examining every document and process and questioning its current or future usefulness, then eliminating as much as possible will help develop and maintain clear and clean workflows. Once the initial work is done, there should be an ongoing project to try to find and reduce waste and improve processes and eliminate documentation. ISO relies heavily on documentation and structured processes, but a good quality assurance system needs fewer rather than more documents.

REDUCE DOCUMENTATION

There are only a few reasons to have documentation: the customer wants it, it is required for ISO or some regulatory requirement, it satisfies specific safety requirements, or it supports tasks infrequently done by untrained employees. Some ways to reduce documentation and reduce or simplify processes include:

- Push procedures down to work instructions whenever possible.
- Use flowcharts rather than lengthy verbiage in procedures.
- Avoid complex processes by breaking large tasks into small ones.
- Avoid unrealistic and grandiose documentation plans.

BENCHMARK AND COMPARE

Benchmarking is an important part of the Baldrige criteria, and baseline assessments are part of the ISO implementation process. Both provide new ideas, serve as examples of what works well and what works less well, and—importantly—provides context. It is especially useful for organizations to look outside their own borders and take a wider view. Like continuous improvement, benchmarking must be an ongoing activity.

ISO 9000 AND MBNQA

EXPAND THE CUSTOMER BASE

Make a concerted effort to expand the training function to serve more individuals and departments within the organization. Too frequently training functions are limited to one primary trainee group or one or two levels of employees. Finding ways to expand the training function both internally and externally will help improve the quality of training because it will challenge trainers to move outside their comfort zone, master new content areas, and develop their own new SKAs.

A Final Thought

Implementing a quality and performance program requires a substantial investment of time, energy, and financial and human resources. Like any other large project, especially a transformation project, it involves risk. This risk is individual and collective. Advocates and implementers always will have to deal with some individuals who feel threatened by change or who have another vision. If the naysayers are in senior management, jobs or promotion might be jeopardized. But, as I have argued, the benefits clearly outweigh the costs. Implementing a quality and performance program is a way to make a demonstrable difference to the training or education function, your customers, and the larger organization.

The ISO standard and Baldrige criteria contain requirements that help sustain quality and performance initiatives over the long term. Neither allows trainers the luxury of resting on their laurels. ISO's ongoing internal audits and Baldrige's continuous improvement encourage trainers and educators to continue to look for ways to develop cleaner workflows and structure processes to ensure effective, efficient, and high quality training. Improved training will improve relationships with customers and vendors and gain management support and resources for training functions.

I am confident you will find your journey to quality and performance through ISO 9000 or the Malcolm Baldrige worth your investment. Good fortune to you.

Index of Terms

Academic freedom, 125
Acceptance criteria, 77, 79, 84, 119, 127-129
Accreditation, 10, 12, 25-26, 80, 310
American Society for Quality Control, 31, 34
Analysis
  Gap, 19, 34-35
  Job-task, 19-20, 68-70, 72-73, 84-85, 93, 214, 216, 248, 252-253, 312
  Root cause, 314
  Statistical, 20, 52, 55, 120, 132, 136, 140, 157-160, 162, 171, 198-204, 306, 313, 329
  Test-item, 20
Application plans, 195
Approach, 207, 221, 239
Assessment report, 81, 87
Attitudes, 16-17, 19-20, 70-71, 110, 140, 153, 195, 216, 236, 244, 251, 254, 256, 282
Audiovisual aids, 129, 149, 152, 167-169

Audit
  Compliance, 25-27
  External, 26-27, 318-320
  Extrinsic, 26-27,
  First-party, 27
  Internal quality, 27, 44-46, 154-156, 161-163, 175-177, 179, 181, 183, 200, 309, 315-316, 322
  Pre-assessment, 26
  Registration, 8, 10, 12-13, 25-26, 30, 35-37, 307, 328
  Second-party, 27
  Surveillance, 26
  Systems, 25-27, 148, 316
  Third-party, 25, 27
Auditor, ISO
  Lead auditor, 24
  Provisional auditor, 24
Award schemata, 12
Award visit, 30, 36
Benchmarking, 38, 212, 230, 233-234, 236, 265-266, 268-269, 271-272, 275, 281, 285, 331
Best of class, 11
Best practices, 43, 265
Board of Examiners, 24

Business drivers, 231-232, 239-242, 249

Calibration, 136-141

Capability, 19, 47, 66, 72, 100, 119-120, 124, 199, 246, 255, 282

Checklist, 28, 83, 158, 180-181, 319

Checkpoint, 126

Communication, 6, 34, 47, 51, 54, 64-66, 72, 76, 79-80, 88, 117, 162, 182, 186, 198, 249-250, 269-271, 274, 284, 286, 324

Company-level data, 234

Compliance audit, 25-27, 59

Concurrent engineering, 214

Consultants, 34-35, 48, 75, 82, 85-86, 103, 105, 151-152, 284

Continuous improvement, 7, 98, 117, 155, 160, 162, 211-212, 218-219, 258, 263, 270, 277, 287-288, 299, 308, 316, 320-321, 329, 331, 333

Contract review, 47, 64-76, 79, 99, 101, 157, 171, 194

Control
  Customer-Supplied Product, 47, 101, 106-107, 109
  Design, 16-18, 47-48,, 55, 73-88
  Document and Data, 45-46, 61-62, 89-91
  Process, 16-29, 42-43, 45, 60-62, 75-76, 78-88, 115-128, 239-243, 258-271, 273-278
  Quality Records, 45-46, 89, 170-171, 173-174

Core values
  Continuous improvement and learning, 211, 218
  Corporate responsibility and citizenship, 216
  Customer-driven quality, 209-210

Design quality and prevention, 213

Employee participation and development, 212

Faculty and staff participation and development, 212

Fast response, 213

Leadership, 6, 32, 50, 88, 210-211, 222-225, 227-229, 257-258, 284

Learning-centered education, 209

Long-range view of the future, 214

Management by fact, 214-215

Partnership development, 215-216

Results orientation, 216-217

Corporate
  Goals, 4, 123, 160, 246, 267, 304
  Responsibility, 216

Corrective and preventive action, 45-46, 51, 154-155, 157-163, 175, 200, 315

Correlation, 20, 139, 202

Counseling services, 285

Course descriptions, 65, 70, 103

Customer
  Focus and satisfaction, 243, 289, 291, 293, 295, 297, 299, 301
  Needs, 9-10, 67, 71, 75-76, 82, 85, 99-100, 155, 157, 213, 223, 232, 241-243, 260-261, 274, 278, 290
  Service, 17, 230, 293-294, 299-300, 311, 314, 330

Customer-supplied product, 47, 101, 106-107, 109

Deliverables, 72, 189

Department of Commerce, 11, 38, 206-207

339

Order Form

ISO 9000 and Malcolm Baldrige in Training and Education
by C.W. Russ Russo

Telephone orders: Call Toll Free 1-800-589-9009 Please have your Visa or
                     MasterCard ready.

Fax orders: (913) 865-4311

Postal Orders: Charro Publishers, Inc., 4700 Carmel Court, Lawrence, KS
                     66047-1842

Name: _____

Company: _____

Address: _____

City _____ State: _____ Zip _____

Phone: _____ Fax: _____

Please send _____ books @ $49.95, plus shipping $3.50 per copy.

☐ Check   ☐ Credit card: ☐ Visa   ☐ MasterCard

Card number: _____

Name on card: _____

Signature: _____ Card Expiration date: _____

We ship within 24 hours of order receipt. However, postal shipping time may take three weeks. Add $3.00 to shipping cost for second day air.

Cost @ $ 49.95	$ _____
Shipping @ $ 3.50	$ _____
Second Day Air @ $6.50	$ _____
Kansas residents please add 4.9%.	$ _____
Total Order	$ _____

☐ Yes, send me information about the ISO 9000 and Malcolm Baldrige in Training and Education Seminar.

343

*You have read the book, now attend
this seminar and gain practical experience to implement
ISO and Baldrige in your organization.*

Transforming Training and Education: Implementing ISO 9000 and Malcolm Baldrige A 5-Day Intensive Workshop

Develop a workable project plan with detailed task
agenda to transform your training organization into an
award winning service for your company.

Learn strategies and tactics to

- Align training and education practices to corporate and community goals.
- Provide excellent customer service to trainees and students.
- Design superior training that meets participants' practical needs.
- Gain management buy-in and support for training activities.
- Generate enthusiasm and participation from internal and external customers.
- Win credibility for training and education efforts.
- Demonstrate the training function's role as an organizational profit center.

**For more information about public seminars or how to
bring this workshop into your own organization.**

Call Toll Free for additional information or fax:
1-800-598-9009 • 1-913-865-4311

Name: _____

Address: _____

City: _____ State _____ Zip _____

Phone: _____ Fax: _____